SOCIAL WORK

SAGE has been part of the global academic community since 1965, supporting high quality research and learning that transforms society and our understanding of individuals, groups and cultures. SAGE is the independent, innovative, natural home for authors, editors and societies who share our commitment and passion for the social sciences.

Find out more at: **www.sagepublications.com**

SOCIAL WORK
A CRITICAL APPROACH TO PRACTICE
Second Edition
Jan Fook

Los Angeles | London | New Delhi
Singapore | Washington DC

First edition published in 2002. Reprinted in 2003, 2005, 2007, 2008, 2009 and twice in 2010
This edition first published 2012

SAGE Publications Ltd
1 Oliver's Yard
55 City Road
London EC1Y 1SP

SAGE Publications Inc.
2455 Teller Road
Thousand Oaks, California 91320

SAGE Publications India Pvt Ltd
B 1/I 1 Mohan Cooperative Industrial Area
Mathura Road
New Delhi 110 044

SAGE Publications Asia-Pacific Pte Ltd
3 Church Street
#10-04 Samsung Hub
Singapore 049483

Library of Congress Control Number: 2011934508

British Library Cataloguing in Publication data

A catalogue record for this book is available from the British Library

ISBN 978-1-4462-0051-3
ISBN 978-1-4462-0052-0 (pbk)

Typeset by C&M Digitals (P) Ltd, Chennai, India
Printed by MPG Books Group, Bodmin, Cornwall
Printed on paper from sustainable resources

CONTENTS

About the Author   xii
Preface   xiii
Acknowledgements   xv

Part 1 Critical Potential and Current Challenges   1

1   The Critical Tradition of Social Work   3

2   Current Contexts of Practice: Challenges and Possibilities   21

Part 2 Rethinking Ideas   37

3   New Ways of Knowing   39

4   Power   53

5   Discourse, Language and Narrative   65

6   Identity and Difference   82

Part 3 Redeveloping Practices   101

7   Critical Deconstruction and Reconstruction   103

8   Empowerment   119

9   Problem Conceptualisation and Assessment   132

10   Narrative Strategies   150

11   Contextual Practice: Strategies for Working in and with Contexts   161

12   Ongoing Learning   178

Glossary   193
References   197
Index   209

DETAILED CONTENTS

About the Author   xii
Preface   xiii
Acknowledgements   xv

Part 1 Critical Potential and Current Challenges   1

1 The Critical Tradition of Social Work   3
   Does social work have a critical tradition?   3
   Critical origins – the social context   3
   Radical critique – the social structure   5
   Disquiet about structural theories   6
   Postmodern and poststructural social work possibilities   12
   Doubts about postmodernism   15
   A critical approach to social work   17
   Contextualising other critical perspectives on critical social work   18
   Chapter summary   19
   Further reading   20

2 Current Contexts of Practice: Challenges and Possibilities   21
   The current context   21
   Economic aspects   22
   Technological aspects   24
   Theoretical aspects   25
   Political, social and cultural ramifications   26
   The critical challenges for social work   28
   Challenges to the profession   28
     Labour market   30
     Broader social and cultural contributions   31
   The critical possibilities   31
     Changing views of professional practice and professionalism   32
     Inclusivity   33
     Complexity and context   33
     Redeveloping critical social work   33
   Chapter summary   34
   Further reading   35

Part 2 Rethinking Ideas   37

3   New Ways of Knowing   39
    The nature of knowledge and knowledge generation   39
    Professional knowledge and power   42
    Theory and practice   43
    Critical reflection   45
        Origins of the reflective approach   45
        Similarities between the reflective approach, feminism and
            postmodernism   46
        What is a critical reflective approach to practice?   46
        Processes of critical reflection   48
    Reflexivity, reflective practice and contextuality   49
    Other perspectives on critical reflection   50
    Rethinking research and educational practice   50
        Towards inclusivity   50
    Chapter summary   51
    Further reading   52

4   Power   53
    Reflecting on power   53
    Criticisms of the empowerment model   55
    Problems in conceptions of power and empowerment   56
        Power as commodity   56
        Binary oppositional relations   57
        Allowance for difference   58
        Accounting for contradictions   58
        The disempowering experience of empowerment   59
    Reformulating the concept of power   60
    Reformulating the concept of empowerment   61
    Chapter summary   63
    Further reading   63

5   Discourse, Language and Narrative   65
    Ideology   66
    Limitations of the concept of ideology   69
        False consciousness – truth/falsity distinction   69
        Clear split between interests and awareness (dualism of action
            and consciousness)   70
        Directionality (in favour of some, not of others)   70
        Overarching superstructure   71
        Lack of plurality/contradiction   72

Ideology and discourse   72
Discourse   72
Language   73
Language, discourse and power   75
Narrative   76
Interpretive approaches   77
Revisiting theory   78
Chapter summary   79
Further reading   80

6 Identity and Difference   82
   What is self and identity?   82
   Criticisms of traditional concepts of self and identity   83
   Dichotomous thinking   84
   Reformulating the ideas of self and identity   86
   Self and identity in reflexive modernity   88
   The whole self   89
   Constructions of the self in social work   90
   Making difference and 'othering'   92
   Difference, diversity and inclusivity   95
   The dilemma of difference   95
   Identity politics and critical possibilities   97
   Chapter summary   98
   Further reading   99

Part 3 Redeveloping Practices   101

7 Critical Deconstruction and Reconstruction   103
   Unsettling dominant discourses   103
      Discourse analysis and possibilities for critical resistance,
         challenge and change   103
      Deconstructive methods and discourse analysis in practice 104
   The critical reconstructive process   106
      Deconstruction   106
      Resistance   109
      Challenge   110
      Reconstruction   111
   Critical reflection and de/reconstruction   112
   Critical incident technique   113
      Description of the critical incident   114
      Analysis of the incident   114
   Creating practice theory   115
   Other approaches to critical reflection   116
   Chapter summary   117
   Further reading   117

8   Empowerment   119
    New notions of power and empowerment   119
    Deconstructing and reconstructing power   120
        A process of empowerment   120
        Deconstructing power and power relations   121
        Resistance   122
        Challenge   122
        Reconstruction   123
    Common constructions of power in social work practice   123
        Social workers' constructions of themselves   124
        Constructing the enemy   125
    Must power be structural?   126
    The only change is total change   127
    Participating in our own disempowerment   127
    Change and responsibility   128
    Other assumptions which relate to power   128
    Reconstructing ourselves and service users   129
    Constructing our own theories of power and empowerment   129
    Chapter summary   130
    Further reading   131

9   Problem Conceptualisation and Assessment   132
    Criticisms of traditional notions of assessment and problems   132
    An alternative approach: assessment as 'construction of
        professional narratives'   135
    Problematising   136
    Establishing the appropriate climate and process   137
    Research orientation and strategies   138
    Politics and context   139
    The integrated and changing nature of constructing professional narratives   141
    Reframing major concepts and language   142
    The main elements of a professional narrative   142
        Service user perspectives/story   143
        The perspectives of other players   143
        Contexts and changes   143
        How the narrative will be interpreted and enacted in the
            professional context of the worker   143
        Constructing a narrative to be effective in this context   144
    Strategies   145
        Ethnographic and observational methods   145
        Biographical methods   145
        Reflexive methods   146
        Other unobtrusive methods   147
    Chapter summary   148
    Further reading   148

10   Narrative Strategies   150
      What is narrative?   150
      Elements of narratives   151
      The broad uses of narrative strategies – narrative reconstruction   153
        Identity reconstruction and identity politics   154
        Action research   155
        Narrative therapy   155
      The processes of narrative reconstruction   156
      Techniques of narrative reconstruction   157
        Uncovering the narratives   157
        Challenging assumptions that are unhelpful   157
        Externalising the problem narrative   157
        Shifting the story to narratives that are enabling or empowering   158
        Creating an audience   159
        Other narrative techniques   159
      Chapter summary   160
      Further reading   160

11   Contextual Practice: Strategies for Working in and with Contexts   161
      A new way of conceptualising social work practice:
        contextual practice   162
      The nature of contexts   162
      Positionality   164
      Working with whole contexts   165
      Transferability   165
      Reframing skills in contextual terms – contextual competence   166
      Resisting dominant cultural contexts   167
      Bureaucratic practice   168
        Reconstructing roles and identities   168
        Challenging dichotomies and impossible dilemmas   169
        Critical case management   170
      Advocacy   171
      Constructing enemies and allies   172
      Supervision, management, education and organisational change   173
      Education – establishing the appropriate learning climate   174
        Deconstructing educational practices   175
      Chapter summary   176
      Further reading   177

12   Ongoing Learning   178
      Working critically in uncertainty   178
      Critical reflection: linking reflection, evaluation and research   179
      Linking learning, therapy and research   180
      A grounded and transcendent vision   181
      Unity in diversity?   182

Relativism?   183
Critical practice in hostile environments?   184
  Reframing our practice as contextual   184
  Challenge and resistance in a variety of ways   185
  Expropriating and translating the discourse   185
  Identifying contradictions, complexities and points of alliance   186
Contributing to change while being part of the problem?   187
Handling differences in an accepting way   188
  Creating a climate of critical acceptance   188
Politicising service users?   190
Structural or personal power?   190
Celebrating social work   191
Further reading   191

Glossary   193
References   197
Index   209

ABOUT THE AUTHOR

Jan Fook has been a social worker and academic for 30 years. She is currently Director, School of Social Work, Faculty of Health Professions, Dalhousie University, Nova Scotia, Canada. She was recently Professor of Professional Practice Research and Director of the Interprofessional Institute at the South West London Academic Network (Royal Holloway, St Georges (University of London) and Kingston University), UK. She has born and educated in Australia where she has worked most of her life. She has held a variety of academic positions in Australia, the UK and Norway (including professorial positions at Deakin, La Trobe and Southampton Universities, and Diakonhjemmet College, Oslo) but has an ongoing interest in professional education and practice research. Over the last 15 years she has focused on developing critical reflection, and has conducted many workshops with professionals across Australia and in Europe, the UK, Asia and Canada.

She is probably most well known for her work on critical social work and critical reflection. Her research work involves the empirical research of professional practice, and developing better methods for representing the complexity of this. In particular, she is currently engaged in developing critical reflection as a method for researching experience. She has published approximately 80 book chapters and articles. Her 13 books include: *Radical Casework* (Allen & Unwin); *Professional Expertise* (with Martin Ryan & Linette Hawkins, Whiting & Birch); *Social Work: Critical Theory and Practice* (Sage), and *Practising Critical Reflection* (with Fiona Gardner, Open University Press).

PREFACE

Many of you, like me, will have entered the profession of social work because we were interested, quite simply, in 'helping people'. Unfortunately, this is a set of activities which is not quite so straightforward as it sounds. Depending on what country you live in, and what historical period you entered social work, what attracted you to social work may be quite different. For some of you, social work may mean counselling, case management, or the dispensing of emergency assistance and tackling poverty. For others it might mean working to change social policies or communities. Still others might be motivated by a mission of working against social problems such as child abuse. Some of you may still hold ideals of 'changing the world'. Whatever your motivations, interests or expertise, most social work practice textbooks you have read will talk about the 'social justice' mission of social work, the commitment to some kind of social reform or change, a concern about social disadvantage and those who experience it. Where does this ideal sit, in the complex array of practices and values which are said to be part of social work today? And how do our theories and ideals assist us in the everyday practices and settings which are, and often seem, beyond our control?

Many social workers believe that work and employment contexts are so restricted that they do not allow us to practise in empowering ways. As we settle into a new millennium, and much is made of the damaging effects of globalisation and the spread of capitalism, it is indeed difficult to imagine that employers would pay social workers to bring about social change. However, there are many complexities involved in these issues and ideals and theories can be translated in many different ways, in different contexts and by different players. The critical tradition of social work, as ever, involves a complex set of understandings and practices. In responding to new contexts, new practices may evolve. It is my aim in this book to begin to flesh out some of these possibilities for critical practices in changing contexts.

I have organised the book into three parts. The first part, 'Critical Potential and Current Challenges', sets the historical and current contexts for critical social work in the first two chapters. The second part, 'Rethinking Ideas', covers the major concepts associated with critical social work and how these need to be rethought in new contexts, in Chapters 3 to 6. The last part, 'Redeveloping Practices', illustrates how these new ideas might inform new practices, in Chapters 7 to 12.

I have written the book in a number of styles which reflect a number of different ways of engaging with the ideas. In places I have incorporated reflective exercises, which I hope will assist you in making connections between the ideas I discuss and your own thinking and experiences. I have also included some of my own experiences, to help illustrate at first hand how some of the intellectual and theoretical dilemmas have a personal and emotional face. In this way I think we are better able to connect with the very real life tensions for which words in academic textbooks can only ever provide a pale likeness.

I wrote the first edition of this book whilst living and working in Australia, where I was born and raised. I am writing this second edition from the UK, where I moved in 2006, and by the time this second edition is published, I will in fact be living and working in Canada. Whilst I believe that critical approaches to social work are relevant across the Western world, the changes in this second edition to some extent reflect my ongoing awareness of how context influences our conceptualisations of social work. Therefore in this second edition, I have tried to contextualise some of the ideas more, in keeping with the principle of 'contextuality' that I develop in the book. As we march solidly into the twenty-first century, I am aware that some of the ideals of critical social work, and of social justice, may seem even more remote than when I wrote the first edition, nearly ten years ago now. I have bowed to the more pragmatic concerns of our cash-strapped age, and included more summaries and additional readings, to make the book more student-friendly. My purpose, however, has remained constant – to provoke a glimmer of hope that as individuals, and as a profession, we can still make a difference. My hope is that from this book, you as readers can take some small inspiration for the ever-important endeavour that is social work.

Jan Fook
Salisbury, UK
July, 2011

ACKNOWLEDGEMENTS

Some of the material in this book is loosely based on material previously published as Fook, J. (1998) *Critical Social Work Practice*, Deakin University, Geelong.

PART 1

CRITICAL POTENTIAL AND CURRENT CHALLENGES

1

THE CRITICAL TRADITION OF SOCIAL WORK

DOES SOCIAL WORK HAVE A CRITICAL TRADITION?

There is still a lot of argument about whether social work is essentially a conservative profession, one which primarily serves the interests of the dominant groups in society. There is even debate about whether or not social work is a profession (Payne, 2006; Dominelli, 2009: 20). I do not think there is much mileage in debates couched in these terms. A profession comprises many elements – its values; practices and practitioners; theories, knowledge and espoused ideals; institutions and social functions; community perceptions and status; its embedded culture and discourses. It is also a function of, and response to, the many different contexts in which it operates (Ife, 1997: 3). Many of these diverse elements and contexts seem entirely contradictory including the possibilities for both conservative or politically progressive agendas to be met. What is more important, therefore, is what radical potential exists and how and whether these possibilities are played out. Is there, among these elements, the possibility for engaging in social practices which enable people to participate in and create more caring and inclusive social environments? What forms might such practices take and in what contexts? These are the primary issues at stake.

In this first chapter I focus on the critical potential inherent in social work's tradition. In many ways the rest of the book will be about the practices which might emanate from such potential.

CRITICAL ORIGINS – THE SOCIAL CONTEXT

The contemporary profession of social work, from its Western origins (Mary Richmond, 1922, in England and Jane Addams, 1910, in the USA), always emphasised the social side of human existence, the influence of social context in the lives of individuals. From the beginning, the ethos of the social work version of 'helping people' had something to do with the social environment in which people lived and was never simply focused on personal traits. An experience from the autobiography of Jane Addams (Conway, 1992) illustrates some of the long-lasting and critical principles of the social work tradition.

In 1889 Jane Addams set up Hull House in Chicago, a settlement house to bridge the gap between middle and working class, the propertied and the poor, the native born and the immigrants. I find the following passage moving, not the least because I can imagine the well-meaning, perhaps over-zealous Jane, humbled by an incident which could have happened to any of us more than a century later:

> A ... beginning was then made towards a Bureau of Organised Charities, the main office being put in charge of a young man recently come from Boston, who lived at Hull House. But to employ scientific methods for the first time at such a moment involved difficulties, and the most painful episode of the winter for me came from an attempt on my part to conform to carefully received instructions. A shipping clerk whom I had known for a long time had lost his place, as so many people had that year, and came to the relief station established at Hull House four or five times to secure help for his family. I told him one day of the opportunity for work on the drainage canal and intimated that if any employment were obtainable, he ought to exhaust that possibility before asking for help. The man replied that he had always worked indoors and that he could not endure outside work during winter. I am grateful to remember that I was too uncertain to be severe, although I held to my instructions. He did not come again for relief, but worked for two days digging on the canal, where he contracted pneumonia and died a week later. I have never lost trace of the two little children he left behind him, although I cannot see them without a bitter consciousness that it was at their expense I learned that life cannot be administered by definite rules and regulations; that wisdom to deal with a man's [sic] difficulties comes only through knowledge of his life and habits as a whole; and that to treat an isolated episode is almost sure to invite blundering. (Conway, 1992: 518–19)

This early awareness of individual lives, buffeted by social and economic conditions, invites a more holistic and contextual (as opposed to rule-bound) approach to individual suffering and hardship. Awareness of social context and its importance in understanding individual experience and informing practice is therefore one of the earliest principles which holds critical potential for social work. The concept which probably best sums it up is Hamilton's 'person-in-situation' (Mailick, 1977: 407).

As social work developed as a profession, with the elements of social legitimation this entailed (Torstendahl, 1990), professional knowledge was developed in ways which allowed it to be taught, and appear acceptable, in traditional contexts (the university). Thus we can argue that it was the need to scientise our knowledge, so that it was acceptable in essentially masculinist environments, which motivated social workers to adopt models and ways of conceptualising our practical knowledge from more masculinist (Hearn, 1987) traditions, such as psychoanalysis and psychology. We can also argue that in this masculinising process we lost our way as a caring women's profession. These models focused so squarely on the individual and intrapsychic explanations for behaviour and personal problems, that the idea of social context was either abandoned or, at worst, undeveloped. However, in the 1960s the emergence of radical critique put the issue of social context back on the agenda and broadened it to include understandings of how the socio-economic structure and historical conditions also influenced individual experience (Fook, 1993).

RADICAL CRITIQUE – THE SOCIAL STRUCTURE

Radical and structural approaches to social work practice were developed between the 1960s and 1980s in Britain by Bailey and Brake (1975, 1980) and Corrigan and Leonard (1978); in the USA by Galper (1980); and in Australia by Throssell (1975), Rees (1991), De Maria (1993) and Fook (1993). Radical critiques initially criticised traditional social work (casework) for the emphasis on individualised forms of helping and, by implication, individualised notions of personal problems. Coming at the same issue from a different angle, structural social work emphasised the structural nature of individual and social problems. The Canadians Maurice Moreau (1979) and Bob Mullaly (1993, 1997, 2007) are generally credited with the development of the structural approach.

In broad terms, feminists (Brook and Davis, 1985; Dominelli and McLeod, 1989; Marchant and Wearing, 1986) agreed with the analysis of both radicals and structuralists, but added the dimension of gender as a structural concern in influencing individual lives. Feminist social work models, in particular, focused more on developing the links between analysis and practice and personal and political experience, both of which dimensions were largely ignored (or poorly developed) in earlier radical formulations.

This main concern with social structure, and with not 'blaming' the individual 'victim' for problems is a cornerstone of these radical, structural and feminist approaches. This principle entails some related ideas which include a critique of existing social arrangements and social work's complicity, and a corresponding emphasis on emancipation and social change.

We can therefore summarise the basic elements of a critical approach as embodied in radical, feminist and structural writings as follows:

- a commitment to a structural analysis of social, and personally experienced problems, i.e. an understanding of how personal problems might be traced to socio-economic structures, and that the 'personal' and 'political' realms are inextricably linked;
- a commitment to emancipatory forms of analysis and action (incorporating both anti-oppressive and anti-exploitative stances);

SUMMARY

- a stance of social critique (including an acknowledgement and critique of the social control functions of the social work profession and the welfare system);
- a commitment to social change.

DISQUIET ABOUT STRUCTURAL THEORIES

The social justice goals and mission of social work, from its earliest times, seem clearly reaffirmed by these more recent critiques and reformulations of social work to include a structural dimension in the understanding of social context and its influence in human experience. Yet many people noticed problems with the ways in which these structural approaches were practised and experienced. A few years ago I began to reflect on my own experience as these doubts emerged. What follows are several extracts from a talk I delivered some years ago:

I trained as a young social worker in the mid-1970s. I began the four-year course with a firm commitment to practise as a caseworker. In fact, I was not really aware there was a choice. However, by my final year, my class of students had split into two distinct groups – radicals and conservatives, or community workers and caseworkers – the latter group being somewhat patronised by the former. I still belonged firmly to the latter group. I remember being somewhat chagrined, after the first day at my community development placement, at being told to go home and change my only respectable dress for a pair of jeans. Even then I felt there was something vaguely limited about an ideology which had to be so clearly marked by the way one dressed.

I actually did well at the placement, which became a project to set up, among other things, a community garden in Darlinghurst, inner city Sydney. I recall, somewhat incongruously it felt, planting tomatoes with an 'alky', and door knocking sex workers for the garden roster. (Incidentally, the garden is still there, some twenty years later, but with a high wall and locked gate.) I came away with a healthy respect for community work, but wondered why it felt like it had to be at the expense of casework.

Luckily my first job was 'generic' – I counselled, caseworked and community developed people with intellectual disabilities and their families. In my work I found that there was a desperate need for many methods and approaches. Indeed, it was often the clientele themselves who demanded one-to-one sessions, thereby feeling that they were worth the personal attention. In some of my community development projects, parents worked with me effectively as activists and volunteers, yet at the same time needed sensitive counselling to see them through some of the more traumatic experiences they encountered in their work and personal lives. Was I being 'conservative' because I indulged in some micro work?

This issue took on a larger significance for me when I took up my next job, in 1981, teaching introductory welfare to social welfare students. On the one hand I was teaching about the welfare state, and I became firmly committed to the many sociological critiques of social work's appalling role in social control. Yet at the same time I felt that much of what I had done as a social worker had actually felt like helping people, and that as well, the people I had worked with felt like they'd been helped. I didn't think, even then, that I was a particularly special social worker. It just seemed that there was this huge disparity between macro critiques and individual people's perceptions of their experience. Surely it must be possible to continue to help individual people, yet not automatically act as an agent of social control, I reasoned. If one held a firm critical analysis of social work's function in society, then surely this must affect the way in which one assisted individual people?

What to do?

Enrol in a postgraduate degree. Research the problem.

Needless to say, there was not much written on the problem, except to acknowledge that there was this problem. Sure, we still need people to provide the casework, put on the bandages, wipe the tears from the eyes, and sweep up the broken glass. (Very noble, I thought.) But, so the argument ran, if you want to do the real work, it is in collective and structural action. Don't just sweep up the glass and replace the window so it can be broken again. Get a whole new building!

Unfortunately, in the course on which I enrolled there were a number of youngish and enthusiastic (male) sociologists teaching. We class of slightly older (female) social workers sat there taking serious notes, on Althusser I think it was, whilst I kept thinking (as I later discovered so did others) but what does it all mean for practice? The social and experiential contrasts between the teachers and the taught, the sociologists and the social workers, the male academics and the female practitioner-students seemed ludicrously stark. I remember the class was jubilant when someone provided a copy of Stanley Cohen's famous 1975 'It's Alright for you to Talk' article. It acknowledged the difficulties of practice, and the sometimes patronising attitudes assumed by sociological critics towards practising social workers.

It was clear to me that whilst radical approaches to social work big-heartedly acknowledged the need for individual work, and personal care, the development of detailed models and strategies for practice remained token. There was an implicit devaluing of personalised aspects of radical social work, and to me, this also constituted an implicit devaluing of much of social work, in particular much of women's work within social work. (Fook, 1995: 2–4)

Let me stop at this point and summarise some of these early doubts about social work radicalism. First, there was the quite clear and distinctive split between social work student radicals and conservatives, apparently able to be identified by the methods one practised (community work or casework) and possibly also in the way one dressed. Second, this almost simplistic valuing of collective approaches seemed to me to deny, overlook and devalue the personal experiences of myself as a social worker, and the people I worked to assist. Third, this was borne out in my subsequent experience as a postgraduate student, when it seemed that academic sociological answers were only peddled (by people who seemed to share little of the social work experience) in order to obtain our conversion to a higher order of thinking, rather than to assist in transforming our practice. I got the message early on that most academic theory, including radical, sometimes termed structural social work perspectives, also denied and devalued some of the experiences of workers.

Exercise

It might be useful to stop at this point and reflect on some of your own experiences in encountering radical, feminist and structural approaches in social work.

- Who taught these and how were they taught to you?
- What 'hidden' messages did you pick up about these theories?
- Compare your experiences with mine. Are they similar or different?
- What reasons might there be for this?

SUMMARY

My experience thus points to three major criticisms of the way structural theory was enacted and taught, in that it actually functioned in contradictory ways to the ideals it claimed to uphold.

1 Structural perspectives implied a status differential between men and women. The men were the sociologist theorists and teachers, the women were the social worker practitioners and students. It seemed that radical approaches to social work reinforced gender status differences, rather than making them more egalitarian.
2 Structural theory also implied a gendered nature of the value differences between 'macro' and 'micro' work, implied by the radical perspective – 'micro' work, the traditional area of work for women, was relatively devalued in a radical perspective.
3 Structural thinking supports a relative devaluing of social work practice experience as against radical and sociological theory.

Now let me continue some of my reminiscences as I tried to address some of these implied imbalances:

It was against this background of thinking that I developed and later published my ideas about how radical social work could be practised at the individual level (Fook, 1993). This practice model was based on the assumption that theory could be applied, in a direct and deductive manner, to practice. Although this nice little framework proved useful and meaningful for some time, I wondered about some of the reasons people put forward for liking it. Many students like it for its clarity, and practitioners like it because it reaffirms what they already do. I'm not sure I feel these are necessarily good reasons to like a work. I suppose I had hoped, like my sociological teachers of postgraduate days, that students and workers would become converted to radicalism, but I had to acknowledge that it appeared to be meeting some expressed need, which might be just as important. I have had to recognise that unless a work is meaningful to a person's experience, it is unlikely to be used. And at least I am constantly reminded that our work is probably never used in the way we intended!

I have found that in the course of teaching radical casework and working with like-minded colleagues many other doubts and queries have arisen for me about the limiting ways in which radical approaches to practice are conceptualised.

For instance, although much radical and feminist literature states otherwise, many of my student, academic and professional colleagues still seem to assume that politically correct work is macro work, and that only the unenlightened still willingly practise at micro level. This uncritical equation of collective work with political practice bespeaks another intellectual oversimplification, present in some radical thought, which is the notion that a radical analysis or theory necessitates new and specific radical skills, techniques or strategies. In other words, one's radicalism can be defined solely through one's actions. The popularity of empowerment techniques and the empowerment approach is one which concerns me a little in relation to this point. Instead of just asking how we empower, I still think we need to ask and address the harder questions like empowerment for what and for whom?

Related to this type of thinking are limitations in the way we have conceptualised the relationship between theory and practice. My own work is guilty of perpetuating the dominance of the deductive relationship between theory and practice – the idea that generalised theory can be applied in a linear fashion to deduce specific practices. This view is implicit in the idea that for every radical idea there is an equivalent radical practice. This can lead to the assumption, which I have seen many students make, that there has to be a new radical practice skill waiting out there somewhere in the ether. This often leads to noble *in*action, because they reject many quite serviceable strategies simply because they already know about them so, by definition, they must be conservative!

Focusing ultimately on identifying the 'radicalness' of our practice strategies can also lead us to devalue the unintended outcomes which might occur in the process of engaging in our work. For instance, I have seen my own postgraduate students talk of some marvellous piece of practice, only to end by belittling it because they thought it was not 'radical' enough! I wonder sometimes whether we have constructed some unattainable ideal of radical practice, which only serves to devalue the change efforts that we do make.

Another question my students often ask is what to do if the person/people they are helping doesn't want 'radicalism' or 'feminism' dished up to them, as if these ways of seeing the world are some sort of treatment package. They speak about theories, our ways of seeing the world, as if they are some type of objective mantle which can simply be thrown on or off as the occasion warrants.

This relates to one of the big questions my teaching of the deductive application of radical theory has raised. This is about what I have termed the 'commodification' of theory, as if theory, radical in particular, consists of a material set of ideas which can easily be transferred from one person to another. Although I think it is true to say that radical social work has wholeheartedly adopted Freierian educational principles (that it is not objective knowledge which is learnt or 'banked', but rather an empowering way of engaging with the world of ideas), I do think 'banking' models of education underpin some of our conceptualisations of radical theory, in that we do assume or hope that people will be 'converted' to our way of thinking. We hope that they will cross the great divide, become conscientised and empowered, politically aware and active, and that in the course of this process they will agree with and become like us. They will have arrived. They have the keys to the bank.

This 'commodification' concept also applies to the way in which power is often perceived in a radical social work perspective, as if there is some finite pool of power from which the radical worker draws to distribute to the disadvantaged. The danger is that if the worker draws some for her or himself, there is automatically less left for the disadvantaged person, thereby effectively disempowering them. So any empowering of workers automatically becomes a disempowering of the disadvantaged people with whom they work. This type of thinking can function to potentially disempower workers. Another *disempowering* aspect of this type of thinking is that disadvantaged groups are characterised *by definition* as disempowered, thus denying any power they might have. Much attention has been drawn of late to the potential such views have of constructing a passive 'victim' identity amongst the disadvantaged. It is hard to act in one's personal world, when all the causes of your problem are located well outside and beyond your reach.

Such 'black and white' views hold an inherent potential for determinism which may not allow room for people to have complex, changing and conflicting identities when operating with a framework which persists in categorising people in terms of binary opposites – disadvantaged or advantaged, oppressed or non-oppressed and so on. These potentially deterministic views also fail to allow for the contradictions of people participating in their own oppression – the feminist in public who does all the ironing at home, the meek-seeming woman who rules the household in private, the dominant male executive who is still mother's boy. This is almost a common sense view to which it is easy to become blinded – people's identities and behaviour differ in different situations and contexts.

I am worried by what I see as a type of moral and technical absolutism fostered in myself, students and colleagues by the culture of radicalism and structural perspectives, which flies in the face of the intended traditional social work values of flexibility, tolerance, non-judgementalism and acceptance. Radical ideals of the 60s and 70s and feminist ideals of the 80s were clear. We sought a changed world of social equity and justice, welfare for all, and structured opportunities so that all classes, cultures, races, genders and sexualities, ages and abilities could attain personal and social fulfilment. Whilst I would still wholeheartedly subscribe to these ideals, I am concerned that if our present-day notions of how this is to be achieved rest on past-day notions of what sort of people and society we are, then the potential to achieve this might be limited.

This can be applied to some of the more epistemological questions. The way in which our past notions of radical theorising and practice have been conceptualised can be dangerously positivistic and scientistic in the ways in which theories and practices have been distinguished and oppositionally characterised. Such views automatically value the knowledge created by 'scientific', often male, academic researchers, and discount the learning which arises from practical experience, the reflective process in which ideas are created, as well as developed. They also function to discount the learning and experience of ordinary practitioners and service users. (Fook, 1995: 5–8)

Exercise

- Why do radical, feminist or structural approaches appeal to you? (Try to think of all kinds of reasons, both personal and professional.)
- What does your understanding of these theories and the way they are practised imply about yourself and the people you work with?
- How do you think the people you worked with would have perceived you, and how would they have experienced your use of such theories?

I wrote my reminiscences about five years ago, and in the meantime have found that many students, workers and other colleagues agree with me. These experiences cover a lot of ground so it is worthwhile summarising the main points again. The aspects of the experience of teaching and developing radical and structural theory for practice created disquiet in me for a number of reasons:

1 The assumption that workers could or should 'be radical' solely through their actions, and that new practices should be the sole defining feature of radical social work, often led to a stultifying inaction. (See Ife, 1997: 178–9 for a further discussion of this issue.)
2 The seemingly oversimplified, one-way, deductive view of how 'theory' relates to 'practice'.
3 The idea that to be an effective 'radical practitioner' you had to undergo a type of 'conversion' seemed a little too much like a type of ideological oppression of another kind.
4 Related to the above, the implicit assumption that if any client were to be effectively helped, they too had to undergo a conversion and take on board the new radical theory.
5 Radical perspectives seemed to have very limited and oversimplified conceptions of 'power' and 'identity', which did not seem to cover the multitude of situations in which both clients and workers operate, and indeed may lock disadvantaged people into disempowered identities.
6 Radical theories seemed to imply a very deterministic view of people and the possibilities for change and transformation. They almost seemed to have an 'alienating' rather than an empowering effect, denying people personal agency, rather than creating the power to effect change.

Exercise

Using your responses to the last two exercises, construct your own list of advantages and disadvantages of radical, feminist and structural approaches.

These were some of the issues with which I struggled when applying and teaching radical social work, but they also reflect some of my social experiences from mixing with colleagues who were both sympathetic and unsympathetic to radical approaches.

In short, I experienced some discomfort over the ways in which radical social work manifested itself culturally. There seemed to be a rather large disparity between the expressed empowering ideals of the radical tradition, and how people lived and experienced it. Is there a better way?

POSTMODERN AND POSTSTRUCTURAL SOCIAL WORK POSSIBILITIES

I found postmodern thinking initially attractive in addressing these problems because of its critique of theories or views which claim to be universal and total, and therefore its allowance of multiple perspectives. Yet more than a way of thinking, it is also a way of labelling this particular period in global history (Fawcett and Featherstone, 2000: 8). It is therefore helpful to understand the phenomenon of 'postmodernism' in relation to the period of 'modernism' which it is said to have succeeded.

The characterising feature of the modernist world is the belief that conditions can be progressively improved through the establishment of reliable, universal and generalisable knowledge, developed through the use of reason and scientific methods. Knowledge in this sense is cumulatively developed, in a linear sequence, and disciplinary knowledge is clearly bounded and controlled. Strict hierarchies, structures and rules govern the ways in which knowledge is legitimated and enacted. The nation-state and professional institutions are two examples of modernist organisations believed to be the appropriate structures to maintain such modernist ideals.

Postmodernism, in its simplest sense, involves a critique of totalising theories and the structures, boundaries and hierarchies which maintain and enact them. It represents both (in a theoretical sense) a critique of these structures and (in a pragmatic sense) an actual fragmentation of them. Postmodernism is both a theory and a descriptive framework. Postmodernism (in theory and practice) represents a recognition that the traditional (modernist) organising frameworks are no longer valued or relevant, and that we must now acknowledge the existence of diverse and multiple frameworks or discourses. Our meaning (and therefore our reality) is constructed out of the language of our (multiple) discourses about it. In this way, there is no one universal truth or reality, but instead 'reality' is constructed out of a multiplicity of diverse and fragmented stories. In this sense, the 'grand narratives' like Science or Reason, which sought to provide a universal explanation and basis for human action and inquiry, are now deconstructed and seen to be a mass of conflicting ways of making sense of different experiences from different perspectives.

Poststructural thinking is related to postmodernism and is most easily understood as referring more particularly to the language and discourse elements of postmodernism (Healy and Fook, 1994). Poststructuralism is associated with

French social theorists such as Derrida, Lacan and Foucault (Featherstone and Fawcett, 1995). Poststructural thinking challenges broad structural thinking (for example, Marx, Freud) which essentially assumed that observable phenomena could be best explained by underlying structures or relations. Whereas structuralists might view meaning as fixed, poststructuralists would argue that meaning, because it is produced within a language or discourse, is therefore multiple, unstable and open to interpretation (Weedon, 1987). Language (and therefore meaning) must be interpreted in relation to specific contexts (social, historical, political). Discourses are therefore situated (socially, historically and politically).

Sands and Nuccio (1992) summarise the six main themes of poststructuralism as follows:

1   A critique of logocentrism (the belief that there is a fixed, singular and logical order): there are no essentialist qualities, since these vary in relation to context and are mediated through our use of language (discourses).
2   Dichotomous thinking: also involved in logocentrism. The way we represent our 'reality' through language is based on the tendency to order our world (make meaning) by categorising phenomena into polar or binary opposites. These are mutually exclusive, oppositional and hierarchical, and not seen as interdependent. The categories we create have only two subsets which are mutually exclusive of each other, cast in opposing terms, with one set valued over the other and not believed to be dependent on each other for definition (e.g. 'male vs female').
3   The idea of difference: because logocentric thinking supports the use of binary opposites, the way differences are defined is problematic. Binary opposites do not allow for a wealth of diverse meanings, experiences and identities to be represented in our discourse. Instead, the experiences of the marginal are often defined (and lumped together) in relation to the mainstream, thus perpetuating dominant discourses. In this process marginal people are often 'othered' or perhaps even silenced or ignored in relation to some ideal of mainstream experience. Derrida (1978) used the term 'difference' to refer to meanings which do not fit into this dichotomous way of categorising – meanings may be 'neither' or 'both-and' or something else entirely.
4   Deconstruction: because logocentric thinking dominates our language, it is important to deconstruct discourses in order to uncover hidden, contextual or marginalised and multiple other meanings. In this way, deconstruction decentres (i.e. upsets) dominant thinking, giving prominence to formerly suppressed perspectives.
5   Multiple discourses: since it is possible, by deconstruction, to uncover the many other possible voices which may be implicit or missing from the text (or discourse), it is important to recognise that any one reading or interpretation of a text may only uncover a partial narrative. It is therefore important to be aware of multiple (and diverse) discourses which could be crucial in understanding any one text.
6   Situated subjectivity: since meanings and discourses are context-dependent, a person's idea of her or himself, or subjectivity, is also socially constructed. It is therefore 'precarious, contradictory and in process, constantly being reconstituted in discourse each time we think and speak' (Weedon, 1987: 33). It may also be multifaceted, depending on the changing contexts.

Exercise

Compare these characteristics of postmodern thinking with the concerns regarding structural social work which we noted earlier.

There are therefore many possibilities for postmodern and poststructural thinking to address some of the concerns about structural approaches in social work. I shall outline them in point form, since there are quite a few:

1   The emphasis on social context and the constant connection of this with individual experience (e.g. situated subjectivity) provides a more detailed theoretical understanding of the individual in social context, and also considerably develops our understanding of how the social structure is part of everyday experience. It provides a stronger theoretical basis for practice at the point of intersection between 'person-in-situation'.
2   The analysis of dichotomous thinking provides an excellent basis for a critique of gender-biased thinking and related practices.
3   The recognition of multiple discourses adds a complexity of understanding to the multifaceted situations in which social workers find themselves. This should allow for more effective practice.
4   The recognition of how 'difference' is constructed provides an alternative way of conceptualising marginality and redefining it in empowering ways.
5   The allowance for changing subjectivities and identities represents a little more of the complexity of human life, and the ways in which living is mediated continuously by context. This may allow us to match our understanding of people's lives more closely with their own perceptions and experiences.
6   The understanding of how knowledge is produced and 'hierarchised' provides an alternative way to reconceptualise and value the 'marginal' voices of service users and practitioners.
7   The upending of the 'theory/practice' binary leads to the revaluing of practice and lived experience as ways of knowing. This also potentially empowers previously marginal people, because it acknowledges and legitimises their experiences and identities. It also allows for more complex forms of theory which incorporate new perspectives to be developed.
8   The possibilities for knowledge and theory to be generated and used in multiple ways make for potentially more flexible practice.
9   The critique (deconstruction) of mainstream practices potentially upends taken-for-granted hierarchies and power differences, and allows for the possibility of new forms of empowerment.

These are some of the major ways in which postmodern perspectives can potentially enrich our thinking and practice so that it is more complex, flexible and empowering. I have found the adoption of postmodern perspectives to be empowering in my own work, particularly in relation to my relationship with theory. I am much more aware of using theory consciously in different kinds of ways and of developing a process of creating my own theory. In my more 'radical' days, I felt more of a 'slave' to theory, that I had to 'get it right', before applying it accurately, and that therefore there could only be limited ways that it could be applied. For me, now, the crucial question is not whether a theory or practice is 'radical' (or structural or critical) but whether and how it can embody and enact critical possibilities. I participate as an active player in a much more creative process in which I use ideas to develop critical possibilities, and thereby develop practice theories. This is the process I hope to demonstrate in this book.

DOUBTS ABOUT POSTMODERNISM

Although I argue that postmodern and poststructural thinking can be practised and experienced in potentially more empowering ways than structural theories, I also believe these types of thinking need to be examined to ensure that multiple perspectives are taken into account in formulating a sound and complex approach to critical practice. What, then, are some of the doubts about postmodernism?

Many social workers are concerned that postmodern thinking supports a moral relativism which potentially undermines the strong social justice, indeed the critical ideals, of social work (Ife, 1999: 215; Piele and McCouat, 1997). In this sense, while it provides an attractive framework for the incorporation of multiple and marginal perspectives, it is argued that there still needs to be a privileging of a single perspective, in order to make decisions about how (and why) to act. Having a guide for action implies a moral framework which justifies that action. Many people feel that postmodern thinking fragments this framework, and therefore provides no clear basis for action.

As well, such a 'moral vacuum' can easily leave the door open for actions and ideologies to be co-opted by more sinister political interests, or can at the very least provide an excuse for moral *in*action. So one of the potential strengths of postmodernism, its openness to diverse perspectives, is also a potential weakness, in that it leaves the door open to perspectives which may work against a critical agenda. Political neutrality may not, in fact, be possible.

Amy Rossiter (2001) raises this question very pertinently in relation to social work education, when she questions whether there is any such thing as 'innocent' knowledge. How can social work educators hope to help students learn in an open way when we, as social workers, are already implicated by the very fact that we make choices about which knowledge (perspectives) to present and how we present it? These choices are necessarily made from our own subjective position and so, in this sense, our knowledge can never be 'pure', but is in fact unavoidably 'tainted' by the position from which we see and speak. Since everyone speaks from a particular position, no knowledge is ever innocent or free of perspective. So the very advantage of postmodern thinking is also its weakness. Pointing up that every perspective is 'positioned' in fact removes the privilege of any position. Therefore postmodern analysis does not provide guidance about appropriate or desirable knowledge and ways to act.

So while postmodernism might embody a relativistic stance and appear politically neutral, in fact it points up that there can never be pure political neutrality, since all positions (including a postmodern one) and actions embody a moral perspective. Ironically, however, postmodernism, with its emphasis on fragmentation, multiplicity, diversity and contextuality, does not supply this clear perspective.

Yet at the same time, it would seem desirable, within the traditions on which social work was founded, that we value the principles which postmodernism emphasises – certainly the ideas of multiplicity, diversity and contextuality sit perfectly within a social work frame of reference. So is there a way out of the maze?

Foucault provides a starting point for the way out: 'My point is not that everything is bad, but that everything is dangerous' (1984: 343). The issue at stake is to focus on the potential ('dangerousness') of practices and situations, rather than starting with the assumption that they are inherently 'good' or 'bad'. The way I like to understand the contribution of postmodernism is that the value of ideas is in how they are enacted or expressed in a given situation or context, rather than in any inherent value in the ideas themselves, regardless of context. Of course, the expression of an idea (discourse surrounding an idea) may carry certain associations of 'badness' or 'goodness', which may produce particular effects; in which case it may be important to focus on these associated functions and how they are managed. Postmodernism provides a beginning for an understanding of how certain discourses might carry and enact particular effects.

In this sense, postmodernism is more particularly a theory about ways of knowing, rather than a theory about what sort of society we should have and how people should behave within it. It is an epistemological theory, rather than a moral theory. Radical, structural and feminist theories would fit into this latter moral category. Of course, this is a reasonably simplistic categorisation, but it does provide the beginnings for us to see how it may be possible to couple ideas about how we know with ideas about what we should be. It provides a simple starting point to picture how we might combine postmodern thinking with a structural theory.

If we take this idea as a starting point, it is meaningless to compare postmodernism and, say for example, Marxism, because they are theories about different types of things. Indeed, Marxism is characterised as a *structural* (and in this sense a *modernist*) theory in that it is about trying to find particular underlying causes or explanations (or structures). Postmodern (or poststructural) perspectives are about focusing on the fact that we do search for underlying explanations. In this sense, postmodernism holds much more critical potential, since it opens up all realms of thinking for scrutiny as to how they are constructed, enacted and expressed in any given situation. Presumably we need to combine both types of theorising in order to begin to understand our complex world and the plethora of experiences within it.

Since we have established a basis for the possiblity of combining postmodern thinking with critical perspectives, let us now turn our attention to critical theory and how it might be applicable in social work.

A CRITICAL APPROACH TO SOCIAL WORK

A critical approach to social work has only been explicitly talked about in social work relatively recently (Healy, 2000; Ife, 1997; Rossiter, 1996). It is therefore useful to revisit the idea, and its meaning in the broader social sciences, before we develop our ideas about what it means in social work.

Below is a summary of the main thinking in critical social theory, as outlined by Agger (1991, 1998: 4–5).

1 'Domination' is structural, yet also personally experienced. It is achieved by ruling groups through a mixture of external exploitation *plus* an internal self-discipline or self-deception. This is the idea that people also participate in their own oppression. As some feminists might term it, people hold and perpetuate 'self-defeating' beliefs and customs.

2 Thus the notion of 'false consciousness' is important. There is a recognition that a process of false consciousness operates within capitalist societies so that members of the society cannot recognise that social relations are in fact historically constructed, and therefore transformable.

3 A critique of positivism as a major ideology, since this encourages passivity and attitudes of fatalism. Social members see themselves as removed from, disengaged or alienated from the power to act on and in their situation. Therefore there is a need to develop a consciousness which is able to view 'facts' as pieces of history which can be changed. 'This emphasises the power of agency, both personal and collective, to transform society' (Agger, 1998: 5).

4 The possibility for progress is inherent in critical social theory. It is political in that it sees a role for critical social theory in raising awareness about domination and the possibilities for social change. Because it links this awareness of structural domination with everyday experience, critical social theory is *voluntaristic* rather than *deterministic*.

5 As part of the critique of positivism, there is a recognition that knowledge is not simply a reflection of 'empirical reality', but is also actively constructed by those studying it. There is therefore a need to distinguish between knowledge which comes from causal analysis and that which comes from self-reflection and interaction. This means that there needs to be a reliance on communication as a major transformative process.

SUMMARY

There are clearly many points of similarity between postmodern thinking and a critical approach:

- the recognition of interactive and reflective ways of knowing;
- the recognition of the connections between structural domination and personal self-limitations;
- the recognition of possibilities for both personal and social change.

Such an approach might incorporate an understanding of how social realities are constructed both externally and internally. The emancipatory possibilities are opened up through a critical analysis of the interactions between individuals and society which situates the interest group and power relations operating in both external structures and constructed ways of thinking (discourses). Resistance and change therefore lies in challenging power relations and structures that are constructed in these ways. Furthermore, it is through a process of dialogue and interaction, self-reflection and analysis, in conjunction with knowledge obtained empirically, that an understanding of how power relations are specifically expressed and used in a particular situation will be achieved.

How then might we characterise a postmodern and critical approach to social work? A postmodern and critical social work practice is primarily concerned with practising in ways which further a society without domination, exploitation and oppression. It will focus both on how structures dominate, but also on how people construct and are constructed by changing social structures and relations, recognising that there may be multiple and diverse constructions of ostensibly similar situations. Such an understanding of social relations and structures can be used to disrupt dominant understandings and structures, and as a basis for changing these so that they are more inclusive of different interest groups.

Knowledge to inform this understanding is derived in different ways. Empirical knowledge is needed in order to understand how material structures shape lives. Processes of self-reflection are crucial in ensuring that dominant structures and relations are challenged in the way they are implicitly enacted in everyday life. Communication and dialogue are necessary in order to ensure that diverse perspectives are included in forging new and inclusive ways. Thus, in a postmodern and critical social work both the kinds of social changes that are sought, and the ways in which they are enacted, are important. Outcome and process are integral to each other.

CONTEXTUALISING OTHER CRITICAL PERSPECTIVES ON CRITICAL SOCIAL WORK

In the last few years perspectives on critical social work have developed further. These developments have taken on slightly different dimensions, in different national contexts. In the UK, for instance (where I am currently writing) anti-oppressive (Dalrymple and Burke, 2006; Dominelli, 2002a, 2002b) and anti-discriminatory practice (Thompson, 2006) are more commonly spoken about. The term 'critical' social work is also used in a broader way in the UK, to refer to work which is significant or crucial in some way (Adams et al., 2009a, b, c). The book by Jones et al. (2008) attempts to contribute to the critical social work tradition by illustrating examples of best practice.

Interestingly, in the UK, there has been a recent resurgence of neo-Marxist traditions exemplified in the work of Iain Ferguson (2008) who calls for a re-establishment of structural analysis in approaching social problems. Indeed, it may be fair to say that postmodern approaches to social work are not predominant in the UK. In fact there appears to be little open peddling of postmodernism in social work in the UK. Social constructionism (e.g. Parton and O'Byrne, 2000) seems more commonly preferred.

I have found it interesting to observe, since moving to the UK from Australia, how the 'modernising agenda' of New Labour policies in the UK may have influenced this preference for more structural approaches. Despite the ostensible goals to make bureaucracy more flexible and efficient, modernisation appears to have been experienced in a top down and inflexible way (Parton, 2004), ironically tending towards greater control and privileging of managerialist agendas (Payne, 2009). In such an environment, 'anti-' approaches may seem more effective in resisting this more centralised control of professional services.

From living and working in the UK, I have also gained a greater appreciation of how anti-oppressive approaches to practice may be more embedded in the political identity of the social work profession. Anti-oppressive value positions, for instance, give a greater profile for the distinctiveness of social work, and stake a claim for distinctive knowledge and practices based on those values.

In Australia, and perhaps to a lesser extent in Canada, there has been more of a mix of different approaches. Allan et al. (2009) attest to the variety of perspectives covered under the rubric of 'critical' in the Australian literature. Human rights perspectives (Nipperss and Briskman, 2009) are included on this overview. In Canada, anti-oppressive approaches incorporate both structural and critical perspectives (Baines, 2007; Carniol, 2010).

The use of postmodern (and social constructionist) perspectives has also continued to be criticised from several countries, and several writers have put forward different types of theories to bridge the gap between the relativist thinking of postmodern perspectives and the fundamental value position of more critical perspectives. Examples of these are de Montigny (2005) who proposes a 'reflexive materialist' position, and Stan Houston (2001), who introduces critical realism as an alternative framework.

Exercise

Think about your own country context and which type of 'critical' approach you have some sympathy with. What is it about your own experience and your own context which might have influenced this sympathy?

Chapter summary

In this chapter we began with the long-standing social justice ideals of social work and its commitment to understanding and helping people in their social contexts. We traced how these ideals have changed and developed, with the introduction of Marxist and structuralist then

(Cont'd)

feminist frameworks. We also discussed how the essential ideals of social work might have been seen to be compromised to some extent through the need to politically legitimate social work as a women's profession in a man's world. We also traced how the search for a relevant theoretical framework for critical social work continues with the application of postmodern ideas, and how there is continuing criticism and development of this perspective, which differs somewhat depending on the country context. Clearly the task of developing a critical approach to social work will continue to change in relation to evolving contexts.

FURTHER READING

Allan, J., Briskman, L. and Pease, B. (eds) (2009) *Critical Social Work: Theories and Practices for a Socially Just World*. Crows Nest: Allen & Unwin.

Very comprehensive (Australian) collection of up-to-date chapters on all aspects of critical social work.

Ife, J., Healy, K., Spratt, T. and Solomon, B. (2005) 'Current understandings of critical social work', in S. Hick, J. Fook and R. Pozzuto (eds), *Social Work: A Critical Turn*. Toronto: Thompson Educational Publishing. Ch. 1, pp. 3–24.

This chapter provides some excellent dialogue about the concept of critical social work. The authors come from Australia, Canada, the UK and the USA and illustrate their own different perspectives, as well as perspectives from different countries. This gives a good flavour of how social work is developed in relation to its context.

Hick, S. (2005) 'Reconceptualising critical social work', in S. Hick, J. Fook and R. Pozzuto (eds), *Social Work: A Critical Turn*. Toronto: Thompson Educational Publishing. Ch. 3, pp. 39–51.

An excellent alternative account of how critical social work developed and the current challenges.

McBeath, G. and Webb, S. (2005) 'Post-critical social work analytics', in S. Hick, J. Fook and R. Pozzuto (eds), *Social Work: A Critical Turn*. Toronto: Thompson Educational Publishing. Ch. 11, pp. 167–86.

Provides some critique of some critical social work theorists, and develops the contribution of Foucault and Deleuze.

Houston, S. (2001) 'Beyond social constructionism: critical realism and social work', *British Journal of Social Work*, 31: 845–61.

A good introduction to critical realism and its possible application to social work.

2

CURRENT CONTEXTS OF PRACTICE
CHALLENGES AND POSSIBILITIES

Because of the emphasis placed on working in context, social work is a profession, perhaps more than any other, which is shaped by its many contexts – material, social, political, economic and cultural. It is therefore important that we understand in broad terms the main features of this context and what they mean for critical practice – both the potential for positive changes and the challenges to past ideals. In the last chapter we examined the context of historical changes in thinking which have influenced the current trends in social work theory. In this chapter we examine these theoretical changes within the broader context of social and economic changes. I will begin by outlining the broad changes and then move on to discussing the specific challenges they pose for social work. I end the chapter by pointing to the possibilities posed for critical social work.

THE CURRENT CONTEXT

Processes of globalisation (Payne and Askeland, 2008; Harrison and Melville, 2010) are said to characterise the current world economy. In summary, globalisation refers to the 'compressing' of the world through economic and technological means (Robertson, 1992) and there are also political and cultural repercussions of this. As international economies become more interdependent and communication and transport systems more efficient, consciousness of the world as a whole intensifies (Robertson, 1992: 8). An upside of this is the breakdown of boundaries and parochial thinking, allowing new expressions of identities, and a broader awareness of global responsibilities (Midgley, 2001: 15). A downside is fragmentation of old certainties and structures, leading to outbreaks of conflicts between differentiated groups. Another downside is that globalisation can be seen as a type of 'capitalist imperialism' in which the economic and political structures of the West are imposed on the rest of the world in the guise of 'development' (Hogan, 1996: 282). Elements of both these positive and negative views of globalisation are echoed by social workers internationally (Rowe et al., 2000).

In a more recent analysis, Dominelli (2009: 14) points up how globalisation is now associated with neo-liberalism which represents a deepening of capitalist social relations. This has an effect on all aspects of everyday life. She summarises some of these effects for social workers: privatisation of public services and managerial control of the workforce; promoting nationally developed forms of practice as if they have universal applicability; colonising processes; responding to natural and human-made disasters; fostering developments in local practices; having an impact on the international stage; and being part of a migratory workforce.

I will discuss some of these effects in more detail in the following sections. It is important to note here however that these new situations are complex, and the way they are seen and addressed will be a reflection of the many different perspectives on globalisation and its interwoven effects. One of the difficulties, yet challenges, of understanding globalisation is recognising how vast world-scale changes have different and contradictory expressions in different contexts. The resulting tensions and differences in perspective allows for exploring the possibilities for critical practice in a context which seems initially to be overarching and unchallengeable. As Pugh and Gould (2000) suggest, to see globalisation as inevitable pre-empts possibilities for change and oversimplifies the realities of how politics operates. Let us therefore examine in more detail the different aspects of the effects of globalisation – economic, technological, theoretical and political.

ECONOMIC ASPECTS

Social work in the Western world depends to a large extent on publicly funded employment. Unfortunately, it is commonly noted that the 'welfare state' is dying (Fabricant and Burghardt, 1992; Ife, 1997; Johnson, 1987; Leonard, 1997; Mullaly, 1993; Parton, 1994). This is associated with a general downsizing in public spending, particularly on services such as welfare, which are traditionally recognised as non-profit making. A major concern is that such public downsizing leads to far greater inequalities and there is much evidence to support this on a world wide scale (Carniol, 2010: 6). This privatisation of public infrastructures (Ernst, 1996) threatens the livelihood of welfare-related professions, which are under threat of collapse, or at the very least of major transformation (Parton, 1994).

Dominelli (1996) and Dominelli and Hoogevelt (1996) argued that internationally processes of globalisation have resulted in increased economic competition between service providers. In order to be more competitive, skills must be technocratised (broken down and expressed in concrete terms), so that they can be more easily measured and marketed. This results in a disaggregation and a subsequent devaluing of professional knowledge and skills – elsewhere referred to as a proletarianisation (Fabricant and Burghardt, 1992: 85). It also functions to deprofessionalise jobs, since the power to define jobs shifts from the professionals as their managers seize control of the language of how skills are framed.

In line with the tendency to privatise, the 'purchaser–provider split' has also become one of the main organising features of service provision under a globalised economy. According to this principle, the 'purchaser' (for example, the government) buys specific services from 'providers' (for example, community-based, non-government, private or business organisations), who compete for service provision contracts. This split between purchaser and provider effectively allows the government purchaser to maintain centralised control (because it controls levels of funding, as well as the criteria and methods for its provision), while effectively decentralising service provision, through devolving it to localised providers. Moreover, the purchaser potentially increases its relative levels of control, since by contrast providers are fragmented and their interests split and divided through competition with each other. The purchaser argues that this system is more accountable since funding is tied to specific contracts, with specific measures of success. Similarly, efficiency is ensured through the competitive process.

The net effect of such marketised contractual arrangements means that specialised professional skills are devalued for their inherent worth and must be costed and measured in terms of more 'objective' outcomes. This effectively places the power for decision making about quality services and desired outcomes in the hands of purchasing funding bodies, which are distanced from the site of service provision. Policy development and regulation of services thus becomes separated from the grounded operation of services. Practising professionals who implement services are thus not only alienated from policy and decision making, and the means of changing services, but also lose considerable autonomy in the day-to-day decision making of their practice.

Using this type of model, services become more fragmented, intensified and specialist (Fabricant and Burghardt, 1992). Professional practice therefore becomes programme based, and skills and knowledge are potentially conceptualised in relation to specific services, rather than in terms of more generic professional orientations.

Global economic changes are correlated with the culture of what is termed 'economic rationalism' in Australia (managerialism in the UK (Payne, 2009)). In simple terms, economic rationalism is based on the belief that there should be minimal regulation of economic activity and that in such a climate the most efficient organisations will flourish because they will be the most competitive. In this type of 'survival of the fittest' arrangement, it is argued that the market selects for excellence but is also just (Carroll, 1992: 7–8). 'Excellence, efficiency and effectiveness' are therefore key terms in an economic rationalist paradigm.

Economic rationalism is associated with managerialist culture (Howe, 1986), which Ingersoll and Adams (1986) claim involves three core components: work processes can be rationalised (broken into constituent parts and thereby controlled); the means for attaining organisational objectives take priority over the objectives themselves (objectives may become lost or forgotten); efficiency and predictability take precedence over any other considerations.

In Britain, similar policies have given rise to what is termed the 'enterprise culture' (Cannan, 1994), seen as an alternative to a culture of dependence, fostered under the welfare state. Alternatively, the enterprise culture: 'denotes a self characterised by autonomy, responsibility, initiative, self-reliance, independence and willingness to take risks, to "go for it", see opportunities, and take responsibility for one's own actions . . . it is individualistic, masculine and voluntaristic' (Cannan, 1994: 7).

Ironically, as Jordan (1998) argues, this new politics of welfare ignores the fact that the welfare of its citizens is dependent on global markets. Instead, the 'third way' of New Labour administrations emphasises that efficiency and justice can be reconciled by social institutions within nation states. Jordan (2009) has recently extended his analysis, commenting on how the new 'contract' culture potentially undermines social work's culture of valuing relationships and well being. In an ironic twist, the new (2010) Tory ('coalition') government in the UK has put a new spin on community relations with its exhortations about the 'Big Society', whereby individuals are encouraged to take more responsibilities for the welfare of each other through community and voluntary involvement. Interestingly such policies and rhetoric have been criticised as a way of masking severely reduced government spending. However it is also another good example of how globalisation brings a mixed bag of changes.

TECHNOLOGICAL ASPECTS

Changes in information and communication technologies have revolutionised the contexts in which professionals operate. The plethora of new technologies available now means there are a multitude of new ways in which everyday life and relations can be conducted. There are mixed views on whether such technologies present an advantage for social work practitioners. Steyaert and Gould (2009) observe that social workers seem reluctant to embrace the opportunities afforded, and have tended to critique the effect technology can have on social work practice. For example, Parton (2008) argues that social work is changing from a 'social' perspective to a more 'informational' culture.

Social workers also decry the possibilities for managerial control which are afforded by new technologies. For example, Hough (1994) argues that technological advances have fed into managerial powers, in that managers are better able to monitor workers' performance, either through direct surveillance or through more efficient data collection methods. Uttley (1994) echoes the fears of many, in seeing the potential for machines, particularly computers, to appropriate the skills of professionals. Technology, in these senses, is a distinct threat to professional expertise and autonomy. At the very least, if technology does not result in the expropriation of professional work, professionals who cannot use technology will be vulnerable.

Another argument against technological development is that in broad terms it may be said that new inequalities have been created, as the 'digital divide' separates those who can afford (or have access to) new technologies (Harrison and Melville, 2010), potentially creating new forms of exclusion. On the other hand, communication technologies may also provide new forms of inclusion, such as advances in distance education for rural and isolated populations (Steyaert, 2005).

Continuing on this more positive note, advances in communication and information technologies also open up new avenues for the provision of services and allow better access to previously isolated people more generally (albeit still only for those who have access to the technologies). Expertise and knowledge can be shared across the boundaries of geography and culture. Better standards of service provision are possible. As well, the potential to create new communities, based on the electronic sharing of information and experience, is exciting, not least for the promise of reducing social isolation.

As ideas of space and distance change, our ideas about access also change. There is potential for both new 'advantaged' and 'disadvantaged' groups to be created, as new types of access for some simultaneously create new barriers for others.

Similar possibilities apply in relation to the organisation of services. Some may become more 'centralised' as possibilities for the electronic delivery of information increase. For instance, many services may provide telephone information or counselling from one centre in a large country. This may result in a decrease of staff in smaller regions. So while telephone access is increased for some people, face-to-face services may be reduced for others.

The nature of professional expertise and the relationships between professionals and service users will necessarily change as a result of these sorts of developments. How professionals engage with and use technology to enhance delivery of services is a crucial issue, as is the question of how new technologies can be used in inclusive, rather than exclusive, ways.

THEORETICAL ASPECTS

In discussing globalisation, most social policy analysts have focused on the economic aspects, and thereby tended to emphasise the deleterious effects (Pugh and Gould, 2000; Midgley, 2001: 26). Yet it is equally important to examine the concomitant changes in thinking, often loosely labelled as 'postmodern'. In fact social theorists have tended to characterise the current age as 'postmodern', and postmodern theorising has thus been used to understand the vast amount of social and economic change taking place (Healy and Fook, 1994; Parton, 1994; Fawcett, 2009). The main proposition is that the welfare state, and associated notions of government intervention and responsibility for the public good, are features of 'modernist' thinking. They can be seen as ideals which are part of a modernist valuing of generalisable and unified ideas of the progressive 'good'. By contrast, in postmodern times, the attainability of these totalising ideals and structures is questioned, and we recognise that knowledge and ways of organising are fragmented. In addition, there is a recognition that global economies and technologies have changed the traditional modernist ideas of the 'nation-state'. Globalisation and technology are thus responsible for fragmentation and the associated emergence of different cultural identities.

In postmodern thinking, with the breakdown of organising structures, there is also a breakdown of hierarchies, so that traditional divisions between elite and lower status groups are questioned. From this point of view, the authority and dominance of the professional practitioner is questioned, as consumer and lay perspectives become relatively better valued.

In line with this way of thinking, traditional rationalist ways of knowing are also questioned. The object of such 'scientistic' thinking is to produce, in a deductive manner, generalisable, unassailable and unified knowledge which is researched in an objective fashion. The idea of professional expertise, based upon and legitimised by a specialist set of elite knowledge, arrived at through rationalist means, is therefore a modernist idea. In postmodern terms, there is a move to recognise the knowledge derived from the on-the-ground work of the practitioner, rather than the elite, distanced researcher.

The postmodern recognition of multiple ways of knowing and constructing meaning therefore places an emphasis on diversity – both in accepting that there are many different perspectives, but also in validating perspectives which are relatively unknown or undervalued. In this sense, it is the diverse perspectives and experiences of the 'ordinary' person or group who has not previously claimed privileged status, which gain recognition in a postmodern age.

This discussion of changes in thinking needs to also incorporate the associated ideas of 'uncertainty' and 'risk' (Fook, 2007).

POLITICAL, SOCIAL AND CULTURAL RAMIFICATIONS

These economic and technological changes, and the related changes in thinking, have of course been paralleled by changes in these other aspects of our global world. On a world scale the fragmentation of national organising structures has led to geopolitical changes resulting in massive displacements of populations, and even wars (Hoogeveldt, 2009). The resultant breakdown of community structures adds to the problem of how such fragmentation is to be addressed (Dominelli, 2009). The problem of refugees, of what global responsibility should be taken in local affairs which have resulted from global changes, is of extreme concern. Issues of race, ethnic identity, how we accommodate any difference with more fluid structures, become paramount.

In a postcolonial world, indigenous issues also take on new importance. How is reparation made to colonised populations, and how are these groups accommodated fruitfully in cultures and structures which are not of their making? These questions are part of the broader issue of how to create societies that nurture and celebrate difference without the conflict, tensions and violence which could result.

In a postcolonial world, postcolonial ways of understanding and appreciating relations between ex-colonial countries and colonising countries, as well as how identities have been constructed, become important. To quote Harrison and Melville (2010: 18): 'postcolonialism refers to a broad range of critical scholarship that seeks to rewrite colonial relations in order to offer alternative insights into the complexity of these relationships in both their historical and continuing forms'. The work of Edward Said is informative (1978, 1993, 1995) with his analysis of how colonising 'white' populations developed a concept of 'orientalism' which effectively categorised, devalued and inferiorised the cultures and people of the colonised groups. Such frameworks become part of a postcolonial approach to understanding and studying identities. In this sense, identity politics needs to be integrated into our thinking as an important approach to empowerment and the achievement of inclusion.

Another important aspect of postcolonial ways of thinking about race, ethnicity and identity is the study of whiteness. This is based on the idea that in order to understand how disadvantage is created, there is a need to also understand how advantage is created. It is therefore vital to include a focus on privilege, and how it is constructed and maintained against categories of non-privilege. Yee (2005) makes this point clearly in relation to the study of race and racism in social work.

The idea of social exclusion is of growing importance in the postmodern world. Powell (2001: 91) describes social exclusion as originating from the idea of poverty arising from a more divided society. The poor are not able to exercise their full rights as social, cultural and political citizens. Global changes create different forms of exclusions, ironically at a time when the inclusion of difference is becoming valued. Much has been written, for instance, about how new economic practices not only accentuate the position of the existing poor (for instance, by creating long-term unemployed groups), but create new classes of poor as well (younger unemployed) (Leonard, 1997: 131–2). The disparities between developed and developing economies are becoming more pronounced, incorporating new forms of cultural dominations. The idea of cultural and social injustice (Fraser in Powell, 2001: 92) illustrates these new kinds of exclusions:

- *Cultural domination* – some people are excluded because they are subjected to ways of inter-preting or communicating which originate from a culture which is not their own, and which may be alien or hostile to them.
- *Non-recognition* – some people are excluded because they are effectively rendered invisible by the dominant cultural practices.
- *Cultural disrespect* – some people are excluded because they are routinely devalued by the stere-otyping of public representations or everyday interactions within the dominant cultural context.

Social exclusion and inclusion therefore become much more than issues of poverty, referring also to the many ways in which 'difference' is excluded from mainstream opportunities and experiences.

Exercise

Think about who you are, and the sort of person you see yourself as. How do you think globalisation has affected your life chances? It may be interesting to compare your own experiences of getting employment with, say, that of your parents or your own children. Does globalisation help explain some of the differences?

THE CRITICAL CHALLENGES FOR SOCIAL WORK

What is particularly interesting about our foregoing analysis of postmodernism is that it does not function as a totalising analysis. It points up many types of contradictions in the current state of affairs. For instance, globalisation can be seen as responsible for greater unifying and compressing of differences on the one hand, and on the other for a greater social fragmentation. It creates new exclusions at the same time as it opens up possibilities for differences. Even in the more immediate field of professional practice, there are clear tensions between increasing managerial 'scientistic' regulation and a growing culture which recognises more personal and holistic ways of understanding experience.

How do we reconcile and integrate these tensions in a meaningful way? These are the sorts of challenges which a postmodern understanding of our global world poses. What are the specific issues for social work inherent in these challenges?

Exercise

Given our foregoing outline and discussion of the influence of globalisation on our current world, how reasonable do you think it is to try to find a 'universal' social work? What might be some of the issues involved in trying to do this?

CHALLENGES TO THE PROFESSION

As we discussed earlier, the autonomy of all professionals is challenged in the current context. Increased managerialism and changed funding arrangements effectively place more control of professional practice within the hands of managers or bureaucrats. Not only are types of practices more controlled, but the ways in which practice is defined are also more controlled from outside. Add to this the increased postmodern value on 'lay' views and rights and the relatively elite position of professional knowledge is also under siege.

In summary, the professions of today operate in a context which potentially undercuts the assumptions upon which much of their ethos are based. Professions are a feature of modernist times. They are based on notions of the common good and unified, identifiable disciplines, or separate and clear bodies of knowledge which define them. Members are socialised and accepted into a tight professional community.

Professions in this sense are an elite group, trusted to practise autonomously because of the specialist nature of their expertise and knowledge. Professional power is exercised because of the ability to claim expert knowledge, and to maintain tight controls over who is able to gain access to it (Leonard, 1997: 170). According to Uttley, professions also have a kind of pact with the state, in that many depend on state patronage to maintain elite positions. In this sense professionals are by their nature conservative, socialised to comply with employing organisations (1994: 191).

We can summarise the current position of professionals as follows:

- Professional skill and knowledge is devalued.
- Professional skill and knowledge is disaggregated and decontextualised so it can be measured and evaluated.
- Professional knowledge is represented in terms *other than* the professionals' own; i.e. it is represented in terms of managerial, rather than professional discourse.
- Professional autonomy and control are lessened; professionals are increasingly distanced from sources of policy and decision making.
- Professional identities are undermined and professional boundaries are weakened.
- Jobs are represented in fragmented skill or programme based terms, rather than in holistic professional terms.
- Domain boundaries between professional groupings are less clear, as discourse shifts to aggregations of skills for specific programmes, rather than orientations of value bases and approaches.
- Competition between different professional groups potentially increases as each struggles for territory and ascendancy.

SUMMARY

The current challenge (and irony) for professionals is that the very state which legitimates them is now effectively eroding their position. Simultaneously, the consumer population whose allegiance is integral to sustaining their position is questioning the legitimacy of their expertise.

For social workers, these issues are perhaps more poignant than for many other professionals. For instance, social workers in much of the Western world rely strongly upon either state legitimation or consumer need. Social workers on the one hand represent the 'conscience' of the state, but on the other like to see themselves as representing the interests of the individual. In particular the social justice value base of social work is often regarded as a defining feature of the profession. In addition, for social workers the whole idea of professionalism is contested territory. On the one hand it is seen as a route to better social recognition and therefore better service provision. On the other it is seen as a grab for power at the expense of service users. So it has never been clear whether it is a good thing to foster and develop a professional social work identity. Yet current economic conditions create the situation in which a weak professional identity might mean the demise of the profession.

Appreciation of these challenges has given rise to the idea of the 'new professionalism' (Leicht and Fennell, 2001) which is essentially a more accountable professionalism, committed to ongoing self-evaluation and transparency. This type of stance may also need to involve new ways of generating professional knowledge that is relevant to different and changing contexts.

An associated movement is the call for increased service user involvement and empowerment. In the UK in particular, the involvement of service users in social work education and research is becoming increasingly important (Dominelli, 2009; Charnley et al., 2009). In turn, the call for service user involvement can also be associated with more interest in partnership working, which extends from working in partnership with service users, to working with other professional groups (Lymbery and Millward, 2000). In this way, interprofessional working is very high on the current UK agenda, especially with more recent calls for integrated children's services as a response to high profile reviews of child death cases.

LABOUR MARKET

How do these current conditions actually play out in terms of labour market opportunities for social workers? The challenges to professional autonomy and identity posed by the changing economic climate mean that jobs are characterised in new and fragmented ways. They are more short term and it is likely that in the normal course of a career a person will hold a number of different jobs (Raber, 1996). Positions that once required particular professional qualifications may now draw from a multiple array of professional qualifications. Specific qualifications may not be so closely tied to specific employment destinations, which indicates a need to prepare for a range of occupational settings (DEET, 1995: 96). Alternatively, jobs may not be characterised in professional terms at all. For example, Clarke suggests that in his vision for social services of the future in Britain, the job title 'social worker' will not exist (1996: 56).

There may also be a downgrading of professional qualifications, in that graduates may seek and gain employment which is below their skill level. For example, some Australian research (Hawkins et al., 2000) indicates that although social workers are still maintaining good levels of employment, many of their positions are not designated as 'social worker'. Furthermore, the increasing number of jobs available in Australia does not always require social work levels of qualifications (MacDonald, 1999). This may be part of a broader trend, a result of a general increase in skill level (DEET, 1995).

In the UK, Parton (1998: 80) characterises the changing role of social workers: 'No longer are social workers constituted as caseworkers, drawing on their therapeutic skills in human relationships, but as case managers who assess need and risk and operationalise packages of care in an individualised way.' Four elements are identified:

- increased specialisation re. population groups;
- separation of assessment and care management from direct service provision;
- division of roles – professionally qualified staff focus on assessment and care management, other services are provided by unqualified staff;
- attempts to shift power between service user and professional.

It is also crucial to note that the workplace itself has become more busy and stressful. Carniol (2010: 7) quotes from the findings of a Canadian study of social service employees:

Increased workloads, having to do more with less, and service users who are experiencing more intense, multi-dimensional challenges to their social, psychological and economic survival – all contribute significantly to making social service employment extremely demanding and sometimes very dispiriting.

BROADER SOCIAL AND CULTURAL CONTRIBUTIONS

Social workers are both professionals and employees. We are also citizens, community participants in global and local contexts. How, as professionals, employees, citizens and community members, do we meet the broader challenges inherent in the contexts in which we live?

These are the challenges of participating in the creation of a social service system and a society in which differences are valued and integrated, yet one in which social justice is furthered and domination resisted. How do we work, live and practise so that new inclusions are created and old exclusions are demolished? How do we uphold the interests of competing groups in climates which foster tensions and contradictions? How do we forge new concepts of responsibilities at global and local levels? Last, the age-old question for social work: how do we work against poverty in local situations, when the seeds of it are sown at global levels?

What kinds of things do we need to do on daily levels in our different jobs to address these issues? How do we need to conceptualise our practice and our roles and identities in order to take our place as responsible participants in our communities and society? These are the questions which encapsulate the current challenges for us as social workers.

THE CRITICAL POSSIBILITIES

I end this chapter with a broad overview of the major types of possibilities which the foregoing analysis indicates. If we frame the challenges in these terms, it is possible to conceptualise some broad ways in which we might begin to approach our practice.

CHANGING VIEWS OF PROFESSIONAL PRACTICE AND PROFESSIONALISM

We need to change the ways in which we conceptualise our skills. In broad terms I would term this an emphasis on context, on the ability to transfer knowledge and expertise successfully so that it is applicable in different settings.

The work of Reich (1991) is useful in illustrating an alternative framework of this type. In Reich's framework there are three broad categories of workers: routine production workers, in-person service workers and symbolic analysts. Routine workers are those involved in simple routine and repetitive work. They include blue-collar workers and clerical workers. The work of this group is vulnerable to replacement by technological innovation and therefore also vulnerable to global competition. In-person service workers perform repetitive tasks which must be delivered person to person. Symbolic analysts work with information in solving problems and strategic decision making. The category includes managers and professionals.

Reich's framework is interesting because it reconceptualises occupations on the basis of process skills (that is, the way products are organised or delivered), rather than in terms of more domain-specific categories (work setting or type of skill involved), as in more traditional conceptions. His framework also reconceptualises the work of the professional in the twenty-first century. In the old economy, the professional person was one who practised from a particular body of knowledge and from a particular value system involving specialist expertise. This is threatened in the new economy, where specialist knowledge is easily accessible to all who have access to the new information technology. What becomes crucial in differentiating professionals from others is the ability to use information in particular settings. Professionalism, therefore, if it is to be viable in the new economy, must be reconceptualised as the ability to produce knowledge in ways that are applicable to specific settings. Reich notes that communication skills are one of the essential sets of skills in transmitting knowledge in different situations.

The implications of this framework for social work are obvious. Social workers are well grounded in (and often come with a personal history of) interpersonal relations and communication. They are also well attuned to practising within the vagaries of different contexts, being one of the few professions based on knowledge of the 'person-in-situation' (Hamilton, 1951).

We may also need to revisit and recreate our identity as social workers, constantly redeveloping how our value base is expressed and practised within different settings. This may mean understanding and incorporating different perspectives into the way we communicate about ourselves and the sorts of things we can offer to our service users, managers, colleagues and community members. As critical social workers we need constantly to translate and communicate about what the values and goals of social justice mean to different people and groups.

INCLUSIVITY

As social workers we have always had a responsibility to represent the interests and perspectives of marginal and excluded people. A postmodern analysis of our global context makes this principle even more imperative. An appreciation of the politics of identity and difference making is crucial to understanding and improving our practice. This includes an ability to use and incorporate different cultural ways of knowing and being. Our ways of practising and knowing about our work need to be inclusive of different methods and approaches. We may need to incorporate modes of working and technologies which are more congruent across local and national boundaries. Social development approaches may be more applicable than traditional clinical approaches. In addition, the idea of international social work (Midgley, 2001) takes on significance as we develop global perspectives in our practice.

COMPLEXITY AND CONTEXT

Globalisation is expressed in many different ways, in different contexts and at different levels. Our practice needs to be able to incorporate the contradictions and tensions which may exist between experiences for different groups. This involves an awareness of the possibilities for both inclusion and exclusion of any one act or situation and an ability to practise to minimise the exclusionary effects.

In addition, understanding context involves understanding how experiences, ideas and practices are very much an artefact of the context in which they are developed and played out. For social workers, this includes applying this understanding to their own work, as well as that of the people with whom they work. The whole principle of contextuality therefore becomes integral to the work of social workers in a global era.

REDEVELOPING CRITICAL SOCIAL WORK

Last, a postmodern and global analysis, by pointing up the complexities and contradictions of experience, indicates that we need to be able continually to redevelop our critical practice so that it is relevant and responsive to both global and local contexts. We need, therefore, to be prepared continually to revise our understandings of power and its expression, our place and role in this, and our responsibilities to the possibilities it opens up. In this book these main possibilities for critical practice underlie the following chapters. The ideas and practices discussed in the book are designed to be responsive to, and to work effectively in, the changing contexts discussed in this chapter.

Globalisation also of course poses new challenges on a structural and material level. Critical social workers also need to be mindful of how different ways of collectivising may be necessary to challenge the ways global power operates on broader national and international levels.

Exercise

Choose one particular global issue that interests you (e.g. The problem of the fragmentation of professional expertise; or the need to challenge white privilege). How do you think you might go about working with this issue as:

- An individual social worker in a particular job;
- A member of the social work profession in your country;
- A member of the social work profession on an international scale.

Chapter summary

In this chapter we have outlined the main features of globalisation, in particular discussing the economic, technological, theoretical, and social, political and cultural implications for social work. This has raised a series of challenges for social work, with quite radical possibilities for the way it needs to be repositioned to meet these challenges.

In brief, globalisation is said to both 'compress' the world through greater accessibility in both travel and communication, but at the same time fragment it, by breaking down established barriers and boundaries. This is associated with a more exaggerated form of capitalism, resulting in more intense economic competition, and further resulting in greater gaps between rich and poor. In this climate power differentials shift, and the role and power of professionals is seriously undermined as the relative economic and social importance of professional autonomy becomes less valued. In addition, social fragmentation gives rise to more complex understandings of social difference and therefore social inclusion. When these trends are understood and addressed on global levels, new postcolonial ways of working with international differences must also be taken into account. Today's social workers must therefore meet challenges of risk and uncertainty in their everyday jobs, but also be mindful of how different contexts may influence their understanding and practice, and on a series of levels.

FURTHER READING

GLOBALISATION AND SOCIAL WORK

Dominelli, L. (ed.) (2009) *Revitalising Communities in a Globalising World*. Aldershot: Ashgate.

Good introduction to globalisation and also specific chapters on key aspects of globalisation.

Harrison, G. and Melville, R. (2010) *Rethinking Social Work in a Global World*. Basingstoke: Palgrave Macmillan.

Excellent introduction and coverage of all the main aspects of globalisation as they apply to social work.

Payne, M. and Askeland, G.A. (2008) *Globalisation and International Social Work*. Aldershot: Ashgate.

Excellent introduction to the concept of globalisation. Chapter 2 is an especially good discussion of postmodernism and postcolonialism.

OTHER ISSUES

Gray, M. and Fook, J. (2004) 'The quest for a universal social work: some issues and implications', *Social Work Education*, 23 (5): 625–44.

Illustrates some of the issues in trying to impose Western views of social work more universally.

Yee, J. (2005) 'Critical anti-racism praxis: the concept of whiteness implicated', in S. Hick, J. Fook and R. Pozzuto (eds), *Social Work: A Critical Turn*. Toronto: Thompson Edcuation Publishing. pp. 87–103.

Excellent introduction to the concept of whiteness.

Rossiter, R. (2005) 'Where in the world are we? More on the need for a social work response to global power', in S. Hick, J. Fook and R. Pozzuto (eds), *Social Work: A Critical Turn*, Toronto: Thompson Education Press. pp. 189–202.

Discussion of further challenges for social work in globalisation.

Fook, J. (2007) 'Uncertainty: the defining characteristic of social work?', in M. Lymbery and K. Postle (eds), *Social Work: A Companion to Learning*. London: Sage. pp. 30–9.

Good overview of concepts of uncertainty and risk and implications for reconceptualisation of some of the fundamentals of social work.

ACKNOWLEDGEMENTS

Some of the ideas in this chapter have been previously published in Fook, J., Ryan, M. and Hawkins, L. (2000) *Professional Expertise: Practice, Theory and Education for Working in Uncertainty*. London: Whiting and Birch and Fook, J. (2000a) 'Deconstructing and reconstructing professional expertise' in B. Fawcett, B. Featherstone, J. Fook and A. Rossiter (eds), *Practice and Research in Social Work*. London: Routledge. pp. 104–17.

PART 2

RETHINKING IDEAS

3

NEW WAYS OF KNOWING

As we discussed in Chapter 2, the broad changes associated with globalisation and postmodern thinking have significant implications for the way we understand and make sense of our world. In this chapter we look more closely at how these changes influence the way we think about knowledge and the way it is formed, influence our understandings of what it is to be professional and to practise in responsive and effective ways.

One of the very interesting challenges of postmodern and poststructural thinking is the way in which it makes us question not just what we know, but also how we know it. In this sense, this newer way of thinking is very different from more modernist or 'structural' ways of thinking in that modernist thinking tends to assume that there is an underlying 'structure' which explains the 'causes' of a phenomenon (Healy and Fook, 1994). Postmodern and poststructural ideas are in some ways more concerned with how and why we search for underlying causes or explanations, rather than what those causes might be, and whether one explanation is more accurate or better than another. In some ways they are theories of knowledge (epistemologies), rather than theories of being (ontologies). They are about different sorts of concerns. Yet on the other hand, 'knowing' is an integral part of 'being', so it is important to understand how what we know affects how we act and practise.

THE NATURE OF KNOWLEDGE AND KNOWLEDGE GENERATION

In modernist ways of thinking, knowledge is believed to be made up of sets of ideas which have attained some sort of objective status, usually built up through generations of scientific research. Legitimate knowledge is thus linear (built up through a progressive process) and cumulative (built upon preceding knowledge). Acceptable scientific knowledge is thus believed to be generalisable and timeless, applicable across different contexts.

SUMMARY

Postmodern and critical thinking challenge the idea of immutable scientific knowledge in a number of ways:

- by asking what constitutes 'acceptable' knowledge, and whether and why some forms of knowledge are valued over others;
- by focusing on how we know, as well as what we know;
- by drawing attention to different perspectives on what and how we know;
- by drawing attention to the perspective of the knower, and how it influences what is known and how it is known (reflexivity).

These questions are inextricably bound up with each other. What we know is influenced by the medium and processes of how we know it, and how we produce and communicate it. These are inevitably all influenced by who we are, and the contexts which influence how and what we know.

Exercise

For example, it is worth thinking about what I am writing here at this very moment, and what you are reading, here at this very moment.

- What makes what I am writing knowledge?
- Do *you* think it is 'knowledge'?
- How does the form it is written in influence the content of what I am saying?
- Would you think differently about this material if I told you I learnt it from my own experience, or if I copied it from another book written by someone like Foucault?
- How do you think I 'know' what I am writing here?
- Would you think differently about these ideas if you read them 5, 10 or 25 years ago?

The central debates, as we have mentioned in earlier chapters, revolve around issues of what counts as legitimate knowledge, and what and whose knowledge is privileged. It is of course assumed that legitimate knowledge is that produced through legitimate processes, and therefore the only true knowledge or 'facts' is that produced through scientific methods which are both valid and reliable. These methods assume that there is a separate empirical 'reality' waiting to be discovered, and that the making of knowledge simply involves the use of reputable methods in order to uncover new bits of this reality. Moreover, this knowledge can only be discovered by reputable people using reputable methods. So it is that acceptable knowledge is framed as knowledge created by acceptable (reputable) people using acceptable (reputable) methods. It is not hard to work out who these reputable people might be – usually the ones who have attained the social status of 'researcher'. When we think about the sorts of people who might normally make up such a group in Western societies (more likely to be white, middle class, middle aged and male) then we get a picture of whose perspectives dominate in the making of knowledge, and therefore whose knowledge it is which is likely to be seen as legitimate.

The form knowledge takes is also influenced by the way it is expressed and communicated. This is in turn influenced by issues of whose knowledge it is and in what way it was generated.

Exercise

It is worthwhile thinking about all the different ways in which the 'knowledge' communicated in a journal article, for instance, might have been conveyed, and whether this would have changed the nature of the knowledge being discussed.

Would you think differently about the ideas you are reading here if you read them in a book written by Jacques Derrida, or they were told to you by your ageing aunt?

There is in fact a whole range of different ways of seeing what knowledge is, how it is generated, how it is expressed and whose perspectives count. Postmodern thinking allows us first to be aware that these might exist and second to be aware of how and why they might or might not be prominent.

For instance, there are all kinds of different sorts of knowledge needed in relation to different sorts of settings. The settings in which only generalisable and tested theories are useful are in fact quite a minority. Most of the knowledge needed for day-to-day living probably does not fit the criteria for being scientific, yet most of us would swear by it. For instance, the great moral codes could not pass muster as scientific knowledge, yet most of us would never question them. How do we arrive at such knowledge? Usually through a variety of methods, including cultural inheritance. Again, this is not knowledge we would give up lightly, just because it was not scientifically proven.

Different perspectives on knowledge might count differentially according to circumstance and the dictates of context. Changes in fashion and trends in thinking mean that different knowledge will be seen as important at different times. Often quite contradictory knowledge will supersede an established set of thinking. For instance, this is graphically illustrated in relation to the current concerns of Australian Aborigines. It was accepted practice, some decades ago, that Aboriginal children be removed from their families and communities and raised on missions. Now, however, this practice is widely deplored and the need for reconciliation towards this generation of 'stolen children' is regarded as a crucial aspect of Australia's development as an inclusive society.

Also, there are many ways of generating different kinds of knowledge. For instance, you may pick up entirely different ideas about people from observing them at home, as opposed to interviewing them in your office. As well, if you conducted an experiment with family members you might induce entirely different kinds of behaviour. Not the least of these might be some quirky reactions to the experiment itself, a result of the family's reaction to being experimented upon, rather than a reflection of any of their inherent characteristics (Lincoln and Guba, 1985). The many different ways in which you as the social worker interact with people will of course elicit potentially different kinds of behaviour and responses from them. The mode of generating the knowledge and how it is communicated becomes an important part of the knowledge itself. For example, *Women's Ways of Knowing*, the landmark study by Belenky et al. (1986) of how women learn in tertiary education, showed that the way knowledge is presented can affect the way in which people engage with it. Women may feel intimidated by and excluded from the rationalist and distanced ways in which knowledge is formulated in traditional educational settings.

The Belenky study points up that the perspective of the knower will influence not only what type of knowledge is generated and how it is interpreted, but also how it is communicated. Some forms of communication sit more easily with some people and such forms are often culture and context bound as well.

Exercise

Compare the following two passages.

'I find postmodern ideas exciting because they enable me to see how I can act in my immediate situation. They open up possibilities for my practice. I no longer feel a "slave" to theory.'

'The exciting promise of postmodernism is that practitioners are enabled to see what actions may be taken in the immediate situation. Postmodernism opens up possibilities for practice. Theory may potentially "liberate" practitioners, rather than "enslaving" them to a rigid commitment.'

How do you react to each? How/what does each passage communicate about the writer, post-modernism, theory and the practitioner, and how do they relate to each other?

There is a lot of debate about whether the first person active tense (in which the first passage is written) should be used in academic writing, as opposed to third person passive tense (in which the second passage is written). The first passage conveys a sense of the person speaking being personally engaged with postmodern ideas, and active in relation to them. The person is taking responsibility for how she or he is using theory. The second passage implies that post-modern ideas and theory are active in their own right. They act upon practitioners, who are portrayed as passive in the process. It can be argued that using a third person passive tense serves to distance people from the awareness that they can participate in creating ideas and therefore might be used as a tool in knowledge gatekeeping (Webb, 1992).

PROFESSIONAL KNOWLEDGE AND POWER

Since postmodern thinkers question whose knowledge is legitimate and what forms for generating and expressing it are privileged, then they also implicitly question the privilege of professional knowledge. As we said earlier, the professions are to some extent legitimated and maintained through their assumption of specialist knowledge, which is generated and disseminated by them (Fook, 2000a). By controlling the processes of what knowledge counts as professional knowledge, how it is made and how it is communicated, professions maintain their social position. They maintain this control by safeguarding the processes by which novices enter a profession and become eligible for their membership, the sorts of knowledge which are taught to these people through control of course curricula and standards, and what knowledge is transmitted to members of their ranks through professional journals and so forth. By and large, these controls depend on there being a specialist knowledge to safeguard and control, which through these very processes itself becomes defined as specialist. Thus it is that by questioning the supremacy of professional knowledge we significantly undermine the profession's claims to dominance.

The idea of a connection between knowledge and power is a postmodern one, in that it is argued that whatever group controls the way things are seen in some ways also has the power to control the way things are. Whoever's interpretation gets accepted will doubtless control how the idea is enacted. We will discuss these issues in more depth in Chapter 5 through our coverage of the idea of discourse.

Professionals therefore stand to lose quite a bit of power if alternative perspectives are accepted, so a challenge to the exclusive knowledge of professionals is a direct challenge to their power base. Similarly, a challenge to the ways in which professional knowledge is traditionally generated and expressed challenges professional power. These are important questions for the social work profession, which in many ways likes to 'have it both ways': to protect professional boundaries and at the same time to be open to other perspectives.

So who are the legitimate generators of knowledge and whose knowledge is more important, in a profession which prides itself on being closely aligned with its service users (themselves marginal and disenfranchised groups)? What ways of knowing will at the same time legitimate the profession but also speak effectively for and to groups whose culture is radically different from the world of professionals? How is knowledge to be communicated effectively across the very different contexts of researchers, professionals, practitioners and service users?

THEORY AND PRACTICE

Similar dilemmas arise in relation to theory and practice. The separate worlds of theory and practice have been built in this way in line with the hierarchical split between professionals and service users and researchers and practitioners. Constructing theory and practice as separate entities, and privileging one over the other, serves to preserve a dominance of researcher over practitioner views and professional over service user perspectives.

Understood in this way, it therefore becomes important in postmodern thinking to question this rigid and hierarchical division between theory and practice. There are in fact many different kinds of theories, practices, and ways of theorising (making meaning of) practice. It is an important aspect of postmodern thinking to recognise the many different ways of understanding theories and making meaning of practices, so that we can be *inclusionary* (Fook, 2000b) in the way in which we understand the relationship between theory and practice.

Theories can vary from a single concept or idea to a major set of interrelated concepts. Miles and Huberman (1994: 434) note at least five kinds of theory, including models, maps and grand theories. Theories can also vary in the type of generalisability they offer (Gilgun, 1994: 122): one may be more a 'bottom-up' test of relevance and the other more a 'top-down' test of applicability. One illuminates, the other helps predict. Both are crucial to any professional practice.

Practices can also be understood in myriad ways, as can how theories and practices relate to each other. Practice can be understood as holistic experience, or as a set of identifiable techniques and skills. It will be more or less identifiable, more or less observable, more or less concrete. Theories of different types may be embedded in practice, or may sit above it in a guiding fashion. Theories may be modified in line with practice and created as practice is enacted. The two processes may take place in conjunction (as we constantly make sense of situations as we encounter them and act within them), or theorising may take place after a practice event. As well, further theorising (or an attempt to make meaning) may continue well after an event and produce new and different ways of understanding what happened.

What is important to remember is that the relationship between theory and practice is a much more complex and intermingled one than a simple split construction of them suggests. This more complex understanding is crucial to a critical approach to practice in social work.

More recently there have been shifts towards focusing more on practice and in particular the importance of reflective judgement in professional practice (Polkinghorne, 2004). Such discussions also underpin the move towards emphasising the alternative conceptualisations of professional practice. As a result, there are also reciprocal moves towards reconceptualising theory. In later sections we will focus in more detail on reflection and reflective approaches. Suffice it to say here that alternative understandings of theory are also important.

In relation to this, some social scientists (Flyvberg, 2001: 3–5; Polkinghorne, 2004) have been returning to Aristotle's breakdown of three types of intellectual virtues (and therefore three differing types of knowledge) involved in these: namely, episteme, techne and phronesis. This breakdown helps to illustrate the differences between theory (episteme) and practice (techne) by posing a third type of knowledge (phronesis). In brief, episteme refers to the type of 'scientific' knowledge we would traditionally equate with theory – it is generalisable, universal, precise and explanatory, and allows us to reason in a deductive manner. Techne refers to the practical knowledge which is involved in making or crafting artefacts, or producing objects. Phronesis is a type of knowledge that allows practical or wise reasoning, in order to act for the good (praxis) *in a particular context*. Phronesis therefore involves a value and a context element. Both Flyvberg and Polkinghorne argue that a concept of phronesis is necessary to our contemporary understandings of knowledge. Flyvberg argues that it is needed as the basis of a new approach to research in the social sciences, and that to seek to produce epistemic type knowledge or theory is both impossible and undesirable in the social sciences. Polkinghorne argues that an appreciation of professional knowledge or theory as phronetic is the most appropriate way to understand the practice of professionals.

I believe that the concept of phronesis is one useful way to conceptualise an approach to knowledge for the critical social worker in a postmodern age. It is in fact about applying knowledge in a reasoned way, based on values and in relation to context.

CRITICAL REFLECTION

With this in mind, how are we to make sense of this conglomeration of more complicated thinking about knowledge, theory, practice and professional power which is suggested by a postmodern critical approach? How will this more complicated conceptualisation actually assist us in our work as social work practitioners?

The idea of critical reflection is one such approach which can assist us in subjecting our practice to a more critical gaze, at the same time allowing us to integrate our theory and practice in creative and complex ways. Let us examine the concept in more detail by first looking at the reflective approach, then critical perspectives, and how they underpin a critical reflective orientation.

ORIGINS OF THE REFLECTIVE APPROACH

The early development of the reflective approach to education is credited to Argyris and Schön (1976) and has been further developed by Schön (1983, 1987). They argued that there was a crisis in the professions, because the formal theories used by professionals often proved inadequate to the needs of everyday practice. They therefore questioned the usefulness of traditional approaches to knowledge building for professionals, since there often appears to be a large gap between what professionals are taught in formal settings and what they 'do' in practice. The approach is therefore based upon an alternative paradigm to the traditional conceptions about how professionals use and develop knowledge about practice. Traditional approaches (what we would term 'modernist') assume an empirical approach to knowledge generation and use, in that knowledge (and theory) are presumed to be generated 'outside' the practitioner (that is, from an objective standpoint). Practitioners then use this generalised theory, developed through systematic (and often scientific) methods, in a deductive ('top-down') way, to make decisions about action.

The reflective approach recognises that there is another type of theory; these are the ideas which are often implicit in the way professionals act. These ideas may or may not be congruent with the theory they believe themselves to be acting upon, and the practitioner may be more or less aware of them. By becoming aware of these implicit ideas, and by consciously examining and developing them, the practitioner is actually engaged in a process of developing their own practice theory directly from their own practice experience – a 'bottom-up' type of process.

This emphasis on the way theory is developed in use draws attention to the creative and contextual way in which knowledge is generated – it often has to be created in spontaneous response to changing (and often unpredictable) situations. The knowledge or theory created in this way often involves a degree of intuition, because practitioners may be reacting almost unconsciously to barely articulated cues or patterns. It may also involve a degree of artistic ability, in that the practitioner may apply or express their knowledge and experience in ingenious, highly individualised or original ways, in order to suit the situation at hand.

Although early formulations of the reflective approach did not draw explicitly on what we have been discussing, as some of the other alternative approaches to knowledge building, they share many common aspects.

SIMILARITIES BETWEEN THE REFLECTIVE APPROACH, FEMINISM AND POSTMODERNISM

There are two common ideas crucial to reflective, feminist and postmodern thinking about knowledge. The first is that knowledge, and how we know it, is contextually based (situated). The second is that this knowledge is also mediated through the perspective of the knower (is subjective). Expanding on these two points, we find that there are a number of related ideas which are also common to the three perspectives:

SUMMARY

- an inductive approach to theory building;
- a recognition of the use and importance of intuition and artistry in professional practice;
- the importance of context and interpretation;
- the importance of a holistic perspective;
- non-positivist and experiential approaches.

Putting these together, we can say that reflective practitioners are those who can put themselves into the context of the situation and can factor this understanding into the ways in which they practise. This ongoing process of reflection allows for the practitioners to develop their theory directly from their own experience. It also allows them to practise in a way which is 'situated' in the specific context. It allows them to take a holistic perspective, because they must take into account all factors which impinge on the situation at any one time, so that they might accurately interpret their practice relative to its context. In this holistic sense, the practitioner uses a range of skills and perspectives to respond to the particular situation as a whole. (This is different from the more traditional social work 'methods' approach, where predetermined decisions about what skills are appropriate for particular settings or problem types often guide practice.)

WHAT IS A CRITICAL REFLECTIVE APPROACH TO PRACTICE?

How do these ideas fit with the postmodern and critical approach to social work which we discussed earlier?

In Chapter 1 we summarised a postmodern and critical approach to social work practice as the following:

A postmodern and critical social work practice is primarily concerned with practising in ways which further a society without domination, exploitation and oppression. It will focus both on how structures dominate, but also on how people construct and are constructed by changing social structures and relations, recognising that there may be multiple and diverse constructions of ostensibly similar situations. Such an understanding of social relations and structures can be used to disrupt dominant understandings and structures, and as a basis for changing these so that they are more inclusive of different interest groups.

Knowledge to inform this understanding is derived in different ways. Empirical knowledge is needed in order to understand how material structures shape lives. Processes of self-reflection are crucial in ensuring that dominant structures and relations are challenged in the way they are implicitly enacted in everyday life. Communication and dialogue are necessary in order to ensure that diverse perspectives are included in forging new and inclusive ways **of living**. Thus, in a postmodern and critical social work both the kinds of social changes that are sought, and the ways in which they are enacted, are important. Outcome and process are integral to each other.

The key principles of this approach are as follows:

- it challenges domination in three areas: external structures, social relations and personal constructions;
- it recognises multiple and diverse constructions;
- this recognition potentially disrupts dominant constructions;
- knowledge is constructed inclusively, through both empirical and reflexive processes;
- communication and dialogue are important processes in negotiating inclusive structures and relations.

From a critical and postmodern perspective then, the reflective practitioner engages with knowledge that is obtained empirically and through reflection in a way that recognises the processes by which this knowledge (and thus power structures and relations) is maintained. Through deconstructing this knowledge, and unearthing multiple constructions, they are able further to develop (reconstruct) their own practice in inclusive, artistic and intuitive ways which are responsive to the changing (uncertain, unpredictable and fragmented) contexts in which they work; and in ways which can challenge existing power relations and structures.

Being reflective and being critically reflective share important similarities. Both involve a recognition of how we, as knowers, participate in creating and generating the knowledge we use, and an appreciation of how knowledge is therefore contingent upon the holistic context in which it is created. A reflective stance points up the many and diverse perspectives which can be taken on knowledge itself, and the shaping of that knowledge. The important difference is that critical reflection places emphasis and importance on an understanding of how a reflective stance uncovers power relations, and how structures of domination are created and maintained. A purely reflective stance holds the potential for any type of change, including maintenance of existing power relations. A critical reflective approach holds the potential for emancipatory practices (Fook, 1999a) in that it first questions and disrupts dominant structures and relations and lays the ground for change.

PROCESSES OF CRITICAL REFLECTION

We have noted the similarities between a reflective approach and postmodern and critical ways of thinking. There are therefore similarities between the processes which might be used to analyse thinking and practices from each of these perspectives. Several writers have noted how deconstructive techniques are similar to reflective processes (e.g. Francis, 1997; Rossiter, 1996). It is therefore possible to draw up some guidelines for critical reflection based on the two traditions. In the third part of the book we will outline these in much more detail, and illustrate how they might be used directly in practice. Here I will simply give a broad outline of the process.

From a postmodern point of view, all practice or experience can be seen as a 'story', in that it is the speaker's version or perspective on what happened, which might change over time, or according to the context in which the person is speaking. In this sense, each person's story or narrative can be seen as 'text' (Taylor and White, 2000) which can be analysed (similar to the way in which a qualitative researcher might analyse an interview transcript or a reader might interpret a piece of fiction). It is therefore possible to subject this piece of 'text' to reflective analysis, whether or not it happens to be your own text or version of events. Diary records, for example, function in this way – they are an initial exercise in telling your own written story, but they also provide a written record which can be analysed at a later time and perhaps understood in different ways.

Deconstructive questions can be used to assist in reflecting upon written (or verbal) accounts later in time (or even at the same time), in a similar way to how deconstructive researchers might analyse 'texts' (Fook, 1996).

Exercise

For example, try writing up a short diary entry about an incident which happened to you today.

Notice how the process requires a revisiting of the incident you wish to reflect upon. Even in writing this up and retelling it, you are already engaging in a process of reflection. It is important to try to be aware of the choices or selections you make in how you word your experience, and about which aspects you decide to include or emphasise. When you reread the entry, you may find that some words or phrases strike you as odd, or that you wonder why you left some bits out. You are already engaging in a mild form of 'deconstruction'.

SUMMARY

Reflective questions can be designed to help you 'research' your experience, by uncovering the theory implicit in your actions and the construction of the situation. You can reread your practice record or diary entry, for example, looking for gaps, biases, themes and missing themes. In a way, to use a postmodern term, when you respond to such questions you are engaged in a process of 'deconstructing' your experience and the situation. When you try to rebuild your theory and practice, on the basis of what you have uncovered in the deconstructive process, you are then engaged in a process of 'reconstruction'. The process could therefore be summarised as follows:

1 Description of your practice and the situation (or context). (In postmodern terms, 'storying' or 'telling the narrative'.)
2 Reflective questioning, reflection-on-action (or deconstruction), focusing on issues of power and how notions of power are constructed.
3 Redeveloping practice and theory (reconstruction), particularly in relation to how power relations and structures can be changed to be more emancipatory.

The whole process is therefore an *inductive* process in which you are engaged in developing your own theory of practice from this particular piece of practice and situation. In Chapter 7 I will outline in much greater detail the critical reflective process of deconstruction and reconstruction as it applies specifically to practice.

REFLEXIVITY, REFLECTIVE PRACTICE AND CONTEXTUALITY

We touched briefly on the notion of reflexivity earlier, and it is now important to address how the ideas of reflectivity and reflexivity relate to each other. On one level there is a simple answer to this – the two ideas seem to have emerged from different discourses. Reflectivity seems to have emerged from professional practitioner and educational discourse (e.g. Argyris and Schön, 1976). The idea of reflexivity comes more from social science researcher discourse, such as that of qualitative and ethnographic researchers. Reflectivity seems in this sense to refer more to a *process* of reflecting upon practice, whereas reflexivity in the latter sense refers more to a *stance* of being able to locate oneself in the picture, to appreciate how one's own self influences the research act (Fook, 1999b). Taken in this way, reflexivity is potentially more complex than being reflective (Taylor and White, 2000: 198), in that the potential for understanding the myriad ways in which one's own presence and perspective influence the knowledge and actions which are created is potentially more problematic than the simple search for implicit theory. However, a reflective process and a reflexive stance are not mutually exclusive and it is possible that the methods of *reflective* practice, used similarly to deconstructive methods, might aid a person in becoming more *reflexive* (Fook, 1999b).

In this book, I will use the terms interchangeably, assuming that reflective processes will be underpinned by a reflexive stance. In a developed critical practice, practitioners will be both reflective and reflexive, able to use a variety of methods to confront the ways in which their own backgrounds, embodiment, personalities and perspectives intermingle in holistic context.

It is also important to note how the concept of contextuality relates here. A contextual understanding of knowledge, theory and practice is an integral part of being both reflexive and reflective. To take a reflexive stance, you need to be able to appreciate how your own self and social position (i.e. your own subjective context) influences your thinking and actions. You also need such an analysis to be able to practice reflectively. An ability to identify and analyse the influence of context is therefore intertwined with the ability to reflect and be reflexive. The actual details of a contextual appreciation and analysis, and what they mean for practice, will be discussed later in the book.

Exercise

Think about who you are (as a person) reading this book now. What social position/s do you occupy? What social context are you in right now? (Think about both 'macro' (e.g. historical period) and 'micro' (e.g.what room you are in) contexts.) How do each of the above influence how you feel about and interpret what you are reading?

OTHER PERSPECTIVES ON CRITICAL REFLECTION

In this book, I have developed critical reflection mainly from a postmodern critical perspective. It is important to note, however, that there are many different ways of understanding, theorising and practising critical reflection (Fook et al., 2006). Because of its increasing popularity, new perspectives are being developed all the time. These include, for example, using Eastern philosophies (Humphrey, 2009). I have chosen not to develop critical reflection in more complex ways by adding more theoretical perspectives here, as the focus of this book is on postmodern and critical thinking and their application in social work. In other work I have done, I have developed a more integrated approach to critical reflection, which includes a variety of perspectives (see Fook and Gardner, 2007) under the rubric of learning from experience (Fook and Kellehear, 2010). It is simply important to bear in mind, at this point, that critical reflection is a potentially complex concept, and how it is practised will depend very much on how it is theorised. In this book, the postmodern critical approach used indicates a particular process based on deconstructive and reconstructive analysis (see Chapter 7).

RETHINKING RESEARCH AND EDUCATIONAL PRACTICE

TOWARDS INCLUSIVITY

New ways of knowing clearly have implications for how we research and how we learn as practising professionals. Postmodern ways of thinking point up how more modernist conceptions of knowledge have tended to polarise our thinking about knowledge, and about theory and practice. Modernist ideas underpin our assumptions about knowledge as a fixed and objective body of ideas, able to be created only through particular scientific methods. In this way, professional knowledge, as fixed knowledge generated in legitimate ways and safeguarded by the profession, has become a means of legitimising professional power. In this way also 'theory' and 'practice' have become polarised as two separate entities, fixed in a rigid hierarchy in which theory has often been privileged. This polarisation is mirrored in the divisions between researchers and practitioners, between professionals and service users.

A postmodern perspective alerts us to the diverse number of ways in which we can understand and make knowledge, and therefore the many different types of theories and practices which exist, and the many different ways in which they relate to each other. Postmodern thinking not only upsets the traditional hierarchies, but also posits many different and perhaps more complex ways of appreciating knowledge and its creation. In this sense, postmodern thinking does not simply reverse hierarchies (to do so would be to still preserve a modernist construction), but rather it unsettles polarised constructions by positing much more complex ones. I like to term this more complex way of seeing as *inclusive*, in that it is primarily about recognising the many diverse and changing perspectives and ways of understanding, and trying to engage with these in a dynamic way. In order to begin to appreciate these diverse perspectives, there must also be an understanding of how we ourselves are implicated in the ways we see and make knowledge.

Critical and postmodern practice therefore involves recognising different ways of knowing, in particular having a reflexive ability to engage with changing situations. This of course has many implications for the way we understand the role of researcher and teacher, and the way we see ourselves in relation to these

Exercise

Think of an instance in which you were recently in the role of student.

What were you assuming about knowledge – what it is, what kinds there are, where it comes from, how it is generated and learnt, whose knowledge is important?
Might you take on different roles or positions, depending on your view of knowledge?
Is it possible to take on several different types of student roles at one and the same time, or in the one situation? For example, can you both take on knowledge from an authority, at the same time as actively engaging in modifying it?

Chapter summary

In this chapter we began by drawing out the links between our understanding of knowledge and how our beliefs about what counts as legitimate knowledge, who can legitimately create it, and what are legitimate processes for doing so are all issues of power. This analysis clearly has implications for the way professional knowledge is created and valued, and plays out particularly in connection

(Cont'd)

with how the relationship between theory and practice is conceptualised. It is important, in a critical postmodern approach to social work knowledge, to recognise alternative forms of theorising, other than 'top-down' approaches. The value of knowledge created directly from the practice of professionals is also recognised in a critical approach. This poses a much more complex understanding of knowledge, theory and the relationship with practice. It also places value on the role of the practitioner in knowledge creation. This has implications for professional practice as well as research.

We then developed a critically reflective approach to knowledge on this basis, showing the similarities between reflective and critical postmodern and feminist thinking. In this way an approach to critical reflection based on principles of deconstruction and reconstruction was shown to be congruent with the critical postmodern approach taken in this book.

FURTHER READING

KNOWLEDGE

Evans, T. and Hardy, M. (2010) *Evidence and Knowledge for Practice*. Cambridge: Polity. Ch. 1 'Knowledge: philosophy, theory and practice'.

A good introduction and overview to different theories of knowledge.

KNOWLEDGE AND POWER

Brophy, P. (2009) *Narrative-Based Practice*. Ashgate: Farnham & Burlington. Ch. 2 'Theoretical background'.

This chapter is very useful for discussing different approaches to knowledge, and their implications for research.

CONTEXT AND THEORY

Flyvberg, B. (2001) *Making Social Science Matter*. Cambridge: Cambridge University Press. Ch. 4 'Context counts'.

This chapter is useful for developing the concept of context as discussed in social theory, and its implications for our understanding of theory.

REFLECTIVE JUDGEMENT

Polkinghorne, D. (2004) *Practice and the Human Science*. New York: State University of New York Press. Ch. 7 'Reflective understanding and practitioner judgement'.

A good summary of and argument for the reflective basis of professional practice.

4

POWER

An understanding of power inequalities and a commitment to the empowerment of powerless people has been a cornerstone of more modernist critical social work approaches. It is therefore important to revisit these concepts and to examine how they might be reworked from a postmodern and poststructural way of thinking.

REFLECTING ON POWER

Exercise

Consider the following scenario (adapted from Fook et al., 2000: 65):

A community health social worker has organised a group of men who are all recently separated or divorced and engaged in the process of settling maintenance and custody agreements about their children. One member of the group, Theo, a manager with a local government department, seems overly hostile towards female professionals. In group sessions, he has become very angry about several incidents involving female professionals. The group have expressed concern (privately) to the social worker that his behaviour will disrupt the group.

The group has decided to lobby their local politician about the rights of men relating to custody and maintenance. To do this they have decided to amalgamate with another men's group, in order to present a stronger case.

At a joint meeting with this other group, Theo almost comes to blows with Charles, spokesperson for the other group. Charles and Theo disagree about how the approach should be made to the politician. Charles wants to organise a submission and to take it personally to the politician by himself. He argues that he has a personal connection with a friend of the politician, so he

(Cont'd)

can be more effective. Theo thinks there should be a small delegation, who should threaten publicity if the politician refuses to agree with their demands.

Some members of the group are concerned that Theo might jeopardise the mission, since their local politician is a woman. On the other hand, they do not entirely trust Charles, as it is rumoured he is an aspiring politician himself.

Reflect on what assumptions are implicit about the nature of power, who has it and how it is used. Where does power come from? What kinds of things are implied about different groups in relation to power?

At first glance it is easy to say that the power resides with the politician, since that is the person to be lobbied to bring about some social changes. In this case we are assuming that power is structural and that this is perhaps the most important type of power. It is also assumed that there is some kind of 'power of numbers' which is why the two groups are joining forces to lobby the politician. There is also the power of personal connection, perhaps networking, which Charles implies he might use. There is an associated implication of added status of Charles, because of his personal connections. Theo also seems to have some kind of power in that his angry behaviour, although it is of concern, does not appear to be challenged.

There are some implications about power in relation to gender as well. For instance, in a structural sense, it is implied that recently separated/divorced men (fathers) do not have power, because they need to lobby to have their case heard with regard to maintenance and custody.On the other hand, there is concern about a misuse of power between genders, with the worry over Theo's attitudes towards women professionals, in a social position (with power) over him.

Most of these ideas about power rest on a general assumption that power has something to do with the characteristics of each group or person involved. For example, there is the power (or lack of it) associated with the gender group and their special experience (newly separated/divorced). There is also the power associated with Charles's personal connections and the power of Theo's angry behaviour. There is the power of politicians, attained through social position. Hopefully, an awareness of the different types and sources of power might help in working to empower the players concerned.

Exercise

How might you empower the group, if you were the social worker involved? What might be some of the difficulties involved?

In simple terms, if empowerment is about giving power to powerless groups, then it is a straightforward matter of identifying the powerless groups or people in this scenario and ensuring that they have the power to carry out their mission. This presumably would involve the social worker in doing things like helping the men prepare a case for the politician. Yet it is easy to see problems already with this simple goal. For instance, the ways in which the social worker does this might depend on gender, since ways of relating to Theo could be problematic if the social worker is a woman. Is it Theo or the female social worker who needs to become empowered? It is not entirely clear who is the powerless person in this instance.

The same might be said in relation to the female politician, who at the same time belongs to a powerful group (politician) and powerless group (women). The men themselves are in this ambiguous category – belonging to a structurally powerful group (men) but structurally powerless as well (in relation to maintenance and custody issues). And who is powerful and powerless when we consider the argument between Theo and Charles? Whose ideas should prevail, and which perspective needs empowering? It is perhaps easy to surmise that Theo's and Charles's respective approaches might be related to their different cultural backgrounds as well. Should it therefore be a simple matter of empowering the less dominant view and choosing this as the best way to proceed? What about the views of other group members, perhaps lost in the excitement over the argument between Charles and Theo. Should they be empowered, simply because their views might have been relatively silenced?

CRITICISMS OF THE EMPOWERMENT MODEL

In some ways, the idea of empowerment is attractive because it is a relatively easy concept to understand and also promises a ready framework for application in direct practice. Yet as we have seen with our example scenario, it is not so easy to apply in practice. For one thing, the idea of empowerment is used very differently. Some approaches do not even mention the concept of power (Furlong, 1987). People do not fit easily into 'powerful' or 'powerless' groupings, sometimes having membership of both at the same time. As well, members of powerless groups do not necessarily agree on the form of their empowerment. The very same experience can be empowering for some and disempowering for others.

Adams (1996: 12–15) nicely summarises some of the risks associated when the idea of empowerment is put into practice:

- the paradox of empowering without doing people's empowering for them;
- one person's empowerment may be another's disempowerment;
- danger of dilution – from empowerment to enablement;
- dangers of addressing too many target groups and addressing none adequately;
- the ambiguous relationship between self-help and empowerment.

Ward and Mullender (1991) make the point that while empowering people, there still needs to be some kind of social justice perspective (in their terms, the concept of 'oppression') operating. Otherwise there are no guidelines about who is to be empowered and for what ends. Baistow (1994/5) very astutely notes that the ubiquitous use of the empowerment model has both politically conservative as well as radical possibilities, and thus reinforces the idea that we do need to be aware of our broader goals and vision in making decisions about who and how we empower.

Obviously the concept of empowerment is crucial to critical practice, yet there are many dangers in using such a 'one-off' concept without linking it to a broader base of structural analysis (Fook, 1987) and a more complex understanding of power. I still think that when using an empowerment model, unless we ask the more important questions like 'empowerment for what?' and 'for whom?', we are left with the possibility of perpetuating oppressive structures for someone.

What is therefore needed is a more complex understanding of power and how this leads to a more complex practice of empowerment. In addition, any such approach also needs to take into account contextual considerations (Fook and Morley, 2005). Before we develop this, first let us summarise the problems with the concepts of power and empowerment.

PROBLEMS IN CONCEPTIONS OF POWER AND EMPOWERMENT

SUMMARY

There are five major ways in which modernist conceptions of power and empowerment are problematic from a postmodern and poststructural viewpoint:

- power as commodity;
- binary oppositional relations;
- allowance for difference;
- accounting for contradictions;
- the disempowering experience of empowerment.

POWER AS COMMODITY

Modernist notions of power seem to conceptualise power as a 'commodity', that is, as a material entity which can be traded or given away, or transferred from one person or group to another. The problem with this is that empowerment is therefore always at the *expense* of one group or person towards another. If a worker empowers or gives some of their power to a service user, by definition the worker becomes disempowered. This type of conception has the potential of setting people or groups against each other, in *oppositional* relationships to each other. For example, in relation to our scenario of the men's groups, if the female worker empowers Theo, she therefore disempowers herself. If she supports Charles, she disempowers Theo and some other members of the group.

Using this commodified notion of power assumes that there is only a finite amount of power as well, so that only one group or person can be empowered. It implies that we have to make choices about who can be empowered and the priority often implied is that whoever is the most disadvantaged, oppressed or marginal should be the chosen group. This overly simplistic approach does not allow for the idea that often it is marginal or oppressed groups themselves who can be least sympathetic towards members of other disadvantaged groups. In our scenario, members of Theo's group are not very sympathetic towards him, even though he has presumably experienced similar disempowerment to them. They are worried that his non-conforming behaviour might jeopardise the greater group interests.

BINARY OPPOSITIONAL RELATIONS

Such notions of power therefore seem to split the world into two oppositional groups – the *powerful* and the *powerless* – with the accompanying assumption that they are two mutually exclusive groups. One of the problems for service users is that if they are characterised as members of the powerless group, and the divide between the two groups is insurmountable, then the process of becoming powerful can seem unachievable. With the shifting of power from one group to another, there is often a shifting of blame and responsibility the other way. This can have the effect of locating the responsibility (and hence 'agency', or sense of a capacity to act effectively) away from the group needing empowerment and, ironically, back in the lap of the dominant group. In this sense, defining one's identity as 'powerless' can have a disempowering effect.

Karen Crinall (1999) makes this point in relation to young women who resisted the identity of powerlessness and 'victimhood'. In many ways such an identity is ascribed from outside, usually from those more powerful, and therefore can function to disempower those who are so labelled, since it is not a label of their own choosing. I will discuss the complex relationship between power and identity in Chapter 5.

In our example scenario, simply putting the 'recently separated/divorced men' as a disadvantaged group against 'recently separated/divorced women' as two clear groups with oppositional interests does little to assist the men to pursue creative ways of changing the situation. In fact directing the blame at another group draws the attention away from problematic social practices and structures which create a difficult situation for both men, women and their children after marriage break-up. Similarly, by locating the problem only within social structures frames it in such a way that the men may feel it is inaccessible for them to change.

ALLOWANCE FOR DIFFERENCE

Modernist notions of power assume that we are striving for equality, that empowerment is about reducing inequality. However, what equality means is often unclear or oversimplified. Often it is assumed that *equality* = *sameness*. Therefore the process of empowerment necessarily means that all people and groups become the same. An example might be the assumption that equality for women means the ability to pursue full-time work and career opportunities, the same as men.

The problem with this type of thinking is that it leaves little room for personal choice and social difference. The experience of being the same as someone else might in fact be disempowering for some people. This might be the case if becoming empowered means attaining goals which are not suitable for the person because of differences in personality, social or cultural background, or present circumstances. In our example scenario, clearly the approach to the politician which is appropriate for Charles would probably not work for Theo, and even the same outcome might be reached in widely divergent ways. Charles and Theo might experience each approach in either empowering or disempowering ways.

Striving for sameness might also have the effect of actually silencing any number of other perspectives, if the tendency is to become like the mainstream. In this case, what could happen is that mainstream perspectives might simply become dominant yet again, by defining the standards to which marginal groups aspire. In this sense one of the paradoxes of empowerment might be that it is effectively about empowering all people to become more like the dominant groups. This may not only devalue (and potentially annihilate) some characteristics of marginal groups which might be desirable, but also serve only to strengthen the power of dominant groups by increasing their hold over what is defined as desirable and normal. This tendency towards cultural orthodoxy is a potential downside of empowerment.

ACCOUNTING FOR CONTRADICTIONS

Such conceptualisations of power are therefore inadequate in accounting for uncertainty, contradictions and difference. In particular they cannot account for the phenomenon of 'complicity with oppression', in that sometimes traditionally disadvantaged people and groups appear willingly to comply with beliefs which work systematically to disadvantage them. Feminists might call these 'self-defeating' beliefs and Marxists might label them 'false consciousness', but in any case traditional modernist conceptions of power are not successful in explaining how some people, when faced with what seems a clear and empowered choice, might still choose a pathway which appears to work against their best interests.

If we were to theorise this phenomenon in a poststructural way, we might surmise that perhaps some people choose apparently self-defeating routes because the choices that are offered are not presented in terms that are meaningful to them. They are part of someone else's discourse, which has not arisen out of their own experience. In the case of feminist belief, for instance, it is often argued that because feminism arose in the West as a white and middle-class movement, many working-class women from non-Anglo backgrounds cannot identify with the cause, and will often choose what seem like 'non-feminist' pathways, because the feminist movement, as currently conceptualised, did not arise from their own experience.

Another explanation for 'complicity with oppression' might be that the choices are not as clear as they seem. In the case of the men's group for instance, while it is supposedly united in its interests to approach the politician, it is not clear which method will achieve their goals, and thus their empowerment. Given that how the politician will react is unpredictable, there is not really a clear choice about what will empower them in this situation. Some group members might choose a less combative route, which may seem less assertive, simply because they are concerned about alienating the politician and burning all their bridges too soon. Others might argue that they are 'selling out', too concerned about their own comfort and not enough about the empowerment of the group more generally. Whatever the rights and wrongs of the argument, it is apparent that there are complex issues involved in empowerment, room for contradictions, changes and difference.

THE DISEMPOWERING EXPERIENCE OF EMPOWERMENT

Being given power may not be experienced as empowering, but in fact may have disempowering effects. Despite the best intentions, our empowerment theory does not always translate well into practice. Sometimes in the attempt to empower, a disempowering climate and culture is set up. I'm sure many of us have experienced someone trying to 'help' us as a patronising and demotivating process. Once I attended some training with a cross-cultural counsellor who insisted that the best way to open an interview with a person from a 'traditional' culture was to ask the meaning of their name. When this was done to me (I happen to be a later generation Australian-born Chinese person, who has only ever had an Anglo first name) I found the experience quite demeaning. It was as if I had been related to in a prejudiced way, on the basis of my appearance rather than who I thought I was. I was in fact being related to on the counsellor's terms, rather than my own.

Of course, to be related to in terms of labels and categories is potentially dehumanising and discriminating, so therefore constantly to define and relate to the 'disempowered' as if that is all they are and ever will be can work contrary to their empowerment. Thus a problem for those wishing to empower others is how to exercise power without creating intimidating or contrary circumstances. For instance, sometimes we need to create service user category groupings so that services can be administered appropriately. But how do we create and use labels for these categories without stigmatising the people who fit into them? Minow labels this problem the 'dilemma of difference' (1985). In the very act of defining disadvantage, in order to empower, we in fact create disadvantage and thus disempower.

In reformulating a critical notion of power and empowerment we are therefore faced with the need to construct ideas which will allow for difference and diversity of experience and perspective, and flexibility in the way power is experienced and communicated in different situations.

Exercise

Look back at your response to the last exercise, about how you might empower the group we referred to at the beginning of this chapter. What approach to power comes across in your suggestions about empowerment? Do you see any evidence of the five problems we just discussed (e.g. seeing power as a commodity)?

REFORMULATING THE CONCEPT OF POWER

SUMMARY

Foucault's understanding of power is widely regarded as helpful in incorporating the different ways in which power is experienced and exercised. Sawicki (1991) summarises the three elements of Foucault's approach to power (Healy, 2000: 43):

- Power is exercised, not possessed.
- Power is both repressive and productive.
- Power comes from the bottom up.

Power is something people use and create rather than simply possess. It is not a commodity, but rather a factor which is given life through processes and structures of social interaction. In this sense it is created out of social relations and is not finite. It is therefore conceivable that both less and more powerful people can work together to create situations in which all experience empowerment. In effect, more power can potentially be created through collaboration.

This also means that power, because it is not located with particular people, groups or structures, may be everywhere. What is important is not where it is located, but how it is used, in different settings and by different people. Different contexts may influence the types of power, how it is practised and exercised (Healy, 2000: 43). With regard to our example scenario, Theo's angry behaviour may be politically effective with the politician, but may function to distance him from the group, effectively removing his base of support.

Power involves the potential to control and restrict, to form and transform. Not only are individuals regulated by state power, but state power gives a life and identity for the individual through providing appropriate categorisations, a fabric through which to live their lives. At the same time that it subjugates, it also provides a creative structure. Thus individuals willingly participate in practices and structures which simultaneously empower and disempower. Power is both a good and bad thing. For example, in our earlier scenario Charles is both disempowered by his identity as a recently divorced man fighting a custody battle over his children, but at the same time this identity holds the seeds of a possibility for a new empowered identity, as politician himself.

Power is expressed in both micro- and macro-level relations and structures. The many manifestations of power at local levels may be more complicated and contradictory than what is apparent at overarching levels. Thus it is important to appreciate both the local expressions of power in specific contexts as well as global structures. This 'bottom-up' view of power encourages looking at how power is expressed in the richness of everyday relations (Healy, 2000: 45). In the scenario, this is well illustrated. Simply seeing the men as a powerless group, subject to structural laws and practices which disadvantage them, does not help us towards empowering them in this particular situation. We need also to take into account the various power plays at different levels, in order to chart an effective plan of action with these particular players.

Every person, despite her or his social status and location, exercises and has the potential to create some form of power. This may vary depending on each context, and changes of context. The key to understanding power in any one context is therefore to appreciate how it is expressed, experienced and created by different people at different levels.

REFORMULATING THE CONCEPT OF EMPOWERMENT

Exercise

Reconsider the example scenario. How might the social worker practise empowerment, taking into account our reformulated concepts of power and empowerment?

Our thinking might roughly follow a path like this:

- Who are we trying to empower?
- For what reasons should they be empowered?
- Are there particular individuals, or the group as a whole (and how is this represented) who should be empowered?
- Is it possible to formulate a consensus on what is at stake for all players?
- What processes might we use to determine this? For example, is it possible that the group, as well as individual members, might all become empowered?
- Can both Charles and Theo have an input which values their respective abilities?

(Cont'd)

- Who is already exercising what types of power, and what types of power might they potentially create?
- Can we identify different ways in which different people might use their power?
- Can we use Charles's skills in different ways to Theo's?
- What are the skills and ideas already inherent in the group?
- Are there other group members who have abilities/ideas which we might put to use?
- Must there only be one way of approaching the politician?
- Can we think of different ways in which the group's goals might be met?

SUMMARY

Let us now try to articulate what a process of empowerment practice might look like from critical and postmodern perspectives:

1   *To analyse/reflect upon (deconstruct)* situations, focusing on how existing power relations and structures are supported and created. For example, what different assumptions about power support the existing state of affairs? How are these expressed and articulated? What types of climate and context are created by these ideas? How does this climate maintain existing power relations? How is this climate experienced by different people and does it function to empower or disempower them?

What are the different interest groups and individuals in the situation? What types of power are used differently by these different people? Whose ideas are dominant, and how are they expressed by, and how do they affect different players? What are some of the contradictions about power which arise for people? How might some players participate in their own disempowerment?

What power do I exercise in the situation? How do I conceptualise it and the power within it and whose interests does this serve?

2   *To redefine and reconceptualise* the power relations and structures in non-oppositional terms, allowing for differences between the different players involved, including yourself. You may need to develop a process of dialogue and communication so that different parties can come to understand how each experiences empowerment or disempowerment.

3   *To negotiate* a changed system of power relations and structures which is experienced as empowering for all parties, including yourself.

4   *To reconstruct and reconceptualise* (include your own as well as others' views) the situation in ways that are more empowering for all parties. How can different players be included in the process of empowerment? How can powerful experiences be indentified and valued? How can an empowering climate be created?

Your initial reaction on reading this might be to question the obvious idealism of it all. I recognise, of course, that many problematic situations arise because all parties have reached an impasse and do experience the situation as oppositional. They are unlikely to be motivated to change their views. The potential of engaging in this type of process, however, is that there might be some unhelpful discourses, held by the oppositional parties themselves, which have gone unquestioned and upon examination by those parties might be changed.

However, there are also many situations which are perhaps more readily open to multiple interpretations, where engaging in this type of process might provide assistance in breaking an impasse. More importantly, I think there is one perspective over which we all do have control – our own – and it is most important to understand, appreciate and change appropriately any of your own thinking which contributes to oppositional and potentially disempowering notions of power.

In Chapter 8 we will explore in more detail this process and some specific empowerment strategies.

Chapter summary

In this chapter we revisited the concepts of power and empowerment and reworked them from a critical postmodern perspective. We started with an exercise about empowerment, a concept which is almost taken-for-granted as underpinning many current approaches to social work. We then discussed five potential problems with the concept of empowerment:

- power as commodity;
- binary oppositional relations;
- allowance for difference;
- accounting for contradictions;
- the disempowering experience of empowerment.

We then reformulated concepts of power along Foucauldian lines, incorporating the notion that power is a more dynamic phenomenon which is exercised, can be used in many different ways (in both controlling and creative ways) and can also be used in bottom-up ways.

We then looked at what a process of empowerment might look like, based on this reformulated view, and showed how it could be based on renegotiating power relations and structures to reformulate them in ways which are inclusive of many different viewpoints and positions. In effect, this could be empowerment for all, not just those traditionally disadvantaged.

FURTHER READING

POWER

Smith, R. (2008) *Social Work and Power*. Basingstoke: Palgrave. Ch. 2 'Ideas about power'.

This chapter provides a useful overview to different approaches to the conceptualisation of power, in a relatively accessible and atheoretical way.

Flyvberg, B. (2001) *Making Social Science Matter*. Cambridge: Cambridge University Press. Ch.7 'The significance of conflict and power to social science'.

This chapter reviews and discusses Habermasian and Foucauldian concepts of power.

EMPOWERMENT

Dalrymple, J. and Burke, B. (2006) *Anti-Oppressive Practice: Social Care and the Law*. Maidenhead: McGraw Hill. Ch. 5 'Empowerment'.

A useful overview and discussion of different approaches to the concept of empowerment. Particularly useful for giving a British perspective in the context of legislation.

Parker, S., Fook, J. and Pease, B. (1999) 'Empowerment: the modernist social work concept *par excellence*', in B. Pease and J. Fook. (eds), *Transforming Social Work Practice*. Sydney: Allen & Unwin. Ch. 10, pp. 150–7.

This chapter critiques modernist approaches to empowerment and suggests a postmodern framework.

Fook, J. and Morley, C. (2005) 'Empowerment: a contextual perspective', in S. Hick, J. Fook and R. Pozzuto (eds), *Social Work: A Critical Turn*. Toronto: Thompson Educational Publishing. Ch. 5, pp. 67–86.

This chapter provides an Australian perspective – the use of empowerment in social work literature is reviewed, and a case application is included.

5

DISCOURSE, LANGUAGE AND NARRATIVE

The ways we think about the world (our knowledge) are related to the ways in which power is made and exercised. This has been a central idea which we have developed in the last two chapters. This is not a new idea. Modernist thinkers (specifically Marxists) are familiar with the concept of ideology, referring to the system of ways in which our ideas about our social world make (and often confine us to) our place within it. In many ways, an understanding of the ideological functions of ideas is crucial to the practice of radical social work. It allows us to make links between the social structure and individual lives, by explaining how people internalise thinking about the social structure and their place within it. In so doing, it provides directions for radical social workers about how and where to challenge inequitable social arrangements through direct practice with individual people.

Postmodern and poststructural thinkers have developed the idea of 'discourse'. This involves an understanding of how the ways we talk about our world, that is, our frameworks for understanding our social worlds, actually also construct it. This is similar to the concept of ideology and might perhaps be seen as a further development of it.

In this chapter I aim to show how ideas about discourse can build upon the concept of ideology and how an understanding of discourses and their operation provides another opening to understanding how power operates. The idea of narrative is also closely related, since narratives are in a sense also discourses – they are specific frameworks or ways of talking about and understanding specific phenomena. So in this chapter I will explore how the three concepts – discourse, language and narrative – can help develop our ideas about critical practice in challenging dominant power arrangements.

IDEOLOGY

There are many variations on the Marxist concept of ideology (Purvis and Hunt, 1993). A definition of ideology which I have found over the years to be the clearest, and at the same time the most complex, is that put forward by Albury (1976). I have used it extensively elsewhere (Fook, 1993) to develop some major practice principles in a radical casework approach. In simple terms, it refers to the totality of processes which form and maintain the social awareness of the individual members of that society. It is about how people's thinking about their social world and their relative place within it is created, developed and sustained. In this sense there are two aspects to ideology – both the content of the ideas themselves and the processes which maintain that thinking. The ideas themselves help define the individual person's social place, and there are also processes (and structures) which ensure that these ideas are built upon and continued. Ideology is therefore a set of ideas and processes which functions to maintain individual people in their social place. In this sense, ideology is directly about power, since it is about how social ideas maintain the social structure (with its inherent power imbalances).

Albury (1976) also helpfully notes that there are three levels to the ways in which ideology is expressed:

- practical;
- theoretical;
- institutional.

The *practical level* refers to the specific behaviours and practices which arise from ideological beliefs. For example, there may be certain customs or roles which are an expected part of membership in a particular group. Social workers, for instance, are expected to dress and behave like 'professionals'.

The *theoretical level* includes the ideas, rationalisations or conceptualisations which explain or underpin these specific behaviours or practices. The idea that 'professionals' should be able to be differentiated from non-professionals because of their specialist status is an example of a theoretical piece of ideology.

The *institutional level* refers to the systematic organisation of these specific ideas and practices which ensures that they are maintained, and in some ways may take on a life of their own. For instance, the ideology of the 'professional' denotes an identifiable set of roles, behaviours and beliefs which helps preserve the superior status of the members of that social group.

This covers the basic Marxist notion of ideology in fairly clear and simple terms. What is crucial to critical social workers about the idea of ideology is that what is important about ideas, in social terms, is not so much the 'truth' of their *content*, but the social (control) *functions* which ideas or sets of ideas perform. 'Ideology' is about the ways in which ideas function to maintain (or upset) the social order. There can of course be different sets and levels of ideologies, held by groups, individuals, cultures, societies, organisations and so forth. 'Ideologies' can exist as single ideas, held by individuals, or as total world views which form the basis of the thinking of whole civilisations. In any case, however extensively they are held, they are usually expressed on a number of levels – as beliefs, actions or in structures.

All societies and groups within them hold different ideologies which function to maintain that group's identity and boundaries and its place in the hierarchy. For instance, social work professionals may hold ideas which differentiate them from those of lesser status (perhaps volunteers). An example might be the belief that professional education allows social workers to make more rational decisions than volunteers. Correspondingly, volunteers might hold views which preserve their identity against professional social workers.

They might believe that it is better to respond to people in need from their own personal experience than through 'book learning'. Social workers might also preserve their place in the professional hierarchy by having beliefs about where they stand in relation to higher status professions, like medicine. 'We care, but they're only interested in money' might be an example. Such an idea almost implicitly acknowledges the superior status of the medical profession, at the same time as providing a rationalisation for the lower position of social work. These views may or may not be true and people may be able to provide varying amounts of evidence for and against them. From an ideological standpoint, this is not the main issue. What is important is whether and how the particular idea in question serves to create or maintain the social boundaries of the people or group.

Exercise

List five common beliefs in social work. Do you think any of them have ideological functions?

Some interesting beliefs to consider are our ideas about appropriate behaviour in social work, such as the idea that we should be objective, or that we should not be emotional, or that we should preserve boundaries. Others might be about theory or knowledge, such as the idea that we should be able to articulate our theoretical framework, or that our work should be evidence-based. It is helpful to think about whose and which power interests are served by each idea.

This relatively simple notion of ideology is crucial to understanding the link between individual people, their thinking and actions and the broader social structure. This understanding is therefore vital in developing a critical approach to social work practice, because it helps us do two things: to analyse the thinking and structures which function to restrict and oppress people; and to locate a starting point for assisting them to challenge the thinking and structures.

Exercise

In no more than three lines, try to describe the sort of person you think you are. Is there any evidence of beliefs about yourself which have ideological functions? In other words, do some of these beliefs serve to ensure that you belong (and perhaps keep belonging) to a particular social grouping? Do they help to sustain your own position or power or that of others?

Some of you might have spoken about yourself in terms like: 'optimistic person'; 'interested in people's problems'; 'have good communication skills'; 'come from a disadvantaged background'; 'easy to get along with'; 'white woman'; 'dog lover'; 'social worker'; 'empathic'; 'have a strong belief in social justice'. I've derived this list from some of the things I've seen people write on application forms for entry to social work courses. On the face of it, it is easy to categorise these characteristics in terms of more social and more personal characteristics and to say that the more 'social' ones (like 'white woman'; 'social worker') are perhaps to do with social grouping. However, on closer inspection it may also be possible to draw links between more personal beliefs about ourselves (like 'optimistic person'; 'have a strong belief in social justice'; 'interested in people's problems') and more social categories (like 'white woman' or 'social worker'). Perhaps we believe that these are the characteristics which should go together. This would say something about our social beliefs about ourselves; perhaps we think that social workers should be optimistic, that women are more interested in people's problems, or that social workers hold social justice values. It may therefore be fair to say that even 'personal' beliefs about ourselves have social ramifications. In its very simplest sense, this is an example of ideas having an ideological function.

Of course, some of these ideas may have 'power' implications as well, that is, may also be tied to issues of power relations and structures. Perhaps, for example, we also believe that women make better social workers, or that social work is a suitable profession for a woman. Such beliefs feed into how we see that status of the profession and the sorts of power its members may have.

Exercise

Look back at the three-line description you wrote of yourself. Is it important to you that what you have said is true of yourself? Can a belief be 'true' and at the same time function in an ideological way?

It may be really important to you to be seen as an empathic person and easy to get along with. Yet at the same time, in striving to keep yourself this way, you may also find that you are not able to assert your needs as well as you might like, or that other people might take advantage of you. This might be an example of a 'true' idea working against you. In a Marxist sense, this would be an example of 'false consciousness', of dearly holding a belief which might also function in self-defeating ways.

Similarly it is true, for instance, that in the Western world social work is a women's profession. It was founded by women and is dominated (in terms of numbers) by women, and works with predominantly a female clientele (Dominelli, 1999: 96–8). Many people see this as a good thing. On the other hand, some people argue that it is this very femaleness of the profession which contributes to its lower status and have argued for the introduction of more men to its ranks (Blanchard et al., 1994). To make the profession more masculine may actually defeat the original mission of the profession, and yet to preserve the profession as predominantly female may mean a trade-off in social standing and therefore power.

What we have unearthed here is the problem of the complex relationship between beliefs and practices and their ideological functions. If ideological beliefs can be either true or false, then we have little direction as to how and what should be changed in order to change power dynamics. This problematic, of the relationship between the ideological functions of beliefs and practices and their 'truth' or 'falsity', is one which potentially limits the usefulness of the concept of ideology. Let us examine these limitations further.

LIMITATIONS OF THE CONCEPT OF IDEOLOGY

FALSE CONSCIOUSNESS – TRUTH/FALSITY DISTINCTION

Some people argue that the idea of 'false consciousness' assumes making a problematic distinction between 'truth' or 'falsity', which itself involves the exercise of power. To label a set of thinking as 'false' implies that there is a set of thinking which is not. How truth is determined and whose idea of truth it is then becomes important. This poses serious questions for critical social workers, since it is usually they who are imposing the label of 'false' upon the ideas of people who are already oppressed and disempowered. To label the thinking of relatively powerless groups as 'false' may only serve to disempower them more.

To imply that certain ideas and practices are self-defeating, and thus mask the social functions that they perform, also implies that there is a 'real' set of social functions which ideology only serves to mystify (Purvis and Hunt, 1993: 478–9). This implies a very simplistic notion of social functions, that they are primarily about preserving inequitable power relations. However, it is possible that there might be several, perhaps contradictory, ways in which ideas function simultaneously. For example, the fact that you believe yourself to be empathic can work in self-defeating ways (it may encourage other people to take you for granted), yet it might at the same time work for you in that the practice of being empathic may mean that you gain power over other people because they are happy to confide in you.

CLEAR SPLIT BETWEEN INTERESTS AND AWARENESS (DUALISM OF ACTION AND CONSCIOUSNESS)

Related to the ideas about the falsity of ideological thinking is the assumption, in Marxist thinking, that people's awareness needs to be changed (that is, their form of consciousness needs to change) in order for them to identify their interests and so act upon them. In early formulations of radical, structural and feminist social work we have become familiar with 'consciousness-raising' as a process whereby people have become aware of how their thinking has served to preserve structures which work against their best interests. Implicit in this view is the idea that people do not necessarily experience, on a daily level, how their interests might or might not be served. Their awareness needs to change in order to be able to distinguish whether their interests are served or not, and how they are acted upon. This dualism underpins the Marxist idea of ideology (Purvis and Hunt, 1993: 476).

It is this dualism, this split between our experience and the awareness/ability to act upon it, which is potentially problematic. It implies a fairly rationalist understanding of experience (that awareness will lead to action), and also devalues the experience itself as an important part of how people understand their interests. For example, you may enjoy being empathic even though you are aware that some people take you for granted because of it.

As well, the relationship between awareness and action may be much more complex than the dualism implies. Just because you are aware that acting empathically may work against you does not mean you can immediately change your behaviour. There may, for instance, be a whole other set of conditions which militate against this, some more personal, some more social. Some of the conditions may involve other sets of decisions which have little to do with the original idea. For instance, you may enjoy being empathic because it is important to you to engage with people and get on with them, even at the risk of them taking advantage of you. Or perhaps your behaviour might normally be interpreted as empathic, because of your social presentation. This is often one of my own difficulties – I present as a fairly soft-spoken woman of Chinese descent. Even when I think I am being decidedly unempathic, such as in an argument with someone, I often find my points are interpreted in softened ways. It is perhaps socially threatening for me to have a differing point of view, so my views are interpreted in diluted ways.

DIRECTIONALITY (IN FAVOUR OF SOME, NOT OF OTHERS)

A further problem with Marxist conceptions of ideology is the implicit assumption that the interests of some groups are always favoured over the interests of others. In advantaging some, others are inevitably disadvantaged. Ideology is in essence a theory about how forms of thinking work to keep subordinate groups subordinated, and how this thinking itself keeps these groups from being aware of their disadvantaged status, and thus from changing their position. In this sense, it is the nature of ideology that it keeps disadvantaged groups from recognising how they participate in their own subordination, and thus from access to the means to do something about it. 'In its simplest and most pervasive form, ideology presents the existing social relations as both natural and inevitable; particular interests come to be disassociated from their specific location and come to appear as universal and neutral' (Purvis and Hunt, 1993: 478).

The problem with this kind of assumption is that disadvantage, or rather the conditions which bring about disadvantage for some and advantage for others, become fixed phenomena, inaccessible to change because they appear all-pervasive and part of our accepted, and therefore assumed benign, reality. This way of thinking increases alienation, a distancing from the ability to act in and upon the situation.

For example, the idea of directionality is inadequate when we apply it to our example of empathic behaviour. Empathic behaviour, and the belief that social workers are and should be empathic, can in fact function both to advantage and disadvantage the social worker and the service user at the same time. Both parties may be empowered through the use of empathy. The social worker obtains power by gaining the confidence of the service user. The service user gains power through having her or his story listened to and legitimated. The social worker loses power through creating the impression that she or he is a 'soft touch'. The service user loses power by becoming vulnerable through confiding personal weaknesses. A whole mixture of functions are served through any one experience, and this mixture of functions can work in several directions at once.

OVERARCHING SUPERSTRUCTURE

The idea of ideology is also problematic because the concept of the social structure has been invested with 'super' powers, which overarch and determine the lives of individuals. Unfortunately this understanding is over-inclusive (Purvis and Hunt, 1993: 481), in that it doesn't allow for a whole range of social phenomena which operate at a more middle level, such as local and cultural institutions. The tendency has been to polarise the phenomena into binary constructions like 'individual/ society', without allowing for a more complex interplay of different types of social groupings and structures.

To return to our empathy example, the overarching idea of the social structure is not helpful in explaining the phenomenon of empathy. In order to understand how it operates ideologically we also need to understand the nature of professions, and the way different people engage with and express professional behaviour. It may be that for some groups and some individuals, within social work, empathy is culturally more appropriate, such as with more expressivist cultures. In order to understand how and why the belief in empathy performs ideological functions in the social work profession, we need to understand more middle-range phenenona, like the history or culture of social work.

LACK OF PLURALITY/CONTRADICTION

There are several polarisations on which the Marxist idea of ideology is based. Clearly the opposition of 'individual/society' is one. The split between mind/body and awareness/action is another. Such rigid polarisations do not allow for complexities involved, for different cultural manifestations of social structures, and for contradictions. For instance, what is disempowering in one culture may be empowering in another. Whereas empathy may be experienced as patronising in one culture, it may be expected of social workers in another. In examining how ideology works, on a mundane level and through lived experience, we need a much more complex understanding that recognises the possibility of contradictions and of variations through context.

IDEOLOGY AND DISCOURSE

In many ways the concept of discourse allows for the complexities which the pure idea of ideology does not. In simple terms, it draws attention to the whole language and cultural context which shapes the way individuals see themselves, and thus their places in society. Both ideology and discourse are to do with the same aspect of social life – how people participate in understanding the social arrangements in which they live (Purvis and Hunt, 1993: 474). Where they differ is in the level of complexitiy and their assumptions about the participation involved.

The concept of ideology tends to assume that clear relations of domination/subordination are produced, and that subordinate groups only participate in these because they are unaware of the subordinating effects. There is an emphasis on social superstructure and how it determines the lives of individuals subjugated to it.

The idea of discourse places emphasis on the context in which individual people live, in particular the linguistic context, and how this not only frames our understandings of our social world, but also how we construct our own identities within it and through social relations. Individual participation is thus seen as a potentially creative and more positive phenomenon, although it is potentially restrictive as well.

DISCOURSE

What is discourse? Discourse refers to the individual social networks of communication through the medium of language or non-verbal sign 'systems' (Purvis and Hunt, 1993: 485). In simple terms, discourse refers to the ways in which we make meaning of and construct our world through the language we use (verbal and non-verbal) to communicate about it. I am using the term 'language' here in its broadest sense, to refer to our many different ways of communicating about ideas. It is a 'vehicle for thought, communication and action' (Purvis and Hunt, 1993: 485) but it is not a passive vehicle. In providing a medium for communication, it also channels and shapes that communication, and hence the meanings derived from it. This is not necessarily a sinister or intentional process. Any one system of thought or communication necessarily allows for some things to be communicated and excludes others.

This problem of communication hinges on the idea that no communication form (speech, writing, actions) can ever perfectly represent a phenomenon. We are therefore naturally limited in expressing ourselves by the medium we use. Our language or form of communication therefore naturally leaves a gap between what we want to convey and what is conveyed, and it is in this gap that there is a lot of room for variation. These variations will be influenced by changes in contexts. Meaning is therefore always contestable (Purvis and Hunt, 1993: 485). I will develop this notion further when we consider the role of language.

Foucault's development of the idea of discourse is probably the most widely used (Healy, 2000; Leonard, 1997; Weedon, 1987). According to Weedon (1987), Foucault sees discourses as being made up of all the ways in which knowledge is constituted in society. As well as expressed beliefs and ideas, this includes:

- the related social practices;
- particular forms of subjectivity;
- the power relations, which are inherent in the knowledge and the relations between different forms of this knowledge.

Because knowledge can only be known through communication of some kind, in this sense discourses might be seen as the whole set of experiences involved in 'knowing about' a phenomenon. Weedon (1987: 108) also makes the point that Foucault sees discourses as being more than ways of thinking and producing meaning. Discourse also constitutes the bodies and feelings of individuals, since these are also a medium involved in the communication and interpretation of meaning.

You will have begun to make connections between the idea of discourse and how we ourselves participate in shaping our 'reality', and the notion of critical reflection (involving our ability to locate ourselves and our personal influence in a situation). In this sense, an analysis of discourse might involve a process of thinking similar to a critical reflection. I will pursue these ideas further in Chapter 6, particularly exploring the practical application of these connections for social workers.

LANGUAGE

As we noted in the earlier section, the gap which exists between the actual phenomenon we are labelling and the label we assign to it provides the basis of room for debate about the meanings of the labels we use. Because there must necessarily be a gap between what we think, see, feel, experience and how we express it, then it implies that there is a choice (whether or not we are aware of it) about how to convey what we think, see, feel or experience to other people. Thus the language, the actual words and the forms in which we use them to communicate, is a crucial component of discourse. The way we talk about phenomena, and the choices which this implies about their nature and relative importance, are crucial in determining how we see, understand, act upon and construct our situations and experiences. The point that many postmodern thinkers make about language, of course, is that the labels we select determine what is emphasised, given importance, recognised, included or silenced. Language labels may carry particular connotations or emotive implications, or may be based on certain assumptions, often unquestioned (or unidentified or not spoken about). Language labels can imply different categories, which in turn often carry implicit hierarchies. (I will discuss binary opposites and dichotomising in the next chapter.)

Exercise

Take another look at the three-line description you wrote about yourself. What labels did you choose and why did you not choose others? What characteristics were you automatically excluding, in making these choices?

For example, if you labelled yourself as 'optimistic', why did you call yourself this rather than 'happy' or 'not pessimistic'? What does your choice imply? Are the categories 'optimistic' and 'pessimistic' necessarily opposite? Is it possible to be both optimistic and pessimistic? If you called yourself a 'white woman' what are the other possible categories that this implies? What aspects of your social identity does this emphasise and why? It is worth also thinking about why you chose to label yourself in these ways, and whether you might have chosen different labels if the circumstances were different (for example, if you labelled yourself at a party or a job interview, rather than as part of a study programme).

There have also been extensive analyses of the ways conversational devices are used to convey particular meanings, usually to work in favour of the person talking. Taylor and White (2000), for instance, discuss the ways in which we create categories which both allow us the privilege of defining the terms of the discussion, and which might also automatically assign particular characteristics to particular categories. For instance, if we want our version of a story to be accepted, we might construct ourselves as a 'passive bystander', with the person we are telling the story about as the 'implicated actor'. Taylor and White (2000: 49–50) use the example of a young woman telling the story of how she discovered her flatmate had a mental illness, by talking about her own passivity (implied 'normal' behaviour) and contrasting this with her flatmate's 'bizarre' behaviour. In this way the conclusion of mental illness is 'forced' on the storyteller and of course, once this category has been applied, explanations for other strange behaviours easily follow.

In a later chapter I will examine these devices in more detail, especially how and where they might be used in defining differences and privilege in the practice of social workers.

LANGUAGE, DISCOURSE AND POWER

Language, therefore is not *neutral*. Our language (and therefore our discourses) will be an expression of a particular attempt to make (or impose) meaning in a situation. Language is therefore about much more than *words* – it is about *power*. The language we use is therefore an indication of which value systems or which groups are dominant. Power, in this sense, is exercised through control of discourses. This accounts for why dominant meaning systems often go unquestioned, and even subordinate groups act against their own self-interest, because they unwittingly comply with the dominant discourse. You will remember that we discussed this in the last chapter, when we looked at the phenomenon of 'complicity with oppression'.

Exercise

Think about the term 'social work' as an example of language use.

- What does the term imply about social work?
- Are there aspects of social work (as you see it) which might be missing or devalued by using such a term?
- What other terms might be used?
- What interest groups might not be represented in using such a term?
- What dominant discourse is implied by using this term?
- What services or disservices do we do ourselves by using the term 'social worker'?

It is interesting to speculate about the different terms which could have been used, such as 'social therapist' or 'social educator'. For instance, in Europe the term 'social pedagogy' is also used. Each implies quite different roles and perhaps different statuses between the professional and the recipient of services. 'Social practitioner' is another possibility which also suggests perhaps a different kind of status. (For instance, consider the difference between talking about a 'medical practitioner' and a 'medical worker'.) Does the word 'social' serve to distinguish the work effectively from other types of professionals, and in what ways?

If you have had any experience working in human service organisations, you will probably have noticed how the meaning of 'social worker' is different from setting to setting, and how indeed the meaning and type of role involved is often questioned. One of the things which I have become quite impatient with over the years is professionals of all backgrounds saying they don't know what social work is. I become particularly annoyed with social workers who say this. This discourse around the term 'social work' functions of course to devalue and silence the social work perspective, and to disarm any challenge social workers might make to dominant ways of thinking in their workplaces. This becomes a very real problem and a threat to the potential contribution that the social work profession might make when social workers take on the discourse of other professional groups, and start to talk about their practice in ways defined by others. For example, Bill Jordan argues that because social workers in Britain have tended to characterise their work as 'counselling' or 'therapy', very much the terms of more psychology-oriented professions, they have lost out because they cannot compete in these terms with professionals better versed in more individualistic orientations. They have therefore participated in their own demise (Jordan and Jordan, 2000).

NARRATIVE

The idea of narrative is clearly linked to concepts of discourse and language. If we can only convey meaning through language, which is changing and contestable, then all accounts or communications are in this sense narratives – they are one person's 'story' of what occurred. I do not mean to suggest that the account is 'untrue' because it is simply a 'story', but that all accounts must be seen as a version of 'reality' coloured by the position and perspective of the person whose story it is, and that this version might change according to the context of time and place.

People also tell stories (construct narratives) to make meaning of incidents, their lives or situations. Moreover, one person might construct a 'story' from a multiple set of perspectives (subject(ive) positions) relative to their changing needs and circumstances. For instance, people might 'reconstruct' their stories, or explanations of their circumstances, as they revise their views in the light of new experiences. In this sense, the story of a person's life can be 'read' as a 'text' which is constructed so as to convey a particular meaning, at a particular time and in a particular context. The role of the 'reader' is therefore one of interpreter.

Exercise

Think about an experience you have had in which you have felt treated unfairly or badly. Now think about the different players in the situation. What 'narratives' might each of these people tell about the situation? What functions might the ideas in each narrative serve?

For me, one of the most telling illustrations of the notion of narrative comes through in a television programme which I find quite addictive. It is a programme produced in the USA, called *Judge Judy*. The programme televises real cases brought to Judge Judy to preside over. These usually involve claims for small amounts of money as a result of disputes between friends or family members or others, perhaps over rental monies owed, damages claimed, or grievances occurring as a result of relationship breakdowns. Each plaintiff and defendant though comes with a 'narrative' about their claims, which they try to embellish, in order to establish the legitmacy of their claims. The narrative on the plaintiff's part typically involves making themselves out to be generous, kind and helpful towards the defendant. The defendant's story often involves an acceptance of the generosity as such, without obligation to 'pay back'. Both sets of narratives require the person to weave a story about the situation, and themselves as people and moral agents within this. Interestingly though, Judge Judy wields the power to determine the narrative, by asking only for 'facts' as they relate to the legality of the sort of agreement or understanding which has been built up between the parties in question. She in effect takes away their power to determine the narrative, and establishes her own powerful narrative of 'factual' legality. This is a very clear illustration of the power of narrative.

Narratives usually have particular structures, which serve to provide some kind of meaning for the teller. For instance, most narratives contain a 'temporal ordering of events' (Mishler, 1986), or a sense of a happening and a consequence which follows. In other words, there is some sense of 'cause and effect', of events that happened which in turn caused others. This appears to be a central concern of most narratives.

The concept of narrative is important in the fields of both practice and research, in that an analysis of narratives is a key avenue towards identifying and understanding how people construct their 'realities' and how they might then be changed for therapeutic purposes. Quite a lot has been written about narratives and the different types of structures involved, which proves useful in the detailed analysis of them. I will explore these more detailed practical uses of narrative analysis in Chapter 10.

INTERPRETIVE APPROACHES

Because of the emphasis on discourse, and the importance of the person's own sub-jective position within discourse, approaches to practice which emphasise the importance of meaning, and hence the interpretation of meaning from different perspectives, are crucial in critical practice. We will cover some specific applications of this in a later chapter, because it suggests a quite different orientation to how we assess problems and make meaning of situations from a number of perspectives. Jones (1990) provides an excellent illustration of how several different theories can be used to interpret the one conversation quite differently.

Because stories and meanings might change over time and context, an interpretive approach is important in that it acknowledges that meanings are made and do not exist independent from the 'reader' (interpreter). What becomes important is an understanding of how meanings are made and how they influence the situation, both from the point of view of the 'teller' and the 'reader'. This is of course congruent with the critical reflective approach we outlined earlier. Both 'teller' and 'reader' can interact in the making (and remaking) of meaning. This is a key element of an interpretive approach to social science as outlined by Jim Ife (1997: 130–1).

REVISITING THEORY

After this discussion of discourse, it is useful to revisit our conceptions of theory, to see how our understanding might have expanded or changed. In Chapter 3 we talked about the inductive relationship between theory and practice (drawing theory out of practice, rather than imposing theory on practice). Over the years of my career, spent largely talking about and working with practice theory, I feel I have developed a much more 'liberated' approach to formal theory, able to bend it to my use, rather than feeling constrained to use it in prescribed ways. My understanding of the operation of discourse, and the ways in which we construct the importance of formal theory, has helped me question the relative importance of formal theory. Annette Riley (1996) makes this point poignantly when she describes her involvement with the case of a mother whose child dies. Riley found formal theory quite useless when confronted with further information and the possibility that the mother might have murdered her child. Her complete anguish and confusion in trying to cope with the mother's changed identity from client to murderer underscored the realisation that there was no formal theory which could guide her thinking or practice in this situation.

From a critical postmodern viewpoint, theory becomes both much more and much less than the formal theories taught in textbooks. This is a less restrictive and at the same time a more inclusive view of theory. In Chapter 3 we talked about 'ways of knowing' rather than 'theories'. This is a much more postmodern type of discourse, a recognition that theory is developed out of the process of making meaning, or of constructing knowledge from and about situations and experience. This language implies an inclusive approach, that there are many ways to know, understand or theorise a particular situation. Formal and more organised textbook theories are one example, but so are the different levels of discourses that might be operating in a given situation. (See Healy, 2005 for a discussion of the discourses which operate in social work.) A particular assumption, a piece of narrative, one hidden idea, which may constitute a particular person's 'subject position', are all examples of ways of knowing, of theories. Your own interpretation will be made from your own subject position and may comprise an amalgam of different types of ideas from your own personal history, formal theories you subscribe to, or your own practice wisdom. Theorising, or trying to analyse and understand a situation, thus becomes much more than simply applying formal theories (although that is part of it).

I make this point for another reason. Students come to the end of classes I have run, where we have spent a significant amount of time trying to understand, analyse and provide explanations for practice situations and I am often totally 'floored' when they say to me, 'But where was the theory? We didn't learn anything about theory!'

When we discuss this concern, it usually transpires that because we didn't use many of the formal theoretical labels, although we were theorising all the time, and because we had worked with their own opinions or thinking or interpretations, they did not feel our conclusions had the same authority or value as formal theory, and therefore felt they didn't 'count'. Perhaps because we did not use the discourse of formal theory, their ideas were devalued. This is a great irony, because it is often practitioners' own theorising which allows them to understand and find effective strategies for working in the situations they discuss. In this sense it is practitioners' own theorising which may make all the difference, and without which formal theories might remain relatively useless in specific situations. It is this sense of different theories and forms of theorising being useful in different ways which is crucial to a critical and postmodern social work practice.

It is useful, therefore, to develop a different way, a critical postmodern way of seeing theory or theories: as our intellectual tools, rather than as rule books. We do, of course, need to refer to formal theories, because they are sets of language and discourses that allow us to communicate more easily with other people. They also provide a beginning frame of reference, from within which to make sense of new situations. However, if we see this as their prime (rather than sole) purpose, they become a useful facility to us, rather than a set of restrictive (and sometimes overly prescriptive) principles.

Sometimes our understanding might be furthered by translating our own theories into the language of formal theories, so that we gain a different perspective and can learn through dialogue and debate with other people. But if formal theories are a substitute for our own thinking and theorising about our own experience, then we are in danger of subjugating our own experience to the dominant discourses of formal theories, developed by other people, in relation to different places and times. We are thus in danger of relying on explanations and discourses which might have only minimal applicability to our own experience and contexts.

Chapter summary

In this chapter we have looked at how the way we speak about phenomena also has to do with power. Specifically this involves understanding how language use, and the way the terms, phrases and ways of speaking, serves to order and categorise our world. The particular concepts of ideology, discourse and narrative are also integral to this understanding. We began by outlining and criticising the Marxist concept of ideology. Ideology is a useful concept for pinpointing how the beliefs we hold, whether they be 'true' or 'false', can also serve social (i.e. power) functions. This means there are reasons for maintaining these beliefs other than whether they are true or not.

(Cont'd)

This provides a useful basis from which to analyse the operation of power. However there are also serious limitations with the concept of ideology, including the inablility to recognise multiple perspectives.

We then discussed the concept of discourse, with its more complex understanding of how power operates in the various ways in which we communicate. Communication can be both verbal and material, and in this way discourses can operate at many different levels and in many different ways. The idea of narrative is thus important, as it recognises that we often create a particular perspective on social phenomena through the way we construct a discourse about them. In other words, people often construct their 'take' according to their own perspective or context, and this may vary according to the circumstances.

An understanding of how discourses and narratives operate can therefore lead us to a more complex understanding of how we interpret ourselves and our world. This invites us to take a different view of theory. If we see theories as particular discourses or narratives, we are able to recognise how they are formed by different contexts or power interests. This allows us to take a more 'liberated' view of theory, and to feel freer about creating our own. I believe such an understanding is crucial to critical social work and also to a critically reflective approach.

FURTHER READING

DISCOURSE

Levin, I. (2007) 'Discourses within and about social work', in L. Dominelli (ed.), *Revitalising Communities in a Globalising World*. Aldershot: Ashgate. Ch. 3, pp. 43–65.

Good definition of discourse and illustration of their operation in social work.

LANGUAGE

Pare, A. (2004) 'Texts and power: towards a critical theory of language', in L. Davies and P. Leonard (eds), *Social Work in a Corporate Era*. Aldershot: Ashgate. pp. 76–90.

Links a theory of language with notions of discourse and power.

THEORY

Brookfield, S.D. (2005) *The Power of Critical Theory*. San Francisco: Jossey-Bass. Ch. 1 'Exploring the meaning of critical theory for adult learning', pp. 1–38.

Very useful discussion of alternative meanings of the idea of theory.

NARRATIVE

Riessman, C.K. (2008) *Narrative Methods for the Human Sciences*. Thousand Oaks, CA: Sage. Ch. 1 'Looking back, looking forward', pp. 1–19.

Good introduction to the concept of narrative in research

Brophy, P. (2009) *Narrative-Based Practice*. Farnham: Ashgate. Ch. 3 'The nature of narrative', pp. 33–50.

Excellent overview of the general idea of narrative as relevant to both practice and research.

6

IDENTITY AND DIFFERENCE

In various forms we have been discussing the idea of personhood, or what constitutes the 'self' or individual person, throughout the last few chapters. For instance, our discussion of ideology and discourse, although primarily about how we construct our worlds, was also about how individuals propagate and participate in this construction, and how this in turn shapes the way individuals act, see themselves and are seen.

In this chapter, however, I want to focus more particularly on how postmodern and critical formulations have changed the way we understand individual identity and its formation within contemporary social structures and contexts. This has important implications for how we actually assess (interpret) individual people, their situations and problems. People's sense of self is integral to their personal and social health and, of course, since many forms of social work assistance might involve some form of personal change for service users, it is important to be aware of and accountable for the types of change involved, and the types of 'selves' we create or are hoping to create. Therefore it also has important implications for how we work with people, and for what ends, since our notions about the ideal, 'normal' or 'healthy' person underpin and are embedded in our everyday practice. Since we are concerned with the ideal or 'normal' development of the self, questions about difference and diversity are inextricably bound to these issues. How we construct the self, and how we understand difference in relation to it are probably among the key questions for social work practitioners. They lie at the heart of postmodern and critical analyses of the nature of social life, the possibilities for changing it and for recreating worlds which support and include many varieties of people and experiences.

WHAT IS SELF AND IDENTITY?

In social work we are most concerned with a sociological view of how the person, self or identity exists or develops in relation to society and social structures, and social groups within it. There are many different formulations about the structures and processes involved in this, and the 'self' which emerges from these. Various conceptions, arising from different disciplinary traditions, emphasise the relative importance of different types of influences, such as early family relationships, or the importance of cultural or historical contexts. Depending on the relative influence of these factors, the sense of self may be more or less changeable. However most formulations have in common the idea that there is some kind of entity or 'I' which interacts with others. As Sands says, most conceptions of self and identity 'converge in their depiction of an internalised relationship between an inner reflective agent and external experiences' (1996: 169).

These two aspects of the self, the 'internal' and the 'external', and the idea that they interact or have the capacity to act back upon and influence each other, is crucial to the social idea of identity. This interactive idea of identity formation entails that there is a sense of the identity being in a constant state of change. Different conceptions of identity place a different emphasis on the degree to which the sense of self might or should change over the course of a lifetime.

Most conceptions acknowledge that a sense of continuation and coherence, of a sense of self built up from a number of sources and encompassing a number of aspects, is also important. Sands poses a useful conception of self and identity as 'an internal sense of personality integration and continuity that encompasses one's life history, accrued identification and values, and relationships with others' (1996: 170).

CRITICISMS OF TRADITIONAL CONCEPTIONS OF SELF AND IDENTITY

Exercise

Write a three-line description of yourself now. Where do you think these views of yourself came from and how were they developed? Now compare it with the earlier one you wrote in Chapter 5. How and why do you think the descriptions have changed?

As discussed earlier, descriptions of ourselves (the discourses which we use and in which we locate ourselves) may serve many purposes or interests, some of which we may or may not have consciously chosen. Many of us will probably have chosen at least some accepted social categories as ways of describing ourselves, such as 'dog lover' or 'white woman'. Many of us would probably feel that the descriptors we used of ourselves do not necessarily do justice to who we think we are or want to be, or at least how we want to be seen. We may feel that we do not have much choice about the social ascriptions we apply to ourselves. This is certainly the case when we fill in bureaucratic forms and have to choose from an often paltry array of categories regarding marital status, for instance.

Many of the criticisms of mainstream conceptions of self and identity relate to these very simple issues – that identity is socially ascribed and is therefore part of and perpetuates the dominant way of seeing. In radical and structural social work, identity is often defined in terms of social structural categories – race, class and gender – seeming to leave little room for variation. Worse, since these identities are fixed in a massive structure located well outside the domain of the individual person, they seem inaccessible to the individual person to change. Worse still, in the social work arena, these ascriptions may take on a stigmatised aspect for those people defined as belonging to marginal or oppressed populations in these categories. Service users might therefore take on a disempowered, marginalised 'victim' identity, because of being assigned to social categories based on fixed social structures. Crinall (1999) discusses, for instance, the experience of young homeless women who resisted this definition of themselves.

The bulk of criticism of traditional conceptions of self and identity originates from feminist thinkers. They argue that the influential conceptions of the healthy personality to date are gender biased. They are based on studies of males (Marcia, 1980) and assume that women's identities are simply derived from a patriarchal system (Sands, 1996). In short, women's identities are defined from a male perspective and may therefore simply represent a male perspective.

In brief, quite an amount of feminist research, through researchers like Carol Gilligan (1982) and Belenky et al. (1986), has developed a picture of women's psychology as more to do with relational characteristics like attachment and caring. This is opposed to more male associated characteristics like autonomy, differentiation and individuation (Sands, 1996: 172). Yet the problem with these earlier feminist critiques was the danger of stereotyping gendered identities into 'either/or' categorisations, which in a sense were still restrictive and devaluing of women.

DICHOTOMOUS THINKING

In this way, one of the most cogent criticisms of modernist constructions of identity lies in the problem of dichotomous thinking (Berlin, 1990). This is the tendency, which we discussed in Chapter 1, for language (and our conceptions of the world) to be constructed as binary opposites, creating forced categories of choices, often opposed to each other, in which one member of the pair is usually privileged. It is easy to think of many examples of this.

Exercise

Refer back to your three-line description of yourself. What binary opposite categories are implied in your descriptions of yourself?

Gender categorisations are often the most obvious (usually a forced choice of man/ woman), but there may be other less obvious ones. For example, the choice of the label 'dog lover' implies the existence of another category 'non-dog lover' or perhaps 'dog hater'. Of course not all categorisations fit this bill. For example, for me the label 'social worker' does not immediately bring to mind an opposite category (although depending on the circumstances I might be tempted sometimes to think about whether people are either social workers or non-social workers, perhaps if I am about to deliver a paper to a mixed professional group).

What is most interesting about such categorisations is that they clearly serve particular interests. In the case of defining social workers or non-social workers, I am safeguarding my own interests in being clear about the possible expectations of the group I am about to speak to, and pre-empting issues on which I might expect criticism or misunderstanding.

Berlin (1990) conducts a thorough analysis of examples of dichotomous thinking (and its unhelpfulness) in social work. A major problem with dichotomous thinking is that it does not allow us to recognise, account for and value difference very well. Dichotomous thinking implies that most phenomena fit into 'binary' and 'oppositional' categories, in which one item of the binary is devalued in relation to the other, and mutually exclusive as well (e.g. you must either be a 'victim' or a 'perpetrator'). Aside from assigning a fixed identity, this has the added effect of devaluing difference, by implying that only one item of the binary is more valuable than the other.

Exercise

Think of some other examples of dichotomous thinking in social work.

Karen Healy (2000: 64) has drawn up a fairly comprehensive list of examples of binary opposites which are constructed in social work, to which I have adapted and added:

- middle class/working class;
- the privileged/the underprivileged;
- technical knowledge/lived experience;
- voice/silence;
- researcher/researched;
- worker/client;
- powerful/powerless;
- researcher/practitioner;
- theory/practice;
- professional/non-professional;

- professional/volunteer;
- voluntary client/involuntary client;
- public/private.

I will return to our discussion of binary oppositional thinking later when we explore the role of such thinking in constructing difference. For the moment however let us summarise the main criticisms of these conceptions of self and identity.

Identities based on social structural categorisations, no matter how many, can be problematic since they do not allow for change. To define people simply in terms of structural categorisations also seems to deny the rich variety of combinations, indeed individuality, arising from the variety of backgrounds, experiences and changes which seem so much a part of the contemporary world of migration, employment, familial instability and global influences. During the course of a lifetime people experience, are influenced by and interact within many different worlds. Locking people into fixed identity categories can also have the effect of fixing power or powerlessness to these categorisations. Therefore marginal groups who are defined by a powerless identity are effectively disempowered through the assignation of this label.

SUMMARY

There are then three main problems with traditional conceptions of self and identity:

1   They deny the possibility of changing identities in response to changing contexts at a number of levels.
2   They deny personal autonomy, the ability to change and reinvent the self in relation to changing contexts.
3   They 'fix' identities in ways which potentially disempower those with marginal identities. From a critical and postmodern perspective, we need a conception of self and identity which incorporates an understanding of changing identities and the ability to empower oneself by participating in making these changes.

REFORMULATING THE IDEAS OF SELF AND IDENTITY

In simple terms, a postmodern view recognises that people's identities are made and understood in context and that therefore they may:

- change;
- be contradictory;
- be multiple.

The postmodern idea of identity, or 'subjectivity' as it is sometimes termed, can be summarised as 'multiple, contradictory and in-process' (Newton, 1988: 99). The idea that identities can only be fully understood in context, which may be fluid and changing, is sometimes referred to as 'situated subjectivity'. Identities and people's own perspectives must be interpreted in the light of changing and specific situations in which they are located. Not only do they change in relation to context and over time, but they may include quite contradictory aspects (presumably because the contexts in which we live can be experienced as contradictory). As well, people may have a number of different identities at any one time, again, because all of us operate in several different contexts even over the course of one day.

Exercise

Review your three-line description of yourself and add any descriptions you think are missing. How many different 'identities' can you identify? Think about how your descriptions of yourself might have changed over time. Do you have a sense of yourself which is continuing, despite all this? How have you arrived at this sense?

In a critical postmodern view, structural categories such as race, class and gender might still have meaning, although a person's self-hood might not automatically be linked to these categories. This is seen as a 'non-essentialist' view – the recognition that although there may be fixed labels and categories with which people identify, the ways in which these are actually enacted and understood might vary according to the situation.

This notion gets us around one of the potential problems with a postmodern approach to identity – that although identities might be fluid, people still experience their sense of self as coherent and often have a need to do so (Sands, 1996: 176). Sands suggests it is better to refer to self-hood, or subjectivity as 'positionality' or 'narrative identity'. Both these terms acknowledge the idea of a sense of self, a need for some coherence in the way people see themselves, but at the same time allow for the relative and changing aspects of identity.

According to Sands, the term 'positionality' assumes that the self/identity both does and does not exist in an essential form. It depends on the context in which we are using the concept. Certain parts of the self might remain constant, others might change and different and multiple identities might co-exist (1996: 176). In simple terms, while a person might not see their own perception of her or himself changing, she or he might recognise that the way other people see them, and therefore the way in which they present themselves, may change from situation to situation.

Sands usess the term 'narrative identity' (borrowed from Ricoeur (1986)) to acknowledge the idea that narratives provide a means for people to integrate potentially adverse experiences into a coherent whole. Because narratives usually carry a cultural requirement to be coherent, people fashion them in these terms, in order to gain acceptance and validation within their own cultural context. It is effectively through constructing culturally appropriate stories then, that identities are made coherent

(Sands, 1996: 178). The idea of narrative identity therefore carries with it the possibilities of both coherence and change, of coherence being remade constantly in relation to experience and context.

This type of conception of identity also addresses another of the major criticisms of traditional modernist conceptions – it restores a sense of agency to the individual. Through participating in constructing their own narratives, people are also effectively taking some responsibility for constructing their own identities. However, they create narratives for social and cultural reasons, and often the form the narrative takes is culturally influenced (Cohler, 1991; Ricoeur, 1986) and certainly infused with and within cultural discourses. This idea that individuals are being constructed, but also engaged in constructing themselves at the same time, is important in a postmodern feminist (Butler, 1995; Fawcett, 2000: 67), and indeed in a critical and postmodern view.

The idea that identity can include contradictions is also important. In an earlier chapter I discussed 'complicity with oppression', the idea that people might seemingly engage in behaviour which works against their own best interests. This might be explained by the suggestion that people operate within a number of different discourses, not all of which might be their own. They may perceive their 'best interests' differently from the way in which accepted discourses define them. For instance, I know of many women – feminists - who still do the bulk of the housework for their male partners. In feminist discourse their behaviour is seen as contradictory. In terms of relationship preservation, however, it might not be. Presumably any feminist, like any woman, also has concerns about relationships, because she lives in a culture and social structure in which they are important. I am not trying to justify here the idea that it is acceptable for men not to do their share of the housework. What I am pointing out is that contradictions exist in identities because contradictions exist in discourses, and identities cannot and do not exist separately from, to use a more jargonish phrase, their 'discursive context'. This aspect of postmodern thinking about the contradictions inherent in identities is important in allowing us to see and appreciate the complexity of people's everyday lived experience. Such a view is therefore important in allowing us to envisage ways in which such experiences might be changed.

SELF AND IDENTITY IN REFLEXIVE MODERNITY

Beck's (1992) concept of reflexive modernity, and Giddens' (1991) concept of 'life politics' are important in understanding these newer approaches to understanding self and identity. 'Reflexive modernity' is Beck's term for the current social period. The main features of reflexive modernity include a breakdown of predictable life stages, norms and rituals, given increased uncertainty in social conditions. The corresponding rise in access to information also contributes to shifts in social boundaries, giving the opportunity to remake them. This then places emphasis on individual identity-making in changing contexts. People derive their sense of community from diverse sources. This however, whilst affording greater opportunity for change, also entails greater risk, given the uncertain conditions. The task of living thus becomes the task of charting a path through these conditions, and this involves finding meaningful constructions of the self. As Giddens says, the self is a reflexive project (1991), as people constantly (re)negotiate their identities.

Thus the experience for the individual person living in reflexive modernity becomes a kind of politics of living or 'life politics' (Giddens, 1991) as people negotiate their own path through sets of unpredictable circumstances. Ferguson (2001) conceptualises life politics as being about how people make a set of *choices* within a set of *chances*. That is, it is about how people engage with the opportunities they encounter. The concept of life politics in effect provides a useful way to understand the concept of individual agency with a social structure which is fragmenting.

A detailed concept of individual agency is also becoming increasingly important to our understanding of how social workers operate as individuals, and also in relation to service users as individuals (Jeffrey, 2011). Reformulating our concepts of self and identity is therefore also important to reformulating our understandings of how individuals exercise power and influence both for themselves and in interactions.

THE WHOLE SELF

An important implication of this more complex view of self and identity is the recognition that there are many aspects to the self made in a social context. As we noted earlier from Sands (1996: 170), there are at least three aspects – life history, accrued values, and relationships with others. If we add to this the three main structural categorisations which are commonly used to define people socially – race, class and gender – we build up an even more complex picture. Of course it is possible to add to these three major categories – ethnicity, age, ablement (dis/ability), health, sexuality – to build up an even more complex picture.

In discussing the role of subjectivity in research, ethnographers like Rosaldo (1993) point out the role of personal weakness and emotions in influencing our interactions, and therefore the knowledge that we see and make from situations. For example, Brigg's ethnographic study of an Eskimo family is partly conducted through the prism of her own emotions. Her depression and need for privacy appeared at great odds to the Eskimo way of living and earned her a loss of status in that community (Briggs in Rosaldo, 1993: 178). She was able to understand something of the Eskimo approach to living, by observing their reactions to her emotional outbursts, but also by comparing her reactions to their living conditions with her own.

Brigg's emotional reactions to the cold temperatures and harsh living conditions of the Eskimos points up the *embodied* nature of the self. Our identities, and the knowledge we make for ourselves and create for others, are mediated through our own physical perceptions and experience. Additionally, our physical appearance carries social connotations and has a role in defining our social place and identity.

While this seems like a self-evident point, there has been much criticism of sociological thinking that has omitted this perspective from our understanding of social interactions (Turner, 1992).

It is not hard to see how an understanding of race, health, age or abled related identities might be integrally concerned with the embodied nature of knowledge and social relations. Leonard (1997: 41–3) also points out how an understanding of identity, from a postmodern perspective, also involves an understanding of the regulation of bodies. For instance, gender categorisations can be seen as based upon a desire to regulate women's bodies and sexuality. Health and medical systems are also based on a desire to regulate and monitor people's bodies:

> It is because people's physical bodies and their subjectivities are fused inextricably together that we might see the body as representing the subject, as a text which the professional observes for certain signs, signs which might be referring to what might be going on 'under the surface'. (Leonard, 1997: 55)

CONSTRUCTIONS OF THE SELF IN SOCIAL WORK

Exercise

Refer back to your last three-line description of yourself. Imagine that your ageing mother has been hospitalised and you have been asked to see the social worker about care options for her.

Think about how the social worker might see you and how you would want to be seen by the social worker. Try to rewrite your three-line description, describing yourself in the terms in which you would like to be seen.

What identities have you constructed for yourself and what identities do you think the social worker will have constructed for you?

Compare the two.

It is useful for us to examine what types of people social work and welfare discourse more generally try to create. What identities should service users have and what identities do we believe them to have? An analysis of this type tells us much about how we participate in constructing ourselves and the people we aim to assist. It is likely that there is quite a bit of discrepancy between how you think the social worker might have seen you and how you would want to be seen. Often we do not want to be seen as service users; not just because we are aware of the loss of status involved and possible disempowerment, but because of the ways in which our lives and identities may be remade to fit the identity of service user. Yet in order for 'good social work' to take place, there may be a need for people to fit the relevant identity categories.

Leonard (1997: 50–2) argues that the New Right movement has constructed the idea of the welfare recipient as 'dependent', a subject position in which 'the individual is likely to experience . . . subjection to a discursive formation which addresses her or him as an object of both negative ethical judgement and moral reform' (p. 51). In this sense, there is an implication both of how the identity of a welfare recipient is seen (negatively judged) and what they should become (reformed). Cannan (1994) makes a similar point when she refers to the 'enterprise culture' governing current conceptions of welfare, in which service users are supposed to become independent and self-reliant. These sentiments are echoed in Jordan and Jordan's (2000) analysis of Britain's New Labour Third Way policies as 'tough love'. Tough love incorporates the following characteristics:

- emphasis on the family and education as sources of norms and discipline;
- demand for more reciprocal effort from those who receive welfare support;
- a tough response to forms of 'disorder' like crime, drug use, begging;
- the prescription of moral standards and obligations;
- support for those in 'genuine' need (Jordan and Jordan, 2000: 26).

These types of conceptions also underpin the more recent developments in neo-liberal thinking (Dominelli, 2009). These conceptions of the identity of the 'welfare service user' have built up over some time. Leonard traces the idea of the 'welfare dependent' to corresponding ideas about the 'culture of poverty', in which the dominant discourse about service users included their construction as being 'trapped' in a pervasive and self-perpetuating way of being and doing which effectively kept them poor. Interestingly, however, current conceptions of the new underclass lump together groups which may have no feelings of group self-identity – for example, 'the poor' may now include single parents, the unemployed and ageing populations (Leonard, 1997: 53). The overarching identity as 'underclass' is clearly one attributed from outside. The contradiction inherent in this attribution of dependency is that it is in fact only dependency on *the state* which is discouraged – dependency on *the market* is in fact encouraged (Leonard, 1997: 53).

Exercise

Identify a field of welfare services in which you have had some experience. What kinds of identities were attributed to the users of that service? How were 'good' and 'bad' service users defined? What corresponding identities did social workers and other professionals have/construct in that service?

Of course different fields may attribute appropriate identities to service users and professionals, depending on the specific characteristics and discourses of that setting.

For instance, in an income security setting, a 'good' service user might be seen as someone who engages in budget planning and counselling and only asks for assistance in extreme emergencies. A 'bad' client might be seen as someone who 'manipulates' the system and takes no responsibility for managing their finances. For example, Moffat (1999) discusses how a social assistance office creates the category of 'welfare client'. In a child protection setting an appropriate service user may be someone who is seen as a 'victim' of their situation. A poor service user may be seen as someone who doesn't have any 'boundaries' and does not respond to discipline. Taylor and White (2000) provide some very useful analyses of the sorts of ways in which service users might construct themselves as 'appropriate clients' by establishing identities as 'credible', 'entitled', with an 'authentic story'. Similarly professionals might seek to establish themselves as impartial, simply 'relating facts' or 'bound by the organisation'.

In Chapter 9 we will explore how these more complex conceptions of self and identity, and the way we construct them in welfare structures and cultures, affect some of the most basic and taken-for-granted practices in social work, like interviewing, assessment and establishing rapport. However, in the second part of this chapter, I want to explore how our reformulated notion of identity affects the idea of difference, and how we make and understand this, from a postmodern and critical standpoint.

MAKING DIFFERENCE AND 'OTHERING'

Earlier we spoke about dichotomous thinking and how the construction of binary oppositional categories could lead to a fixing of identity and an effective disempowering of the individual. Since identities are made in relation to and in interaction with the social world, the making of identity also involves the making of difference.

In simple terms, according to poststructural thinking, the main problem inherent in establishing difference also arises out of the problem of binary constructions in language. Because Western logocentric thinking tends to construct differences in terms of binary oppositions, we tend to define one category against the other, or in terms of the other. Because one member of the pair is usually privileged, it is the characteristics of this privileged member which are used to define and measure the other. Thus, for instance, feminists argue that women's identity is defined in terms of men's (therefore in terms of what they are not) and therefore devalued. As well, because the binaries are constructed as oppositional and mutually exclusive, the characteristics of one cannot (are presumed not to) belong to the other, and are usually couched in the opposite terms. Thus men might be characterised as autonomous and independent and women relational and dependent. Clients may be characterised as powerless and lacking in information and professionals as powerful and informed. Service users might be categorised as potentially manipulative and social workers as objective.

Derrida (1978) however suggested that there are many phenomena and meanings which do not fit into these binary categories. He made a distinction between '*differance*' and 'difference' in order to point up this broad variety of meanings which is often left out of our discourse because language categories do not exist. He used the term '*differance*' to refer to meanings which encompass 'both–and' categories; neither category, or alternative categories (Grosz, 1989; Sands and Nuccio, 1992).

Because difference is often constructed in a binary and oppositional manner, difference categories may become fixed. And because they are often determined by the dominant discourse, then the difference categories that are created often preserve dominant categorisations and hierarchies.

Exercise

Re-examine your earlier exercise in which you described yourself as you thought the hospital social worker might see you, and compare that with how you might wish to be seen.

What kinds of terms did you use to describe yourself and how did they compare with the terms you thought the social worker might use?

What are some of the potential problems with this?

Did you find that you were defining yourself at all using the terminology you thought the social worker might use? If so, this would be an example of using the dominant discourse to define other categories. You may have found that you were quite frustrated because you felt you were defining yourself in someone else's terms. It might have been quite difficult to present yourself in a 'good' light. For example, imagine if the social worker put only two options to you: that your mother live with you to be cared for by you, or that she be placed in a nursing home. If you refuse to have her in your home you are therefore seen as uncaring and selfish. Although you may feel you are quite caring, because you also need to consider the needs of your teenage children, the category for you to be both caring, yet refuse to take your mother in, does not exist. You are therefore limited to being constructed as selfish. In this case, the appropriate number and types of categories do not exist to represent the range of experiences. So you lose out by being defined in a negative way.

This is a really clear example of how *differance* might be constructed as inferior, and of how the service user's perspective might be completely silenced, dismissed or not even recognised, simply because the categories for labelling it do not exist. In simple terms this is how difference is often constructed, and how problems arise because it is usually constructed along the lines of dominant thinking.

This following story from my own experience, which I have referred to earlier (Fook, 2001a), illustrates the problem of difference in another way. I am Australian-born Chinese by descent, being the third generation of my family to be born in

Australia. Although of Chinese appearance, I was raised to speak only English, and in fact speak it with a broad Australian accent. I can well remember my frustration and annoyance when I attended a workshop on cross-cultural counselling, run by a prominent white North American trainer, some years ago. He began the training by informing us that many people in traditional cultures have particular meanings attached to their names, so he thought it was a good idea to begin an interview by asking the meaning of a person's name. We then conducted role-played interviews, starting with this question. I remember thinking I didn't have a clue what my name, 'Janis', meant (unless my parents had deliberately named me after Janis Joplin the rock singer, whose first name is spelt the same as mine). Even worse, I couldn't care less. Not that I thought I was typical of the different cultural groups with whom practising professionals interact, but I was pretty sure I wasn't atypical either. In fact, nearly 20 per cent of the Australian population are second or third generation migrants (Jayasuriya, 1997: 11). What offended me about the example of asking the meaning of a name was its almost innocent assumption of difference, a clear route to 'othering' and distancing a person. I felt I had somehow been assigned an inferior status, constructed as different to and perhaps patronised by my interviewer. Without waiting to find out who I was, in my own terms, the interviewer had assumed my difference and related to me in those terms. He wasn't concerned about finding out *who I thought I was*, only initially relating in terms of *what he thought he saw*.

The cross-cultural trainer had also done several other things which are problematic from a postmodern and critical standpoint. He had made a prejudiced assumption that because I appeared 'non-white' I therefore came from a 'traditional' background. He had assumed only two categories and that I belonged automatically to the 'other' one (that is, not his). Because of my embodied appearance, he had assumed I belonged to a 'different' category, and that this category was automatically inferior. In the discussion immediately following, I voiced some of my concerns (perhaps foolishly). What was interesting was that I felt it was very difficult for me to get my points across, because the only way in which the instructor felt he could make reparation was to instate me to the status of his category. He thought I wanted to be seen like him, in fact to be regarded as 'white', and therefore that his cross-cultural strategies of asking about traditional names did not apply to me. I, on the other hand, was quite comfortable with my racial and ethnic identity, but did not like being patronised. I didn't want to be elevated to his status – I just wanted my own category recognised. But in his thinking, the terms for him to understand this did not exist.

Amy Rossiter (1995) comes to this realisation from the standpoint of a white middle-class, non-racist woman (as she sees herself), who believes that in according her non-white colleague the status of 'friend', she is also according her the status of 'sameness' and equality. In giving this identity category to her colleague, she believes she is also acting in a non-racist way, effectively saying 'you are as good as me' because you are the same as me. Of course there are implicit assumptions here about non-white categories still being racially inferior. As well, the non-recognition of non-white experience being different actually serves to devalue it. Not recognising its existence and legitimacy serves as a way of silencing and dismissing it.

Making difference also involves the concept of 'othering', that is, creating a (binary oppositional) category of different 'other'. People often create categories of 'other' in order to better define and distinguish the groups to which they belong, from people (and groups) who they do not want to be associated with. Said's famous concept of 'orientalism' (1978) is perhaps one of the best known examples of 'othering'. It referred to the tendency of white colonisers to characterise some colonised groups in unfamiliar and therefore undesirable terms vis-à-vis themselves in order to preserve the power distinctions. History is of course replete with examples of 'othering' which have served to justify racist attitudes and discriminatory practices. For instance, in Australia, Chinese people have been deliberately characterised as holding non-Christian values (Fitzgerald, 2007).

Jeffrey (2011: 71) notes that in relation to social work, 'othering' is the antithesis of agency. In other words, the act of 'othering', or creating binary oppositional categories serves to marginalise and disempower certain groups. How we make difference, and whether or not we do it in ways which 'other' certain groups, is integral to our understanding of social inclusion and exclusion.

DIFFERENCE, DIVERSITY AND INCLUSIVITY

How does this understanding of the making of difference help us as critical social work practitioners, and what sorts of dilemmas does it raise? We will discuss these possibilities in some detail in Part 3 of the book, but in this section I wish to refer to some of the broad directions which are indicated by our foregoing analysis.

One of the major challenges in developing a critical postmodern practice is creating meaningful labels and categories which order our world, but which do not at the same time deny or stigmatise the experiences of marginalised groups.

THE DILEMMA OF DIFFERENCE

According to Minow (1985) the 'dilemma of difference' is a major problem in working with people with disabilities. How do we label disability categories, without stigmatising or discriminating against the people defined by the categories? She recognises that in order to name and validate experience we may need to coin labels which bring it to public awareness. So the creation and application of the 'disability' label can make important political gains for people with disabilities. The recognition of difference and the creation of an identity category on the basis of it can have positive effects. At the same time, however, that same process of categorising can have deleterious effects as well. By naming the difference, we also create the possibility of discrimination.

How to recognise and validate difference without discriminating unfairly is a central problem for critical social work practitioners. The main answer she puts forward is to locate the problem of difference squarely in the relationships that define the difference, rather than in the difference itself. The problem is in the way we construct difference, rather than being inherent to the differences we identify. She argues, as Rossiter points out earlier in relation to her non-white colleague, that the problem of ascribing stigma comes about because we equate 'sameness' with 'equality' and 'difference' with 'inequality'. More inclusive formulations might incorporate this understanding that 'difference' and 'equality' are not part of the same categories themselves, nor are they mutually exclusive categories. In fact the attribution of equality may involve the recognition of difference.

Brown takes a slightly different approach to Minow. She argues that postmodern social work should be about 'identifying contradictions, tensions and layers of the ever-changing aspect of social work identities', rather than delineating difference (Brown, 1994: 42). I would take this to mean that rather than actually defining differences as 'differences', perhaps it is better to talk about contradictions, multiple or other perspectives, and changes. The language of our labels for categories needs to reflect these aspects.

Yet another viewpoint is put forward by Williams (1996). She argues that it is meaningful to assert differences. She differentiates between 'differences' and identifies three types:

- diversity, which is the difference claimed because of shared collective experience, which is not necessarily subordinated, e.g. age;
- difference, if there is resistance against subordinate status, e.g. gender;
- division, if the difference is translated into a form of domination and forms an identity which protects a privileged position, e.g. race.

In this breakdown, it is useful from a critical social work standpoint to pursue 'diversity' and its recognition. Difference becomes more problematic when it is associated with the potential for subordination. She also points out usefully that not all discourses about difference necessarily see it as problematic. She identifies three discourses around how difference is addressed:

- the consumer choice discourse;
- the management of diverse needs discourse;
- political and anti-disciminatory discourses.

In the first two sets of discourses, difference is actually constructed as, and might be used quite positively in terms of, responding to community needs.

It is useful to refer to a specific example in illustrating how fixed identity categories and notions of difference can work for or against the political interests of groups defined as 'different'. With regard to the situation of indigenous peoples in Australia, for instance, there is substantial criticism of the essentialist view of Aboriginal culture (Lewin, 1991; Patton, 1995), particularly as one constructed by anthropologists (Finlayson and Anderson, 1996). It is possible to view Aboriginal ethnicity as constructed through harsh state policies of segregation and assimilation – Aborigines were institutionalised (put on missions or reserves), their children removed and their rights to marriage and movement curtailed. While not to deny the injustice of such practices however, there is also an argument that none of these policies could be all-pervasive in the construction of Aboriginal identity – many Aborigines learned both to accommodate and contravene these practices (Finlayson and Anderson, 1996: 53–4).

Taking a more dynamic view of ethnic identity in relation to Aboriginality, Lewin (1991) notes that Aborigines are increasingly taking responsibility for defining Aboriginality, which is not a homogeneous category. Not recognising that Aboriginality is not homogeneous has political consequences. Lewin argues:

> Ideological commitment to the existence of a homogenous culture and its independence from social context prevents recognition of key structural factors, such as Aborigines' and migrants' recognition of their disadvantaged position and their use of those perceptions to mobilise to help redress that disadvantage. (Lewin, 1991: 175)

In other words, an essentialist view of Aboriginality can easily function as a victim-blaming political stance, in which a homogeneous and fixed Aboriginal culture is seen as the cause of the structural disadvantage of Aboriginal peoples. Lewin finishes by arguing that universalist and essentialist ideas of Aboriginality also function to legitimate governmental control over the definition and solution of problems in the Aboriginal community.

IDENTITY POLITICS AND CRITICAL POSSIBILITIES

It is arguments such as Lewin's which give rise to the potential of what is often termed 'identity politics', the possibility of resisting domination through the recognition of difference and the creation of new identity categories as a result (Best and Kellner, 1991: 205).

The key point, for us, as social workers, from this type of analysis, is that the politics of identity construction become integral in resisting and challenging domination. Identity construction plays an important role in the empowerment of disadvantaged groups. For example, Karen Crinall (1999) points out how, although feminist analysis is perceived at one level to be helpful to young homeless women, at another level it can be experienced as disempowering, since it is based on the necessary assumption that young homeless women are powerless victims. It is also the language of middle-class women, a discourse arising from a different set of experiences and positions. With indigenous Australians, as argued above, it is the control over the construction of Aboriginality, as well as the specific constructions, which are important. There are therefore two key issues which have a direct bearing on social work practice in relation to identity politics: the elements of the identity, as well as the control over its construction, are vital in ensuring a critical social work practice with multiple differing groups. Young (1990) notes the politicising effects of a process of control in the construction of identity:

> Assumptions of the universality of the perspective and experience of the privileged are dislodged when the oppressed themselves expose those assumptions by expressing positive images of their experience. By creating their own cultural images they shake up received stereotypes about them. (Young, 1990: 155)

Thus *narrativity* is seen as a route towards a type of social change:

> The postmodern politics of identity defines effective social change as the achievement of self-hoods by group members who tell stories about their own lives and thus do not deny their identities as members of these racial, gender and cultural affinity groups. (Agger, 1998: 73)

We will develop in more detail elements of this narrativity approach and its usefulness as practice strategies for critical social workers in Part 3 of this book.

Chapter summary

In this chapter we have explored how our understandings of personhood, or self and identity, are reformulated from a postmodern and critical perspective. A sense of self, or identity, is typically made up of both 'internal' and 'external' ascriptions i.e. both personally and socially inscribed attributes. Structural perspectives in social work are problematic in that they can over-emphasise identities ascribed through the main structural categories of race, class and gender.

There are three main problems with more traditional conceptions of self and identity:

1 They deny the possibility of changing identities in response to changing contexts at a number of levels.
2 They deny personal autonomy, the ability to change and reinvent the self in relation to changing contexts.
3 They 'fix' identities in ways which potentially disempower those with marginal identities.

However, a postmodern view recognises that people's identities are made and understood in context and that therefore they may:

• change;
• be contradictory;
• be multiple.

The concept of dichotomous thinking is useful in helping us understand how we create binary oppositional categories out of many of our social groupings. This in turn helps us understand how we create difference and 'other' groups who are socially different, thereby contributing to their disempowerment. This in turn points up critical possibilities for creating inclusionary practices, and for empowerment through identity politics.

FURTHER READING

SELF

Mansfield, N. (2000) *Subjectvity: Theories of the Self from Freud to Haraway*. St Leonards: Allen & Unwin. Ch. 12 'The subject and postmodernism', pp. 162–73.

Helpful overview of the postmodern perspective on the self.

Howard, C. (2007) 'Three models of individualized biography', in C. Howard (ed.), *Contested Individualization: Debates about Contemporary Personhood*. New York: Palgrave. Ch. 2, pp. 25–43.

A more contemporary take on current theoretical approaches to understanding the individual in society

IDENTITY POLITICS

Gnanamuttu, M. (2004) 'Whose side are you on? Politicised identitites', in L. Davies and P. Leonard (eds), *Social Work in a Corporate Era*. Aldershot: Ashgate. pp. 60–75.

A very interesting account, incorporating personal experiences and conversations, of the expectations around identity, and consequently the politics involved.

DIFFERENCE AND DISCOURSE

Johnson, K. (2009) 'Disabling discourses and enabling practices in disability politics', in J. Allan, L. Briskman and B. Pease (eds), *Critical Social Work*. Sydney: Allen & Unwin. Ch. 14, pp. 188–200.

This chapter includes a nice analysis of disability discourses and shows the implications of this for working in the disability field.

PART 3

REDEVELOPING PRACTICES

7

CRITICAL DECONSTRUCTION AND RECONSTRUCTION

In Chapter 5 we discussed the idea of discourse, and how our language (the way we frame and communicate our experience and perceptions) both creates and restricts the way we see the world, our social relationships and structures. In this chapter I want to explore in detail some of the ways in which an analysis of discourse might be usefully translated into practice strategies for the critical social worker. In Chapter 3, we also discussed new understandings of knowledge, and its relationship to power. I introduced the idea of critical reflection, and how a postmodern and critical orientation to understanding knowledge underpins one way of approaching critical reflection. In this chapter, I focus particularly on critical deconstruction and reconstruction, as the process derives directly from a postmodern critical theory base. However, as I also mentioned in Chapter 3, critical reflection may be theorised and practised using many different frameworks. I focus here on deconstruction and reconstruction, as they fit most closely with the framework developed in this book.

UNSETTLING DOMINANT DISCOURSES

DISCOURSE ANALYSIS AND POSSIBILITIES FOR CRITICAL RESISTANCE, CHALLENGE AND CHANGE

If we see language (or discourses) as not fixed, that is, as multiple, changing and contestable, as diverse forms of communication, we realise that contradictory messages will often be both given and interpreted. Because of this lack of uniformity, there is an opening for dominant discourses to be *resisted*, simply by recognising that the frameworks of meaning being put forward in any situation do not have to be accepted. This is an extremely important point, and one which holds much potential for the critical social worker who seeks to change dominant power structures and relations. The strength of dominant discourses is at the same time their very weakness. They are powerful often because they are unquestioned and all players, even those who do not benefit, uncritically accept them. In this sense, the power of discourses lies in the degree to which they are unquestioned. However, simply choosing not to accept dominant ideas and pointing up contradictions can work to resist, challenge and change these dominant meaning systems. Therein lies the critical potential of a discourse (and therefore power) analysis.

As well, any one particular discourse will involve a number of perspectives (in Foucault's term 'subject positions'). In other words, any one perspective will come from a particular *subject* (person or group of people) who will hold a particular *position* in the situation. The idea of positioning is therefore important in understanding a situation or discourse, since the very idea of having a position implies the existence of others, or at the very least, a position of reversal. Since there are therefore multiple perspectives or meanings, the possibility of change exists, through the imagining of different positions. Naming (and therefore creating) the possibility of alternative viewpoints and discourses is one step towards critical change.

Analysis of discourses should also take into account how they *operate*, in order to uncover which interests are being served at a particular point in time, and in which particular situations. Weedon (1987) also points out that these interests may be different from those the discourse initially appears to represent. Because discourses are not *fixed* (that is, their meaning is relative to the situation and interpretation, and subjective position), they may operate in different ways, for different purposes and at different times. When analysing discourses, it is therefore crucial to understand how they operate, for whom, and in which particular times and situations. In this way, it is possible to apply resistance, challenge and change strategies much more strategically and effectively by targeting specific sites.

This capacity for unsettling or destabilising commonly held or accepted beliefs is potentially one of the most powerful sets of strategies which arises from a postmodern and critical understanding (Healy, 2000).

DECONSTRUCTIVE METHODS AND DISCOURSE ANALYSIS IN PRACTICE

Deconstructive methods for analysing discourse, which arise out of postmodern and poststructural thinking, have been developed extensively by social researchers (Denzin and Lincoln, 1994; Kellehear, 1993; Reason and Bradbury, 2001; Alvesson and Sköldberg, 2009). Yet a particular advantage of such methods lies in their applicability to practitioners as well. This connection has perhaps been less well developed, but in this chapter I propose to explore it in detail in order to develop the range of strategies which might be used by social work practitioners, both in researching their own practice and in developing a way of approaching practice situations which will allow new practice strategies to be devised. Making such connections will also enable social workers effectively to mine the rich practice strategies inherent in many of the already well-developed research methods.

Much has been made of the links between social work practice and research, particularly the commonalities between qualitative (Padgett, 1998), constructive (Rodwell, 1998) and reflective (Fook, 1996) forms of inquiry and the work of social work. Rodwell, for instance, lists the main aspects that constructivist research and social work have in common:

- the context-bounded nature of reality;
- the interactive nature of knowing and understanding;
- egalitarianism;
- dialogic nature of knowing;
- viability of tacit knowing;
- contextual nature of functional/pragmatic responses;
- consensus on reconstructions needed for lasting change;
- multiple perspectives needed for sense making and meaning making;
- tentative nature of knowledge and goals (Rodwell, 1998: 8–11).

One of the directions which postmodern thinking indicates is that the worlds of practice, theorising and research are much less separate than perhaps more binary-based thinking has assumed (Fook, 1996; Kearney, 2004). This realisation potentially allows a much more holistic (as opposed to fragmented) approach to using and combining methods from both practice and research discourses, in order to improve and create links between our practice, our theorising and our research. An understanding of discourse analysis methods provides a starting point in developing such an approach.

In brief, discourse analysis is based upon an understanding of how discourses shape meaning. Through language, people are involved in constructing their social world. This involves three aspects: (1) people creating accounts using previously existing language; (2) people actively selecting particular words, phrases and constructions from the many available; and (3) the consequences of and responses to the particular modes of expression which are used (Alvesson and Sköldberg, 2009: 232). Discourse analysis therefore involves the uncovering of the ways we talk about and choose to label experience, and also how these shape this experience.

In a practical sense analysing discourse might involve analysis of the *semiotics*. Semiotic analysis 'refers not simply to the uncovering of rules, relations and mentality behind written texts but also to social life and its symbols in general' (Kellehear, 1993: 43). In this sense, the 'text' or material which is analysed may be any aspect of communication in which discourse is inscribed. Thus all aspects of social life become potential 'texts'. In this style of analysis, further to the themes which might emerge from the text, it is also important to uncover what perspectives are missing, which binary categorisations are used, which assumptions are implied but not explicit, or which meanings are distorted or repressed. These might signal some of the ways we have constructed our meaning to preserve particular practices or structures.

SUMMARY

In summary then, the practice of discourse analysis involves:

- themes which emerge from an analysis of the 'text';
- perspectives which are missing;
- binary oppositional categories which are constructed;
- implicit assumptions; and
- meanings which are distorted or repressed.

An analysis of discourse in this way also involves a deconstruction of thinking and examination of how our talk and behaviour contributes to constructing social relations and structures. In the following section I develop in some detail a set of processes based on this approach.

THE CRITICAL RECONSTRUCTIVE PROCESS

I have developed the following based on an earlier formulation of this process (Fook, 2000b).

SUMMARY

In summary it involves four stages:

- deconstruction;
- resistance;
- challenge;
- critical reconstruction.

These four stages broadly trace a process beginning with an analysis of situations which allows for them to be changed or recreated in order for different power relations to be developed.

DECONSTRUCTION

This first stage involves questioning dominant discourses. Sometimes these might be seen as simply 'common sense', or they might be the taken-for-granted assumptions which are a part of our cultural heritage or particular environment. In social work they might be some of the 'grand narratives' which are commonly accepted, such as a belief in social justice or empowerment. Much of what enables discourses to remain dominant lies in the extent to which they go unquestioned. Therefore much of the potential to unsettle that power lies in our readiness to question them, and in the extent to which we are prepared to question them further once they are exposed to scrutiny.

Deconstructing involves searching for contradictions, different perspectives and interpretations. Perspectives which might be missing or glossed over should be uncovered. The presence of binary thinking can also alert us to problematic constructions. Recurring patterns and themes can alert us to dominant ways of thinking. It is helpful to become aware of how different discourses operate (for whom and in what contexts), and to locate the specific sites of operation (through language, beliefs, practices, structures, power relations and different subject positions). Locating our own perspective or subject position in the discourse is also crucial (this is a stance of reflexivity). Analysing how particular aspects of particular discourses preserve power relations and structures in particular situations is also another aspect of deconstruction.

Below is a set of questions that I have devised which helps us deconstruct situations in which we might find ourselves as practitioners or researchers. These are based on another formulation I developed earlier (Fook et al., 2000). The analysis can be conducted on a variety of 'texts', for example, case notes, verbal accounts, or simply our own thinking about situations. The 'text' might emerge through a variety of forms or processes, such as conversations, meetings, manuals and documents. A number of different texts might be analysed in order to develop a broad picture of a situation, or sometimes the analysis might be confined to a particular 'text' in order to achieve a more specific purpose. For example, if you are engaged in a self-reflective exercise you might confine your analysis to your own account of a situation. Later in this chapter I will outline how the following broad process might also be used as a tool for critical reflection.

Deconstructive questions

1 What main themes or patterns emerge from the description? What terms, phrases or patterns of communication reoccur frequently? What labels or categorisations occur? Is there evidence of binary opposites?

2 Who are all the potential players (individuals, groups or organisations) involved in the situation, or potentially affected by it?

3 Whose perspectives are represented and whose are missing?

4 What interpretations or explanations were made and whose were they? How were they represented and how did they influence the situation?

5 How might the situation have been interpreted differently and how might it have been interpreted by different players in the situation?

6 What knowledges and assumptions are implied and used in the account? How do they relate to (for example): practice theory; value and belief systems; paradigms; human behaviour; moral and ethical codes; social and political systems and change; power; gender and cultural considerations? Are they relevant and appropriate to the situation at hand?

7 Where do these assumptions originate? What roles or positions do these assumptions support? What players stand to gain or lose from holding them, and what social and power functions does holding these assumptions perform? What practices, systems or structures are upheld by these assumptions?

8 What holes, gaps or biases are there in the description? What perspectives are missing, distorted or devalued? What actions or assumptions support these biases?

SUMMARY

Exercise

Consider the following scenario.

You are a recently graduated social worker who has just started a new job in a community-based organisation which provides services to people with disabilities. The organisation employs over 100 staff, as well as co-ordinating over 60 volunteers. It provides a range of services including advocacy and support, community education and policy development. At the first staff meeting you are bewildered by an argument which takes place between Thelma (the organisation's director) and Ranjit (the deputy director and also unofficial 'head' social worker). Both Ranjit and Thelma have been employed in the organisation for many years. Apparently there is a history of conflict over whether professional qualifications should define the roles of workers, or whether it is simply a matter of finding the best person for the job. Ranjit argues that social workers are best qualified to co-ordinate volunteer services because they have a broad knowledge of community resources and are used to dealing with a diversity of people. But Thelma is not so sure. You sense that she does not like Ranjit. You become aware that this conflict will really affect your job, as much of it involves working with and training volunteers.

Deconstruct the account of the scenario using the guidelines on the previous page.

The account is constructed as if the main conflict (over 'social workers' vs. 'volunteers') is played out between two main players (Thelma vs. Ranjit). You, the recently graduated social worker, seem to be a relatively passive bystander, as do the service users, volunteers and other staff. These are the perspectives which are missing, or at least downplayed. The debate has been constructed as a binary opposite, in some ways, between the virtues of professional training over personal capabilities. There is an implication that this conflict is a negative thing, because you are 'bewildered' by it and also because you are concerned that it will affect your job. Where your perspective exists, your concerns are couched in terms of Thelma and Ranjit's concerns, rather than perhaps your own. For instance, there is no mention of what you think about the actual issues, your opinion on whether social workers make better volunteer co-ordinators. Is this because you feel the power in the situation lies with Thelma and Ranjit, and that you feel relatively powerless or that your perspective does not matter?

It is also interesting to examine the language used in relation to Thelma's and Ranjit's positions in the organisation. Where Thelma is termed 'the director', Ranjit is given an equivalent (although unofficial title) of 'head' social worker. Is there an attempt here to raise Ranjit's position to equal that of Thelma? What does this say about the perspective of the writer of the account? This might say something about how power might be viewed by the writer of the account. Perhaps official position is important to the writer in ascribing power. It is also emphasised that both Ranjit and Thelma have been at the organisation for some time. Is there an assumption that this also equates with power? It seems that their perspectives are accorded more status because of the length of their service.

There is also a vague hint that the personal dislike between Thelma and Ranjit could be problematic. Again this might indicate an assumption that personal conflict is potentially negative, as it is singled out for mention, in connection with how it might affect your job. It is interesting, for instance, to think about the other kinds of things which could have been mentioned about the situation. For instance, who are the other social workers and how many are there? Who might be potential allies or friends of yours among the existing staff? Why did you want the job and what are the opportunities it affords?

What appears to be a 'neutral' account in fact hides a particular perspective on the situation. This perspective (perhaps it is your *subject position*) does have something to do with power, and it seems to be about constructing yourself as the new social worker who is relatively powerless, with no support, caught up in a situation dominated by two mavericks. You are faced with having to work in a new job which will be adversely affected by the conflict between two people, both of whom are much more powerful than you, partly because they have been at the organisation a long time. You feel relatively powerless as a newcomer.

RESISTANCE

Once you have analysed the ways in which power relations have been constructed in a situation, it becomes possible to identify the ways of thinking that should be questioned, those for which alternatives need to be posited and perhaps not accepted accordingly. This stage of resistance therefore involves refusing to accept or participate in aspects of dominant discourses which work to disempower, or perhaps render a situation unworkable because of this.

In our exercise scenario above, we have automatically resisted the discourse implicit in the account, simply by engaging in a process of deconstructing, or questioning the position or perspective from which the account was written. This is not to suggest that we necessarily disagree with the perspective presented. However, simply through the act of treating the account as a discourse which is presented from a particular position, we have recognised that there might be other ways of seeing it which are not presented. So the very process of deconstruction is in itself an act of resistance, since it assumes a questioning of prevailing perspectives, and an opening of possibilities for other perspectives. This act of opening up is in itself an act of resistance. Some of the views about power which we have exposed for questioning involve implicit assumptions about power. For example, some of these are:

- that it is invested in the two main players, and not in the new social worker;
- that it is related to length of service in the organisation;
- that it has to do with official positions of status within the organisation.

Such views of course function to keep the new social worker in a powerless position, because they support the worker's view that she or he is powerless. In constructing

Thelma and Ranjit as powerful, the implication is that you, as the new social worker, are powerless. Uncovering these assumptions automatically implies that these are questionable and therefore automatically exposes them for scrutiny. Resistance thus involves a stance and willingness to question prevailing and implicit assumptions, particularly for their relevance to power relations.

Exercise

Try to identify any other assumptions about power which you think are operating in the scenario.

CHALLENGE

The third stage is one of challenge. Once prevailing discourses have been questioned and exposed, challenge involves the identification or labelling of both the existence and operation of dominant discourses. This in turn enables us to label other discourses which are hidden, glossed over or assumed.

Putting labels on discourses which are dominant and how they have preserved power relations goes another step towards allowing us to identify and recognise their operation. Naming missing perspectives allows us to value and account for them. Both activities constitute a further step in an ongoing process of not taking for granted the ways in which our ideas and actions are unwittingly influenced by prevailing ways of thinking and acting.

Ways in which we might label prevailing or hidden discourses can be many and varied, perhaps limited only by our imaginations. For example, coining new terms may be a useful technique. Speaking publicly about viewpoints which have not been heard, or are considered unfashionable might also be helpful. Drawing attention to the fact that what you are about to say is unpopular might be another technique. Labelling a perspective for what you think it is might be appropriate.

Exercise

Reconsider the scenario involving Thelma and Ranjit, and also your discourse analysis of it.

Try to label all the different discourses you felt were involved, both the dominant and missing ones.

You might have devised new categories. For instance, we could call one of the dominant perspectives the 'old staff' perspective, or perhaps the 'Thelma vs. Ranjit' perspective. We could even think about the dominant discourse which is presented as the 'non-service user' perspective, since service user points of view do not appear. It is easy to see how naming perspectives in this way puts a potentially different interpretation on them, and perhaps opens the way for other ways of seeing. For instance, to label the dominant perspective as 'old staff' opens the way for questioning whether it should be dominant simply because it is held by long-serving staff. To label a discourse 'Thelma vs. Ranjit' implies that it might simply be based on personal differences and perhaps ought not to become a concern for other staff.

Naming, in the way we have illustrated here, has the power to put a new perspective on discourses and in this sense opens up the way for the creation of new ones.

RECONSTRUCTION

Finally, a stage of reconstruction (change) involves formulating new discourses and structures. Naming existing and hidden discourses allows us to create new ones on this basis. Creating new discourses can involve many different activities. For example, it might include:

- inventing new terms, language or phrases;
- inventing new conversational devices;
- creating new categories;
- modelling new practices;
- creating structures or processes, cultures or climates which allow new discourses to develop and become accepted.

The new discourses we create might be highly specific, or may encompass a number of different practices and ways of seeing. In a sense, existing formal theories are a form of discourse. Our reconstruction might involve changing a small aspect of an existing formal theory or could extend to the formulation of a whole new theoretical approach.

From a critical point of view, discourses need to be reconstructed in ways which change dominant power relations, and in ways which allow marginal and silenced perspectives to be heard. Changing discourses might also involve renegotiating the ways discourses are heard and expressed, and perhaps in renegotiating how these are expressed in relation to each other.

Exercise

Using our example of the discourse in the community-based organisation, how might we reconstruct the discourse and power relations implicit in the account of it?

It is helpful to revisit some of the labels we coined in the third stage of 'challenge'. For instance, by terming the discourse an 'old staff' discourse, we could create a new category of discourse called 'new staff' which would allow us to canvas and value the opinions and interests of new staff. This would unsettle existing power relations and certainly assist you, as a new staff person, to manage your job in a way which might suit your needs and expertise. As well, labelling a discourse 'non-service user' implies the need to find out what the service user perspective is and to include this in deliberations. Conversation devices in staff meetings or other discussions might be used whereby new staff preface their comments by saying, 'Speaking from a new staff person's perspective, I . . .' This also functions to label, create a space for and create legitimacy for a new perspective. Attention might be given to setting up processes which automatically collect the views of service users. Meetings might be structured so that there is a time slot for new staff to speak about their perceptions.

SUMMARY

It is helpful to summarise the four stages of the deconstructive process as follows:

1   Deconstruction (analysis and identification of constructions of power).
2   Resistance (questioning of dominant constructions).
3   Challenge (labelling of dominant and missing constructions).
4   Reconstruction (changing of existing constructions and creation of new ways of seeing and related practices).

CRITICAL REFLECTION AND DE/RECONSTRUCTION

The process of deconstruction I have just outlined can be seen as very similar to the process of critical reflection we outlined in Chapter 3. A deconstructive and reconstructive process can be used as a form of critical reflection, in that critical reflection on our own practice can involve a type of deconstruction of our stories or accounts of our practice. In this way of critically reflecting, we are working towards identifying our assumptions (theories or constructions) about power, and changing these along more empowering lines. Thus, discourse analysis or deconstruction can also be used as a tool for critical reflection, as another process by which practice can be researched and changed along more empowering lines.

In this section I therefore want to outline in some detail an example of a critically reflective process based on deconstructive and reconstructive methods. In doing this, however, it is also important to remember that there is one major potential difference between deconstruction and critical reflection. Deconstruction may be performed on any discourse or set of discourses, whereas the primary focus of critical reflection is on your own personal discourses, and the source of these constructions. Ultimately the same sets of discourses might be unearthed. However, where the primary purpose of deconstruction is to unearth whatever discourses construct our ways of seeing, the prime purpose of critical reflection is to unearth how we ourselves participate in discourses which shape existing power relations. Deconstruction is therefore neither necessarily personal nor critical. The process may be used to focus on any set of discourses for any purpose. Critical reflection utilises a deconstructive process ultimately to analyse and change dominant power relations and structures by analysing and changing the ways we ourselves participate in constructing them. Critical reflection is therefore both personal and critical, and, in the approach I outline here, uses a deconstructive process to enable this. It is important to reiterate here that critical reflection can also be theorised in other ways (Fook et al., 2006). In particular, adult educationalists such as Boud et al. (1985) theorise critical reflection as learning from experience, and such approaches put greater emphasis on the personal nature of the learning. I will discuss these different perspectives, and the deconstructive/reconstructive approach in that context, at the end of the chapter.

With these qualifications in mind I outline a process of critical reflection which slightly refines the deconstructive/reconstructive process outlined above so that it focuses more particularly on the constructions of ourselves, as narrators of the story, rather than necessarily on the discourses of other players.

In other written material I have based this process on the use of the critical incident technique (Fook, 1996; Fook et al., 2000; Fook and Gardner, 2007), which is a well-used educational tool. I will use it again here, because it provides an excellent process for critical reflection and can be applied in a wide variety of ways, most particularly to analyse and research practice in order to make improvements. When used critically, the process of reflection involved in critical incident analysis paves the way for practice and practice theory to be redeveloped in more empowering ways. It is thus a crucial tool for the critical social worker.

CRITICAL INCIDENT TECHNIQUE

Critical incidents have been widely used as research (Benner, 1984) and teaching tools (Brookfield, 1995; Davies and Kinloch, 2000), but in this section I want to develop their usage primarily as a practice tool; a device and process for reconstructing personal practice along more critically empowering lines. In brief, a critical incident is any happening which was significant to a person for whatever reason. It may have been important because it was traumatic, or even because it was so mundane that it encapsulated something crucial about the nature of their work. It may have been remembered because it is unresolved, or posed a dilemma for the person. It may have struck a high point for them, or marked a turning point in their thinking. It is important to remember that the 'incident' should be a description of something concrete which actually happened (and in which the person was involved in some way), rather than a description of a more abstract issue or situation. This is because it is crucial to deconstruct our ideas in their 'rawest' form, and because, if we want to make connections with concrete practice, it is helpful to focus on concrete situations. In order to increase the potential learning, it also helps if the person sees the incident as critical because they are keen to learn something from it.

When using critical incidents as part of a critical reflective process, the incident and its 'telling' become the 'story' of the person which is deconstructed or reflected upon. Their narrative thus becomes a piece of text for deconstruction. This narrative can exist in many forms, for example, as a diary extract, an audio-taped account, a piece of conversation in a supervisory session, an interchange in a meeting, case file notes, a 'debrief' conversation between two colleagues, etc. For a more structured approach to the analysis of critical incidents, it is helpful to construct a narrative, that is, to write a story of a critical incident which can act as the 'text' about your practice to be analysed.

DESCRIPTION OF THE CRITICAL INCIDENT

This 'story' (written) of your incident should be a detailed description of the incident which includes the following:

1   Brief details of the social, organisational and personal context and background of the incident that you see as relevant.
2   Reasons the incident is critical to you, e.g. why you have chosen it; why you want to learn from it.
3   Brief description of the actual incident from your own perspective – the emphasis should be on concrete *description* rather than *analysis*. Try not to be deliberately abstract or theoretical at this stage, but to describe the incident as much from 'off the top of the head' as possible. This has the potential of telling us more about your spontaneous and unexamined assumptions than a more abstract or considered account might do.

ANALYSIS OF THE INCIDENT

The following set of questions should be used to analyse (reflect upon) the written account of your incident. In this stage of the process you become the 'researcher', deconstructing (reflecting upon) your account or narrative in order to identify the assumptions that construct your actions and notions of power. I have adapted these questions from those outlined in the section on deconstruction. You will notice that while the questions are similar in content, the focus here is on your own actions and ways of thinking.

SUMMARY

1   What main themes or patterns emerge from the description and appear important to me? What terms, phrases or patterns of communication do I use frequently? What labels or categorisations do I apply? Is there evidence of binary opposites?
2   Who are all the potential players (individuals, groups or organisations) involved in the situation, or potentially affected by it? Where do I sit in relation to them and how do I see myself in relation to them?

3   Whose perspectives are represented and whose are missing? How do I present my perspective in the story?

4   What interpretations or explanations did I make? Were they all mine or was I influenced by someone else or from elsewhere? Did I present them as mine? How did I represent and how did my interpretations influence the situation?

5   How might I have interpreted the situation differently? How many different interpretations could I have made, and how might it have been interpreted by different players in the situation?

6   What knowledges and assumptions do I imply and use in my account? What do these assumptions have to do with (for example) practice theory; value and belief systems; paradigms; human behaviour; moral and ethical codes; social and political systems and change; power; gender and cultural considerations? Are they relevant and appropriate to the situation at hand?

7   Where do these assumptions originate? Where do they come from? (e.g. family or cultural background? Professional training? A particular experience?) What roles or positions do these assumptions support? What roles or positions of mine do they support? What players stand to gain or lose from holding them, and what social and power functions does holding these assumptions perform, particularly for me? What practices, systems or structures are upheld by these assumptions?

8   What holes, gaps or biases are there in the description? What perspectives are missing, distorted or devalued? What actions or assumptions of mine or others support these biases?

9   What is my 'theory of power' arising from my account? Where does this come from and why have I developed it or taken it on board?

CREATING PRACTICE THEORY

Having undertaken this reflective analysis of the kinds of thinking and constructions which influence our practice, we are now in a position to identify how our thinking needs to change and how our practice theory needs to be redeveloped, so that it supports our empowerment and critical ideals. The following set of questions can assist in helping to redevelop our practice theory. As before, I have adapted these from other material I have written (Fook et al., 2000: 226–8).

SUMMARY

1   How does what happened in my incident compare with what I intended to do, or what I assumed I was doing? Was the theory I claimed to be using different from what was implied by my actions and interpretations? Did my actions fit my theory?

2   How does my experience of this situation compare with past or other experiences? What are common themes and patterns? What aspects of this incident or situation can be applied to others of mine or my colleagues?

3   How do the different types of knowledge and theory I used in this situation relate to each other?

4   What further questions arise out of my theory and practice as a result of this experience and my reflection?

5   What needs to be changed about my assumptions, theory, actions, interpretations, skills, as a result of these reflections?

6   What strategies can I use to make these changes? How do these strategies fit with my changed theories or interpretations?

7   How do the main assumptions which underlie my practice compare with the more formal theoretical perspectives? What do I need to change about the way I see these theories, or the way I use them, as a result of my reflections?

8   How would I label or categorise (or relabel or recategorise) my own theory as a result of this comparison? If I uncovered binary opposites in my story, what is a middle ground (or third or even fourth way) of constructing what was happening? Therefore what might be my version of or my terminology for the theory upon which I practice?

9   What is my reformulated theory of (or assumptions about) power which has/have resulted from my reflection?

10 How can I frame my own practice theory so that what I have learnt from this situation is useable in other contexts?

You can use this last stage of reflective questioning both to develop and improve practice, as well as identifying practice models from concrete practice itself. With this approach, the critical reflective process functions in many ways to evaluate, research and develop practice simultaneously. For the critical social work practitioner its additional value is its usefulness in exposing and developing the notions of power which underpin, construct and restrict our practice.

Exercise

Write an account of your own critical incident as outlined in this chapter, and conduct a reflective analysis of it, using the reflective question guidelines. Keep brief notes and refer back to them as you continue reading this book. As you continue to learn and practise as a social worker, you may like to refer back to this incident and your reflection on it, and note how your formulations of your own theory and practice might change.

OTHER APPROACHES TO CRITICAL REFLECTION

In Chapter 3 I noted that the deconstructive/reconstructive approach to critical reflection is only one way of theorising critical reflection, and that it is the one I have focused on for this book, as it fits most closely with the framework of the book. However in other work of mine on critical reflection, I have begun to develop a more integrated approach, under the broad rubric of learning from experience (e.g. Fook, 2011). I see the reflection (learning from experience) process as being initiated by digging for underlying assumptions (after the Schön reflective practice approach). What makes the reflection critical involves two aspects: (1) the learning needs to be relatively fundamental, so that deep values are reworked and new guidelines for practice/living are developed; and (2) it is based on a critical (as in critical social theory) analysis of how individual and social contexts are linked, and how therefore individual and social power is also linked. Critical reflection is thus transformative in that it allows a reworking of experience and guidelines for living in a more empowering way. There are many different ways in which such a process might be understood, and many theoretical frameworks which might assist in analysing experience so that transformative shifts can take place. Further reading has been included below so that you can follow up some of these different perspectives.

Chapter summary

In this chapter we have focused on how deconstructive methods and discourse analysis might be used by critical social work practitioners in their everyday work, through an analysis of the daily situations forming the context of their practice, to a detailed reflective analysis of how they participate in constructing the power relations integral to the contexts in which they practice. The chapter first develops a deconstructive and reconstructive approach to practice, then further develops this for use as critical reflection. The detailed process for each involves four stages: deconstruction, resistance, challenge and reconstruction. Summaries of each stage of the process, with detailed sets of questions to aid analysis, are covered in the chapter. In Chapter 10 we discuss in more detail how further analysis of narratives might also assist in unearthing specific ways that conversational devices and taken-for-granted ways of speaking might also preserve power relations in the context of the professional workplace.

FURTHER READING

CRITICAL REFLECTION AS DECONSTRUCTION/RECONSTRUCTION

Pockett, R. and Giles, R. (2008) *Critical Reflection: Generating Theory from Practice*. Sydney: Darlington Press.

This whole book contains chapters written by social work students from the University of Sydney. Each chapter is the student's account of their own critical reflection, using the deconstructive/reconstructive model outlined in this chapter. Excellent reading to illustrate the process in detail.

DIFFERENT PERSPECTIVES ON CRITICAL REFLECTION

Fook, J., White, S. and Gardner, F. (2006) 'Critical reflection: a review of contemporary literature and understandings', in S. White, J. Fook and F. Gardner (eds), *Critical Reflection in Health and Social Care*. Maidenhead: Open University Press. pp. 3–20.

This article is useful for a quick overview of the different understandings of critical reflection.

Fook, J. and Gardner, F. (2007) *Practising Critical Reflection: A Resource Handbook*. Maidenhead: Open University Press.

This book provides a detailed theoretical framework and model for practising critical reflection using a variety of perspectives. The on-line teaching resources which are available upon purchase of the book include some in-depth examples of critical reflection written by Master's students.

Humphrey, C. (2009) 'By the light of the Tao', *European Journal of Social Work*, 12 (3): 377–90.

This article is a good example of using a concept from Eastern philosophy to theorise and practise critical reflection.

Ruch, G. (2009) 'Identifying the "critical" in a relationship-based model of reflection', *European Journal of Social Work*, 12 (3): 349–62.

This article presents a relational approach to reflection, and attempts to theorise the critical aspects of this. Useful for providing an alternative to the postmodern critical approach.

Taylor, C. and White, S. (2000) *Practising Reflexivity in Health and Welfare*. Maidenhead: Open University Press.

This book is particularly useful for an in-depth discussion of and model for reflection based upon the concept of reflexivity.

OTHER EXAMPLES OF CRITICAL REFLECTION

Napier, L. and Fook, J. (eds) (2000) *Breakthroughs in Practice: Social Workers Theorise Critical Moments*. London: Whiting & Birch.

The book contains many examples of social workers writing their own reflections on their own experiences. These illustrate many different ways of reflecting.

8

EMPOWERMENT

In Chapter 4 we discussed the concept of power from a postmodern and critical perspective and also reformulated a notion of empowerment based on this. In this chapter I want to discuss this process, some more specific concerns which arise regarding the practice of empowerment and some specific strategies which are possible given this reformulated approach to empowerment.

NEW NOTIONS OF POWER AND EMPOWERMENT

First, let us quickly revisit our reformulated concept of power and what this means in broad terms for our approach to empowerment. We criticised modernist conceptions of power because they tend to see power as being invested in particular people, often by virtue of their position in the social structure. It is 'possessed' rather than 'exercised', and thus is more fixed and less accessible to change. Empowerment of one person or group might automatically mean disempowerment of another, thereby unwittingly setting up binary conflicts. Also, because power is attributed from 'outside', that is, by virtue of position in the social structure, efforts to empower people and groups who are marginalised might actually be experienced as disempowering, since this may not be their own understanding of their experience. The act of empowering involves defining a person or group as 'disempowered', and this process is in fact potentially disempowering. Such blanket definitions also dilute differences between people and situations and do not allow for different identities at different times and in different contexts. Without a complex analysis of how power works in relation to different people and contexts, and a corresponding vision for how it should work in social justice terms, there is a danger that empowerment can simply become a tool to preserve existing power imbalances. In reformulating the concepts of power and empowerment we need to take into account:

- the contextual and changing nature of power;
- how power operates at different levels, often simultaneously and in contradictory ways;

- how power is experienced by different people;
- the creative, as well as controlling, possibilities power entails.

Empowering people therefore involves a complex (multilayered) understanding (which includes their own perspective as well as those of other players) of how power is exercised and how it affects them, but also of how they exercise and create their own power. This includes an understanding of how they might participate in creating their own power*less*ness as well as their own power*ful*ness.

DECONSTRUCTING AND RECONSTRUCTING POWER

A PROCESS OF EMPOWERMENT

In Chapter 7 we outlined in detail a process for analysing (deconstructing) and recreating (reconstructing) situations in ways which lend themselves ultimately to changing power relations. That process can also be applied more generally to change situations more in line with desired ways of thinking and acting, and to allow us to develop our practice theory.

In this chapter it is worthwhile to focus more particularly on how a deconstructive/reconstructive process might be used to empower. In Chapter 4 we outlined a preliminary model for this. In this chapter I want to develop it more fully, using the details of the process outlined in Chapter 7. This process can be used to analyse and change the types of situations in which we might typically work, ranging from the macro-level contexts of economic and global trends, to mid-range national policy and community contexts, to more micro-level organisational workplace settings and interpersonal engagement with service users' environments. The 'text' we analyse in this sense might consist of our 'narrative' of any of these situations in which we practise. Of course, our narrative might involve a complex understanding of how the different levels of contexts interplay to create the situations in which we work.

SUMMARY

The four stages of the deconstructive/reconstructive process in empowerment may be summarised as follows:

1 Deconstruction (of the constructions and operations of power and power relations).
2 Resistance (questioning of dominant constructions of power and power relations).
3 Challenge (labelling of dominant and missing constructions of power and power relations).
4 Reconstructions (changing of existing constructions of power and power relations and creation – and labelling – of new ways of seeing power and related practices).

Overall the process involves an analysis and practice which focuses on the four main aspects of power as outlined below:

1   How is power constructed in this context and climate, and how might it change if some aspects of the context changed?
2   At what different levels does power operate and how might these support or contradict each other?
3   How is power exercised and experienced by different players in the situation?
4   What are both the controlling and the creative potentials of the power involved?

DECONSTRUCTING POWER AND POWER RELATIONS

In this stage, the focus is on identifying the major types and sources of power, and how they are understood and used (perhaps differently) by different players in the situation. The following specific questions might assist you to deconstruct your narrative of the situation. Many of these questions overlap or ask about similar issues in different kinds of ways. I include a variety here to maximise the number of different ways of conceptualising power that might be unearthed.

1   What main themes or patterns emerge from the description of the situation? What terms, phrases or patterns of communication reoccur frequently? What labels or categorisations occur? Is there evidence of binary opposites? Which of these themes, patterns or categorisations involves ideas or assumptions about power? If they are not ostensibly about power, how do they relate to issues of power?
2   Who are all the potential players (individuals, groups or organisations) involved in the situation or potentially affected by it? What are the relative positions of power of each of these players and what are the sources of their power?
3   Are the sources of power related to the context of this particular situation? Would this power change in a different context?
4   How does each player exercise power? How does each player experience the exercise of power?
5   Whose perspectives are represented and whose are missing? What other gaps or biases are present? What does this indicate about power relations?
6   What interpretations or explanations were made and whose were they? How were they represented and how did they influence the situation? What types of power did they imply?
7   How might the situation have been interpreted differently, and how might it have been interpreted by different players in the situation? Why do you think it was not interpreted in these ways and what does this have to do with power relations?
8   How do different players participate in creating or supporting the situation? How do different players participate in ways which empower or disempower them?
9   What knowledges and assumptions are implied and used in the account? How do they relate to (for example): practice theory; value and belief systems; paradigms; human behaviour; moral and ethical codes; social and political systems and change; gender and cultural considerations? Are they relevant and appropriate to the situation at hand? What types of power relations does such knowledge or theory preserve?

10   What are the sources of these assumptions? What roles or positions do these assumptions support? Which players stand to gain or lose from holding them, and what social and power functions does holding these assumptions perform?
11   What practices, cultures, systems or structures are upheld by these assumptions? What power relations are preserved or created by them?
12   What are the 'theories of power' which arise from the analysis? Which ones are dominant? Are my own ideas about power similar or different to these dominant constructions?
13   What power do I exercise in the situation? How do I conceptualise the situation, and the power within it, and whose interests does this serve?

RESISTANCE

In this stage the main focus is on identifying those types of power and techniques of exercise that may need to be changed or resisted in order to change the situation in more empowering ways. The following questions will assist in this stage of the analysis:

1   Which constructions of power should be questioned and further scrutinised and why?
2   Which constructions of power work in disempowering ways and for whom? In what ways do these support or contradict each other?
3   In what ways can we resist, or not participate in, practices, cultures or climates which are disempowering, for ourselves or others?
4   What aspects of the situation or context, if changed, might bring about changes in power relations?
5   What types of power, and the way it is exercised, hold controlling and/or creative potential for which players?
6   Can different players all benefit from a changed situation or must some stand to gain or lose relative to others? Is it possible to change the situation so that all players become relatively empowered?

CHALLENGE

In this stage, we seek to make specific changes to the way we conceptualise power, and thus how we construct the situation and the power relations within it. The following questions will assist with this stage of the process:

1   How can we label or relabel these constructions of power in ways which are more empowering, and for whom?
2   What new types of thinking can we support or create, which will be experienced as empowering, and for whom?
3   How can we support the creative, as opposed to the controlling, aspects of power?
4   How can we change different aspects of the situation or context which might bring about changes in power?
5   What new type of climate, culture, system, structure or situation might be experienced as more empowering, and by which players?

RECONSTRUCTION

In this stage the main focus is to enact the series of changes indicated by the foregoing analysis. This may involve negotiating a changed system of power relations and
structures which is experienced as empowering for all parties, including yourself.
This is an ongoing process, in which constant analysis will indicate ways in which
even supposedly new practices that are more empowering might be scrutinised for
their potentially disempowering effects. Because a process of negotiation between
different players is involved, there may be a series of changes occurring in relation
to each other. Some of the questions which may assist in the reconstructive phase
are as follows:

1 What changes need to be negotiated in order to bring about changed power relations in the
   situation? What different players are involved in these negotiations and how will their positions and
   ways of seeing power need to change?
2 What different strategies can be used to make these changes? How do these strategies fit with the
   changed theories of power we have developed?
3 How can different players be included in the process of empowerment? How can powerful
   experiences be identified and valued? How can an empowering climate be created?
4 How does what is happening in this change process compare to the changed theories or
   conceptualisations of power? What are different players' actual experiences of empowerment?
5 What further questions arise out of this changed situation? How do these relate to my changed
   conceptualisation of power?
6 How would I label or categorise (or relabel or recategorise) my own theory of power as a result
   of this comparison? What is my version of, or my terminology for, the theory upon which I
   practise?
7 What is the reformulated theory of (or assumptions about) power which results from my ongoing
   analysis?
8 How can I frame my own practice theory of power, so that what I have learnt from this situation is
   useable in other contexts?

This model can be used as a framework for analysing and changing the many different situations in which we work, since all situations involve many different layers
of practice ranging from micro intra- and inter-personal interactions, to national
and international contexts. Our focus might be minute or broad, depending on the
arena we wish to focus on and in which we feel we might potentially have influence.

COMMON CONSTRUCTIONS OF POWER IN
SOCIAL WORK PRACTICE

Now that we have outlined a model for the general analysis of power and empowerment possibilities in most situations, it is helpful to examine just how this might
actually be used by social and human service workers, in the many different situations

in which they practise. For instance, how do workers actually construct power in their everyday practice situations?

Exercise

Refer back to your critical incident and your analysis of it from the last chapter. What were your constructions of power implicit in it? How did you construct your own identity in relation to power? What sorts of power did you see yourself as having or exercising?

Many social work students I have taught over the years construct themselves as powerless in relation to their field supervisors, other professional workers on placement, or university teaching staff. Over the last decade I have also been involved with many different groups of workers conducting seminars, workshops and sessions in which we have presented and reflected upon instances in our practice. One of the most burning issues which is always present, particularly as it poses a dilemma in people's practice, is the issue of power. For instance, Napier and Fook (2000) included a number of workers' reflections on their practice and the theme of power was paramount. People were particularly concerned about how much power workers have and should have, and whether it can be exercised to bring about enough change. Many were concerned that what they perceived as their powerlessness meant they could not achieve what they took to be the ideals or values of social work, such as social justice or anti-discrimination.

In this section I want to explore some of the more common conceptions of power which may arise directly from workers' own accounts of their practice.

SOCIAL WORKERS' CONSTRUCTIONS OF THEMSELVES

It is widely acknowledged that social workers feel ambivalent about power or, more accurately, about their own power (Laragy, 1997). While our textbooks write clearly about the use and abuse of structural and personal power by professionals (e.g. Hugman, 1991), the more informal culture within social work in relation to power is much more complex. Accounts from social workers seem to indicate that they feel uncomfortable with the idea of having power and often, therefore, construct themselves as relatively powerless (Okitikpi, 2011).

In my experience I have found this idea of powerlessness is almost universal in accounts of practice in which workers feel they are caught in a dilemma or impasse. For example, in a group of ten workers with whom I conducted a series of critical reflection workshops, this idea was paramount (Fook, 2000c). Workers felt caught underneath the power of a manager or supervisor, the power of bureaucratic rule, or even of agency or community culture.

A major assumption was that the power resided either with the managers, supervisors, recalcitrant colleagues or, in some cases, the community groups with consumer voice. In no instances did workers see themselves as powerful. Either each person had exercised what power they thought they had and it had proved inadequate, or they felt they did not possess enough power to bring about any change. The common themes in the stories we shared showed that we had each constructed ourselves as powerless, denying or minimising the influence of different types of power we might possess. Sometimes we identified as powerless with individual clients for whom we were acting, but in other instances we also invested these people with power we did not have. A major assumption therefore was that *other people had the power, workers did not*. There was almost a sense in which workers saw themselves as victims.

This construction of ourselves as *powerless* is noted elsewhere. For instance, Laragy (1996) notes that caseworkers often identify with their clients, feeling powerless in the same way. Because workers tend to construct themselves as advocates of the client, they automatically become enemies of employers or managers.

While perhaps being an integral part of social work culture, the idea of powerlessness may also be associated with the development of professional expertise. For instance, several different theories of professional expertise posit that as professional practitioners develop, they also develop a sense of connectedness or involvement with situations, in other words a sense of responsibility, of being able to act in and upon a situation (Dreyfus and Dreyfus, 1986; Fook et al., 2000). So a sense of power, certainly of personal ability to influence a situation, might be something which develops with professional experience. On the other hand, the culture of powerlessness within social work might be so pervasive that workers who do manage to develop a sense of themselves as powerful may have learnt not to speak of it in these terms, in order to be accepted by their colleagues.

This basic social work orientation of relative powerlessness is backed up by more recent evaluation research I have conducted on participants in my own critical reflection workshops (Fook and Askeland, 2006). In brief, social workers' sense of powerlessness had to do with such aspects as:

- locating the source of their self-value in their social environment;
- devaluing particular characteristics of themselves (e.g. their emotions) as 'non-professional';
- having split 'personal' and 'professional' identities;
- seeing choices in restricted (often in binary or 'forced choice') terms; and
- a relatively fatalistic frame of reference.

CONSTRUCTING THE ENEMY

In constructing ourselves as powerless, we may conversely construct other people and groups as powerful. Certainly this is the case with regard to managers or employers. However it may also apply to other people or groups whom we see as somehow working contrary to our cause, such as colleagues from other professional groups.

In Fook (2000d) I tell the story of a situation in which I disagreed with a colleague over what I felt was discriminatory practice against an Asian student. I analysed the situation as one which I constructed as 'war', in which there could only be 'enemies' and 'allies', and invariably I saw the disagreeing colleague as an enemy and blamed my failure to change her mind on her deficiencies. So in constructing myself as powerless and my enemy as powerful, I also absolved myself of blame.

Amy Rossiter notes a similar phenomenon in her reflections on transforming a curriculum along more inclusive lines (1995). She is honest about the way she constructs herself as being part of the 'non-racist' camp, and how this therefore clouds her ability to recognise how some of her own attitudes could be experienced as racist by a friend who is a person of colour. Constructing an identity for oneself as non-racist can excuse behaviour which may in fact preserve a racist culture. It also locates the blame and responsibility for doing something about racism squarely away from yourself.

In this sense, constructing our 'enemies' as powerful and our 'allies' as powerless like ourselves can have the effect of excusing us from the responsibility to change.

MUST POWER BE STRUCTURAL?

What types of power and change are implicitly valued by social workers? When the critical reflection group examined ideas about power more closely, it became clear that we were often talking about *structural* power (Fook, 2000c). Group members felt that they did not possess the formal position or authority to bring about change (that is, directly to challenge or cause conflict), even though some of them did hold positions of some authority (team leaders, supervisors). In some cases the power people felt they did not possess was the *cultural* and *personal* power to resist or challenge the embedded culture of their workplace. In any case, all of us constructed ourselves as powerless, even though we possessed varying degrees of different types of power. What this seems to suggest is that less structural types of power expressed at personal or cultural levels within the workplace are somehow seen as less important, since they are factored out when constructing our identities. Despite what power we recognise we may or may not possess, we still see ourselves as powerless.

This tendency of workers not to recognise their own power lies at the heart of Mark Baldwin's (2000a, 2000b) research project with a group of workers investigating the use of discretion in the implementation of policy. Workers began the process relatively certain that there was little room for the use of discretion and therefore the exercise of their own power through the use of their professional judgement. However, during the co-operative inquiry process they came to recognise the relative power of their positions in making differential applications of policy across different cases. It is again interesting in this instance that workers seemed initially to 'factor out' their own power.

Tony Evans' study (2010) of discretion and the operation of street level bureaucracy in social services in the UK also indicates that practice is not necessarily dominated by a unified approach from management, but that professionalism still takes a role in practice.

THE ONLY CHANGE IS TOTAL CHANGE

Related to these assumptions about structural power and powerlessness is the idea that the only worthwhile change is total change. When I deconstructed my own story of my encounter with my colleague who disagreed with me about her assessment of an Asian student, it became apparent to me that I felt the only worthwhile outcome would have been for her to come around completely to my way of thinking and in effect not be 'racist' any more (Fook, 2000d).

I have found this idea of change implicit in many of my other discussions with social workers, when we analyse their own stories of practice. Often the sorts of changes people assume they should be able to make are quite ambitious and far reaching. For example, one worker felt frustrated because she couldn't get the board of management to fire an irresponsible colleague. Another was frustrated at his inability to change agency policy, in the face of incompetent management, so that group homes were efficiently maintained. Still others were annoyed because they couldn't change long-standing policies. In addition, when good work was undertaken and sometimes good outcomes achieved, these were minimised or devalued. For example, support given to clients was often glossed over. Case by case, instances of change were often disregarded. Much of the clarification of assumptions about change revolved around 'how much change is enough change?' and 'how much am I responsible for?'

In discussion with the critical reflection group, we developed the idea that perhaps workers only see structural or, at the very least, organisational change as valuable (Fook, 2000c). I wonder when 'enough' is 'enough'. The bounds seem limitless, as if somehow we have to 'fix' the problems, no matter the scale or extent.

Constructing change in this seemingly unattainable way also functions to ensure that we never attain it, and perhaps makes us feel more comfortable about not doing so (Fook, 2000d). As well, it may be that this way of constructing change, this idealistic view, functions to define ourselves distinctively against other professions. Yet again, it may feed into our powerless identity, excusing at the same time as honouring our inability to change what is unchangeable.

PARTICIPATING IN OUR OWN DISEMPOWERMENT

These constructions of power and change and our own powerless identity are of course ways in which we participate in our own disempowerment and, by implication, preserve the disempowered status of our service users. Although we have not made it explicit in the chapter's discussion so far, it is these elements of oppositional thinking, and the tendency to create constructions and identities that are binaries, which characterise much of this thinking.

Oppositional thinking can therefore function as disempowering if the self, the social work identity (or the identity of service users), is constructed as the *powerless* element of the binary opposite. Similarly, if we have a tendency to construct 'enemies vs. allies' we automatically invest our service user allies with the same powerless identity and status as our own. This can be seen as an example of 'complicity with oppression', in which relatively disadvantaged groups take on 'victim' identities which automatically confer a powerless status (Fook and Pease, 1999: 225).

CHANGE AND RESPONSIBILITY

Similarly, assumptions about power are also related to assumptions about change and responsibility for situations. In the critical reflection group, it was interesting to note that in everyone's story there was an underlying expectation that each person was responsible for change, even though they felt disempowered to bring it about. This is an interesting contradiction which workers constructed for them-selves, a type of 'no-win' situation. This 'responsible yet powerless' identity potentially casts us in the worst possible position, accepting total blame but feel-ing unable to do anything about it. There is almost a 'binary opposite' here, an implicit assumption of 'powerful yet powerless' or 'responsible yet not responsi-ble'. It is almost as if the social work role confers an ability to analyse situations and envision change, but not the associated skills or position to do anything about it.

OTHER ASSUMPTIONS WHICH RELATE TO POWER

I have conducted some more recent analysis of social workers' assumptions about power which arise from written accounts of practice (Fook, 2011). These support the foregoing conceptions, but also make additional observations. In brief, there are four main types of assumptions which emerge regarding power: power and dichoto-mous thinking; the power of theory; power and possibilities for change; and the power of discourse.

With regard to dichotomous thinking, the most common form of thinking appears to involve creating binary oppositional categories of people, and attributing power to the first group, and powerlessness to the second. As mentioned earlier, this often takes the form of 'manager vs. front line worker', or 'social worker vs. service user'. Sometimes however binaries were constructed in relation to ways of working, so that, for instance, 'authoritarian styles' were seen as oppositional and mutually exclusive with 'collegiate styles'.

Practitioners also accord power to theory, in that theory is often seen as useful in controlling people's interpretations, and therefore in controlling situations. In this way it may become a reasonably rigid set of guidelines against which to judge one's own, and others', actions. Theory is also often cast in a binary relationship to practice, so that social workers often feel they have to choose between theory or practice (i.e. to be good at one involves not being good at the other). There is also an implicit valuing of theory in this conception.

There did seem to be a type of fatalism operating regarding change and possibilities for change. This was also related to the worker's identity and sense of personal agency, or ability to influence a situation. Many workers felt they had no power against 'the system', or that they would not be listened to, or were perhaps pawns within a greater set of changes or policies.

Lastly, the power of powerful discourses to operate within a worker's practice, sometimes in a contradictory way, and without the awareness of the worker, also emerged. An example might be a worker who believes themselves to be child-centred, but when they deconstruct their practice they see the operation of adult-centred discourses.

RECONSTRUCTING OURSELVES AND SERVICE USERS

What does this analysis suggest about ways in which we need to reconstruct our thinking and identities so that we can engage in more powerful ways within our practice situations? Again, I pose more questions to help us think through the wealth of possibilities.

1   What kinds of power do we and our service users possess, how do we exercise this and how does it change between situations? Are we able to transfer some types of power from one context to another?
2   What kinds of new identities and labels can we create for ourselves so that we define ourselves, and the people we work with, in non-oppositional terms (e.g. perhaps 'responsible in certain situations'; 'powerful in the interpersonal arena') or our service users (e.g. 'knowledgeable in using services').
3   What kinds of changes are we able to bring about and how can we label and value these?
4   What are the different levels of responsibilities of particular players in the situation, and which aspects can we be responsible for?

CONSTRUCTING OUR OWN THEORIES OF POWER AND EMPOWERMENT

Exercise

Think of an incident from your social work practice in which you either felt powerful or power-less. Write a brief description (one paragraph) of it. What are some of the assumptions you make about power, who has it, where it comes from, what it allows you to do?

I have undertaken this exercise many times with different groups of social workers. They tell stories of incidents in which they were able to change their own views or someone else's way of thinking, times when they felt they gained public recognition of their point of view, or of their own success. Sometimes they were simply aware that they held a position of power over someone else (for example, doing a court report on a client). When they felt powerless, they were often in situations where they were in an unfamiliar environment and/or felt devalued by others.

Their own theories of power embodied notions of power as social and contextual, often ascribed and determined by the situation, as having little to do with their inherent characteristics.

Exercise

In one sentence, describe your own theory of power, derived from your assumptions about power which were implicit in the above description of your incident.

It is useful to look at how we position ourselves in relation to power, and what we think power allows us to do. If we find these assumptions potentially disempowering, then we need to fashion new ways of thinking about power which place ourselves back in the centre of possibilities. For instance, do we see power as coming from an outside authority? If so, does this make us feel less or more powerless? In what situations might we feel more or less powerless with this kind of a view? Sometimes a simple realisation that power can be transferred between situations may function to make us feel less powerless.

Exercise

In one sentence, describe your own theory of empowerment, derived from your above theory of power.

Chapter summary

This chapter began with a summary of postmodern notions of power and empowerment which take into account:

- the contextual and changing nature of power;
- how power operates at different levels, often simultaneously and in contradictory ways;

- how power is experienced by different people;
- the creative, as well as controlling, possibilities power entails.

Then a process of empowerment was outlined, using the four stage framework for deconstruction and reconstruction (deconstruction, resistance, challenge and reconstruction) developed in the previous chapter. The last part of the chapter discussed common social work assumptions about power, such as how we often construct ourselves as powerless, our ambivalence towards power, and devaluing our change efforts by only recognising structural levels of change. These types of assumptions point to how we often participate in creating our own disempowerment, and thus they point to ways in which our disempowerment can be resisted and changed.

FURTHER READING

Okitikpi, T. (ed.) (2011) *Social Control and the Use of Power in Social Work with Childen and Families*. Lyme Regis: Russell House Publishing.

This is an edited volume based on the assumption that the operation of power is complex. Different perspectives are discussed in each chapter.

Fook, J. (2011) 'Critical reflection and power in social work', in T. Okitikpi (ed.), *Social Control and the Use of Power in Social Work with Childen and Families*. Lyme Regis: Russell House Publishing. Ch. 10, pp. 126–40.

This chapter illustrates, from specific accounts, how ideas of power can be transformed through critical reflection.

Fook, J. and Askeland, G. (2006) 'The "critical" in critical reflection', in S. White, J. Fook and F. Gardner (eds), *Critical Reflection in Health and Social Care*. Maidenhead: Open University Press. Ch. 3, pp. 40–53.

This chapter develops the concept of power as used in an approach to critical reflection, and also includes results from an evaluation study of critical reflection, which illustrates the kinds of transformations which have taken place.

Evans, T. (2010) *Professional Discretion in Welfare Services: Beyond Street Level Bureaucracy*. Aldershot: Ashgate.

This book is a contemporary study of practice in social services in the UK. It is a fascinating account of the complex mix of factors in operation, and how managers themselves do not represent a unified group. The concept of professional discretion is very helpful in pinpointing specific ways in which practitioners actually do exercise some control and choice in their day-to-day work.

9

PROBLEM CONCEPTUALISATION AND ASSESSMENT

The ways in which we assess problems, and the ways we describe and define them are of course integrally connected with the ways in which we construct knowledge of our world and more generally our place within it. Therefore our understanding of subjectivity and identity, of the nature of knowledge and constructions of power are bound up with how we conceptualise and assess the 'problems' with which we work. In this chapter I aim to outline in some detail how these particular aspects of postmodern and critical thinking impact on the practice of making assessments in professional social work.

CRITICISMS OF TRADITIONAL NOTIONS OF ASSESSMENT AND PROBLEMS

According to most accepted existing ways of thinking, assessment involves making a professional judgement about the problematic aspects of a situation, in order to act effectively to address the problems with and within the situation. Because a 'scientific' discourse is involved, assessment and conceptualisation of a problem often involve identifying a 'cause', which can then be addressed through 'intervention'. A very linear process beginning with problem identification, which leads to action, is implied. As well, it is assumed that the 'cause' can be determined objectively, through the use of systematic methods of investigation, often obtained from a number of sources. Once the 'truth' is determined, it is a relatively simple matter to work out, by logical and rational means, the sorts of strategies which will 'solve' the problem and its cause. Many social work practice textbooks imply that there is a relatively clear set of procedures by which professionals work, starting with an investigation of the problem (data collection) through to a sorting out of relevant 'facts', to the development of an 'action plan' of goals and strategies (see Compton and Galaway, 1999: ch. 10, as an example).

It is also implied that the professional person making the assessment is a relatively objective and passive party, who simply gathers empirical facts, puts them together and makes a judgement based on what the 'facts' say. Although it is implied that the worker is relatively passive in relation to the 'facts', the worker is usually more powerful than the service user. It is implied that the worker takes responsibility for eliciting the 'right facts' and for making judgements about the relevance or truth of the material presented by different players. For instance, workers are often taught about the possible differences between 'presenting problems' (Compton and Galaway, 1999: 260) and presumably 'real' problems. The implication is that service users may present with what they feel is a socially acceptable problem which may mask an underlying perhaps more serious problem about which they find it more difficult to seek assistance. It is seen as the responsibility of the worker to look beneath this and elicit the issue about which the person feels so uncomfortable.

This judgement in making an assessment might also involve the sorting of the facts into 'categories' or 'labels', depending on the functions of the particular organisation in which the worker is practising. These categories may be more or less predetermined as well, depending on the setting. For instance, in a statutory income security agency the assessment might have to indicate whether a person is 'eligible' or 'ineligible' for certain pension categories. This may not preclude the social worker from forming an opinion about other 'social' aspects of the person's 'problem' such as 'urgency of need', or 'accommodation needs', 'suspected domestic violence', etc. In many settings, workers are required to perform 'risk' assessments or to gather information which may relate to specific health problems, such as psychiatric illness. Some sorts of assessments might involve elaborate checklists. In some settings, the worker's assessment might involve conducting a community profile or needs study, a viability analysis or even market research for a particular programme. What is common to all these activities is a discourse that requires the assessment to frame situations in 'problem' terms which somehow fit the discourses of the groups who hold the resources. This means that 'problems' and the people who experience them ('clients') must somehow be constructed in categories which are non-threatening, powerless or acceptable in some ways to dominant groups.

As an example of this construction of service users in non-threatening ways, I well remember an experience of my own in which I became a type of 'client' within my own employing organisation. Some years ago I was accused of racial discrimination in one of the universities in which I worked. The aggrieved student instituted an elaborate complaint process through the university. I felt that the process was mishandled, particularly in relation to my own rights. However, when I made a complaint in some anger, about this, rather than offering to investigate or redress the complaint, the administrator concerned offered me counselling. The message I took from this was that somehow, as both a respondent and a university employee, 'anger' was not an appropriate reaction from me. Presumably in these roles I was simply expected to submit to university regulations. Therefore my reactions could only be fitted into, or assessed in terms of the categories provided under university rules. The only service available for me was 'counselling'. There was no place within the culture of the university for me or my claims to be treated as powerful. The problem was defined as one of my own emotional coping, rather than the university's responsibility to conduct processes appropriately, simply because there was no category of service to offer me that recognised the validity of my claims.

This example illustrates how the process and criteria of assessment are therefore integral to the process of defining service users in disempowered ways, and of defining problems as the responsibility of disempowered rather than dominant groups; and of defining people with problems as separate or different from dominant groups who do not have problems. Assessment discourses, and the ways in which problems are defined and labelled, are thereby integral to the processes and structures which preserve dominant power relations.

This also means, of course, that 'problems' and those who experience them are often defined in static terms; the problem is assumed to belong to the problematic group, because of some characteristic of that group, rather than being a characteristic of the context in which the group lives. For instance, the 'culture of poverty' idea functions largely in this way to define the problem 'poverty' as being a problem of the group identified as 'poor' because of a culture they have developed which keeps them poor. In this way not only is the 'victim' blamed, but attention is also shifted away from the economic context (and other groups) which might have fostered the conditions for poverty. Another criticism of static identity categories, as discussed in Chapter 6, is that they do not allow for the changes which might occur throughout people's lives, and from one context to another. Nor do they allow for contradictions that some people may experience between different aspects of their identity which have been developed in relation to different contexts.

Exercise

It may be useful to refer back to the exercise in Chapter 6, where you imagined how you would present yourself to the social worker regarding your ageing mother's care options. What choices of self-definition do you think you had in this situation?

SUMMARY

In summary then, existing approaches to assessment and problem conceptualisation involve the following:

- a 'scientific' assumption that problems have identifiable and underlying 'causes';
- a rational and linear process which involves collecting data, identifying the problem, its cause and its 'cure';
- an assumption that the worker conducting the assessment is a passive and objective observer, whose role is simply to collect the relevant empirical 'facts' and establish the 'truth' of the problem;
- the fitting of the problem situation into preconceived categories or labels;

- a discursive function, in that the process undertaken and labels applied tend to reflect (and favour) the discourse of existing powerful groups, rather than the people who are experiencing the 'problem';
- static definitions of problems and identities of people experiencing them, which attribute 'blame' to characteristics of these groups, rather than the contexts which may have created them.

In developing a new approach to assessment and problematising it is important to focus on all aspects of how the discourse operates, and how it is created and maintained. This involves not only an awareness of the processes of assessment, but also the sorts of categories and labels which are constructed in attempting to define 'problems', who experiences them and how they are experienced.

In the following section I outline a broad approach to assessment and problematising, based on this discursive analysis, and then follow with more specific suggestions about how this might be practised.

AN ALTERNATIVE APPROACH: ASSESSMENT AS 'CONSTRUCTION OF PROFESSIONAL NARRATIVES'

A new approach to the understanding and practice of assessment making involves a broad recognition that the act of assessing involves creating a set of meanings which function discursively. Both the content and processes of assessment therefore potentially display all the features of dominant discourses (i.e. they are linear, logocentric, use fixed categories, assume underlying causes of problems, preserve existing power relations). In reformulating the idea and practice of assessment, therefore, we need to allow for multiple and changing understandings which are contextually based and may be contradictory. We also need to acknowledge that the assessment made may primarily represent the perspective of the professional worker making it. Assessment making, in this sense, is no more or less than the professional worker constructing their own version or narrative of the problem situation.

The worker needs to do this in order for the service user to gain assistance within a discursive framework which is not primarily the service user's own, but one controlled by groups dominant in that setting. The role of the professional in assisting service users thus becomes one of translating service user narratives so that they have power in the dominant discourse within that setting. The act of assessment, therefore, from a postmodern and critical perspective, is about the act of constructing professional narratives which function to assist service users in different contexts. In constructing a professional narrative to assist service users we take into account the following ideas:

1 There is not necessarily any one 'cause' of problematic situations. Instead, situations may involve a number of factors, which may be competing and contradictory. These factors may interact with each other, bringing about a complex and changing situation.

SUMMARY

2   The process of constructing a professional narrative may be an ongoing and integrated process. Collecting information does not necessarily precede formulating plans for action. Meanings will change and be constructed and reconstructed as relationships change with service users and new information is gained and interpreted in context.

3   The worker is actively and reflexively involved in the construction of the professional narrative. Their own assumptions and interpretations will influence how and what knowledge is selected and what narrative is created. The narrative produced represents the worker's version or perspective on the situation, which may or may not be used to service users' advantage.

4   Existing labels and categories may need to be resisted as total ways of defining service users or problems. New labels or categories may need to be created, or existing ones modified, in order better to represent the narrative, identity or problem definition which fits the newly constructed narrative.

5   An awareness of the discursive functions of the newly created 'assessment narrative', attempting to construct a narrative which works in favour of service users.

6   Creation of more open ended service user identities and problem categories or definitions, which recognise the influence of changing contexts.

With these broad principles in mind, following are some specific suggestions about how they might be practised.

PROBLEMATISING

If we recognise the complex and multilayered nature of problem situations and how we conceptualise them, then the main principle of problematising, in broad terms, is to look for multiple different ways in which problems might be characterised (Featherstone and Fawcett, 1995; Healy and Fook, 1994). For example, searching for a number of different factors which might be involved is helpful. Looking at the situation from multidisciplinary perspectives and paying particular attention to perspectives which might be missing allows us to recognise not only the dominant, operating discourse but other potential ways of framing the problem.

Allowing for a number of contradictory 'causes' can alert us to possible pitfalls in determining too easy 'solutions'. Recognising that one level of factors operating does not necessarily preclude another (e.g. recognising structural reasons for a person's unemployment doesn't necessarily preclude the possibility that their lack of confidence might also be an inhibiting factor) potentially allows us to be more sensitive to how the situation is experienced. Asking *who the problem is a problem for* alerts us to whose discourse might be dominant and why. Often a problem might be framed in terms of the discourse of whoever seeks to gain from having the problem resolved. This potentially alerts us to some of the political dimensions of the situation, and therefore to other potential ways of seeing the situation.

Exercise

Think about the issue of sexual harassment in the workplace and try to 'problematise' it using the principles we have just outlined, e.g. What are different perspectives? Who is it a problem for and whose discourse is operating?

ESTABLISHING THE APPROPRIATE CLIMATE AND PROCESS

I suggested earlier that assessment is primarily the professional worker's narrative. In saying this, I am not suggesting that the perspectives of service users are denied or even necessarily changed. In fact, their views will need to be understood and respected in order to be *translated* successfully into a professional culture and environment. In order for the professional worker to do this, they will need to participate collaboratively with service users in the assessment making process. What I am suggesting that the worker needs to 'own' (i.e. locate her- or himself reflexively and responsibly in relation to) the narrative which is created jointly between worker and service user. It is the worker's responsibility to create and use this narrative effectively within the professional context. Professionals therefore need to be specifically aware of how they have modified and created this discourse in order to engage with it and use it flexibly.

However, in order to create a joint credible narrative, the climate and culture which encourages this must be established. This involves setting the scene for dialogue, understanding and interpretation, as opposed to a 'fact finding' or data collection interview. If we assume that what we are doing is collaboratively constructing a story of a problem situation which will allow service users to gain appropriate assistance, then this potentially transforms the ways we relate to each other. Additionally, if we conceptualise our role as one of *translation*, then we might see ourselves as exchanging interpretations and perhaps exchanging views on how these interpretations will be treated in the professional culture, rather than trying to elicit 'the facts'. This is not to say that there will or will not be elements of the story which both the worker and the service user do or do not believe to be true. But what is at stake is not the empirical truth or falsity so much as the perceptions of the situation and its problematic potential.

The extent to which and ways in which such collaborations can be established will, of course, vary according to situation. For instance, some service users may be limited in the degree to which they can participate in this process (people with severe intellectual disabilities), or much relevant information may be held by other parties (medical specialists in the case of severe patient injury). Whatever the circumstances, however, the worker aims to build up a complex picture of the whole situation, incorporating a particular appreciation of service users' perspectives and experience. It is therefore crucial that climates and processes are established, in whatever the setting, which encourage maximum exchange of views between the worker and involved parties.

Is it possible to generalise to this extent about the process of how assessments should be constructed collaboratively with service users? This type of view seems to assume that service users are a uniform amorphous group of people with a unified identity. Of course we understand that they are not. But service users do have some agency (Jeffrey, 2011). They are not necessarily always passive recipients of services who need to be completely empowered to receive their entitlements. They may have devised their own ways of working with the welfare system, or they may be in the system because they have contravened the rights of others. Despite being relatively powerless victims of a social structure which disadvantages them, they may still have exercised choice about some aspects of their lives and specifically how and why they are seeing a social worker now, at this point in time. What a broadly collaborative approach to assessment making does allow is for all aspects of service users' experiences to be acknowledged, including the choices or actions they have taken (rightly or wrongly). A climate may be established for maximum respect in exchange of views which does not necessarily mean maximum agreement. The emphasis is on mutual exchange, not necessarily mutual agreement.

RESEARCH ORIENTATION AND STRATEGIES

From a reflexive way of thinking, the process of constructing a professional narrative in assessment making is in many ways little different from conducting research. Both involve the making of meanings from one set of experiences, for translation into different settings. In the world of social work practice, the new settings are usually professional service or care settings, where the new translated meaning will assist directly in providing services. In the research setting, the new settings into which the narratives of research participants are translated may not necessarily involve the direct provision of services, although they might be seen as one step involved in that process. Often the research may have a number of interrelated functions, only some of which may be intentional. For instance, research can function to make public problems which formerly have been kept hidden. The very act of making them public may spur other actions which may work for or against the interests of the original group whose problem was hidden.

The main difference between meaning making for professional assessment and meaning making for research purposes is that the intended consequences may be different. However, the unintended consequences of both activities may be more uncertain and unpredictable. Both processes and the strategies used may be conducted along similar lines, and therefore professional assessment makers can draw on a wealth of research strategies in constructing their professional narratives of problem situations.

For instance, knowledge of how to conduct and construct interviews for different purposes is vital. Whether interviews are formally structured or are more informal conversations will depend on the type of climate which you wish to establish. The types of questions asked and how they are worded will convey different meanings about the relationship between you and your service users, about how you see yourself and how you see them. The types of methods used to elicit an exchange of views will also frame the ways in which views are exchanged, and also the types of meanings constructed from them (see Fook, 2000b). For example, even with as open a mind as possible, it is almost impossible not to sort knowledge into preconceived categories, and thus selectively to sort for that which is already known. Therefore ethnographic and reflexive methods (Fook, 1999b) may be useful in being as open as possible to the unexpected, keeping the bias of one's own vision to a minimum. Observational techniques and principles of pattern recognition (which researchers follow in theorising a situation) are also skills which practitioners use all the time (see Rodwell, 1998). Rodwell even likens the assessment process to one of 'naturalistic inquiry' (1987).

Practitioners conducting professional service user assessments are therefore undertaking a research activity and need to use research skills critically and creatively in so doing. There are myriad ways in which research projects are designed and in which different methods are used to elicit different perspectives on the situation being researched. The same applies to the process of constructing a professional assessment. The sources of different perspectives are many and varied, as are the ways of accessing and processing them. The individual service users' perspectives might only be one aspect in understanding the broad situation of which they are a part. Similarly, community situations may involve a whole array of different perspectives. The research strategies used by professionals making assessments will therefore need to incorporate a wide variety of skills and approaches. In a later section I describe the uses of some specific research techniques in more detail.

POLITICS AND CONTEXT

The politics and context of service users' situations, and the professional contexts in which they and the worker find themselves, will obviously influence both the mutual interpretations made and the narratives constructed. Any assessment making will therefore need also to incorporate an assessment of the contexts involved.

For instance, in forming a picture of service users and their experience, it is important to take into account how they might see themselves in other situations and contexts. How much of their present experience is influenced by the current circumstances, their past experience and assumptions about problems and professional people, for instance? Their own assumptions about you, as the social worker, and how you present as a person and a professional (taking into account your own ways of establishing your identity) may influence their current behaviour and thinking. As well, your own position (subjective and social) may colour the way you interpret them or their behaviour. You are as much a part of their context as they are of yours. At the more micro level as well, there will be aspects of the immediate physical environment which influence perception. I remember a colleague telling about an ageing woman who was seen as paranoid because staff from the nursing home had come to remove her forcibly from her home, all the while telling her they were not going to take her away.

Obviously agency, policy and community contexts influence interpretations of and judgements about certain behaviours and attitudes. Awareness of the influence of some contexts may provide a different perspective on behaviour. For example, I may not judge a sexist 75-year-old man as harshly as I might a 25-year-old. Historical contexts are different and the view of each man in relation to that context is different. As another example, attitudes and behaviours in relation to sexual harassment in the workplace have changed. These are issues highlighted in *The First Stone* by Helen Garner (1995) – an account of a celebrated incident at a university college in which the male head was stood down after suspicion of sexual harassment of a female student. Interestingly, this incident occurred at a time when mores on these matters were changing and unclear. Feminists became divided not about whether the behaviour constituted harassment, but how the student should have dealt with it. Older feminists argued that the student should have dealt with it simply by asserting herself and not making the matter public. They felt sympathetic to the man and argued that the incident was blown out of proportion. Younger feminists argued that the young woman was too vulnerable and needed to resort to public authorities (the police) in order to deal with the situation. The context of historical period was crucial in influencing how this man's behaviour was assessed and treated.

The role of the professional in creating an effective assessment narrative is to size up the influence of these contexts and construct a narrative of service users which works within the one that is currently powerful. This may involve forming a narrative about what is constant about the service user and what has been adversely affected by context and changes. In some instances this may also involve a narrative about how the current professional agency context disadvantages the service user. For example, I well remember a service user I met very early in my career. I was working in an income security organisation and assigned to the case of a man, a suspected alcoholic, who was receiving a pension. He had the habit of coming in a few days before his pension cheque was due to ask for some emergency assistance. When he did this, I would usually arrange for an early payment of his cheque. We would chat for a while and he would go away happy, to reappear a few days before next pension day. One day he came in and I was not there. He spoke to someone on the counter who denied that anything could be done. He became angry and smashed his fist through a glass partition. The police were called.

Exercise

Try to frame an assessment, constructing a 'professional narrative' of this man's situation which you think will work in his favour.

How can I frame an assessment of him which takes context into account? My assessment or professional narrative clearly said that his behaviour when treated differently (i.e. when I chatted with him and worked out a solution) was fine. My narrative said that his angry behaviour was clearly a result of this changed context, of being treated differently. My assessment said that he had a right to have his cheques paid early; that this was an entitlement allowed for under the present regulations; that he had never received extra payments, simply early ones. His 'problem' could therefore be dealt with under the current regime and fitted nicely within it.

THE INTEGRATED AND CHANGING NATURE OF CONSTRUCTING PROFESSIONAL NARRATIVES

If a process of mutual dialogue and exchange of views is established, it is unlikely that this will follow a clear and linear pathway. There is not a clear division between gathering information and assisting and bringing about change based on this information. The collaborative construction of an effective professional narrative involves mutual care and respect. This in itself should bring about some change in the situation by changing something about the way service users see and value themselves at the same time. While working together to change a situation, workers and service users will still be engaged in exchanging views and further constructing a more complex understanding of how and why they are working together. Indeed, people's perceptions of the situation may change as they exchange views about it, so an 'assessment' or constructed narrative may also change as people interact and influence each other. Old experiences may be reassessed in the light of new experiences. Indeed, as in research activity, the process of making meaning of a situation is interactive and reflexive (Fook, 2000b).

As part of a narrative construction process, workers may experiment with different ways of framing a situation, in order to explore multiple perspectives and build up a picture of changing contexts and their influence. These strategies should introduce service users to the possibility of different ways of seeing, without devaluing their own perspectives. They may also begin to build up a sense of their own identity which is not determined by one context, and therefore may create a sense of power and agency. As well, simply having one's story heard and validated can of course be helpful and empowering. The act of externalising (Parton and O'Byrne, 2000: 139) can already introduce an element of resisting the dominant discourse.

Because the narratives which are constructed may change, there is always a degree of uncertainty involved. In this sense narratives are never 'complete' or 'finished'. They are always undergoing a process of construction. Workers simply work with the best available view of the situation at the time and are constantly reviewing these narratives, aware that they are contingent.

REFRAMING MAJOR CONCEPTS AND LANGUAGE

There are some very specific terms and phrases associated with the traditional idea of assessment which we need to consider changing, in line with the new thinking we have developed. Obviously the major suggestion is to frame *making professional assessments* as *constructing professional narratives*. However, there are a number of more specific ones which flow from this.

We have already suggested that the ideas of 'facts' and 'truth' need to be reconsidered. In the discussion so far I have used terms like 'views', 'perspectives' and 'experiences'. In this spirit, terms such as 'knowledge' and 'information' might also be reframed. Similarly, speaking about 'problems' suggests a negative, perhaps oversimplified notion. I prefer to speak about 'situations', 'contexts' or 'circumstances' which convey a more complex understanding, but also draw attention to the contextual and perhaps changing way in which problems are framed or experienced.

The ideas of 'questioning' and 'interviewing', which we often take for granted as tools in eliciting information, might also be reframed in ways more congruent with our approach. For instance, it might be better to ask people to 'tell me about your experience' rather than asking 'why' questions (Featherstone, 2000: 128). We also might think of 'engaging in conversations' with service users rather than interviewing them, although for the benefit of our managers we might still call them 'interviews'. What is valued in one context might not be valued in another.

Rather than speaking about 'causes' of problems, we might like to think instead of 'influences' or 'factors' and how they 'interact', which implies a much less direct or linear relationship.

Last, it is important when framing a professional narrative for the benefit of service users that they can engage with the terminology used. The situation should be framed in empowering and accessible ways. For instance, goals may need to be framed in concrete and behavioural terms so that service users feel change is doable for them. It might also be important to frame their view of themselves in empowered and positive ways. These can be worked out collaboratively. For instance, it might feel more accessible to an unemployed person to think about aiming at 'finding one job per week to apply for' than 'getting a job'. They may feel more empowered to think of themselves as 'a person seeking the right job' than an 'unemployed person'. In relation to this, it is important to remember that empowerment can mean very different things to different people and take many different forms (Fook and Morley, 2005), so the language used to frame goals should reflect specific meanings for that person.

THE MAIN ELEMENTS OF A PROFESSIONAL NARRATIVE

In the earlier sections we focused on the processes and principles involved in making professional assessments of service users and their situations. In this section I outline the basic elements which should form the content of the professional narrative which is constructed. I am using the term 'service user' to refer to any people – groups, individuals, communities, families, organisations – with whom the social worker may be working and in whose interests they are attempting to act.

SERVICE USER PERSPECTIVES/STORY

The first element the professional narrative needs to include is the service user's own perspective or narrative about their situation. Obviously this may include contradictory elements, especially if a group, community, family or organisation is the focus of the social worker's assistance. It may include the initial story of how and why the service user initially sought assistance, and of course this narrative might develop and change as contact with the social worker progresses. This narrative might also include views of the service user's identity, categories or labels which they use to define themselves, or the types of discourses they use about themselves and their situation.

THE PERSPECTIVES OF OTHER PLAYERS

Also important is to identify the other players (again this may be individuals, groups, organisations, communities, interest groups) and include yourself as the social worker as another player. What are the perspectives and interests of these players? Whose discourse is dominant in the situation? Whose discourse defines the situation as problematic?

CONTEXTS AND CHANGES

It is crucial, as we have discussed earlier, to understand the contexts in which you and the service users are situated – how these contexts influence the specific problem situation and how (and what) changes may be involved in association with them. In all the encounters between workers and service users several layers of contexts will be involved, whether broad and global, national and localised, associated with a particular policy or organisation, or interpersonal, micro and material. All these contexts may influence practice, interpretations and behaviour at any one site.

HOW THE NARRATIVE WILL BE INTERPRETED AND ENACTED IN THE PROFESSIONAL CONTEXT OF THE WORKER

It is important to construct and frame an assessment narrative in ways which will allow the service user to access services appropriately, or to have their needs met as effectively as possible. In order for this to happen, the worker may need a sophisticated understanding of the culture and discourse which operate in their organisation or context of services. For instance, they may need to take account of the types of language and categories used within their particular agency or field, and how 'good clients' are defined or rewarded. They may also need to understand how power is made and achieved within their context.

What categories of service users are more successful in attaining services? What are the implicit values and judgements made about service users and their problems? What are seen to be 'acceptable' reasons for problems, and what sorts of service users attract sympathy? Will the service user be seen as 'deserving' or 'undeserving' in this context? Will they be seen as disadvantaged, as a victim? Will they be seen as having helped themselves and therefore worthy of more assistance?

CONSTRUCTING A NARRATIVE TO BE EFFECTIVE IN THIS CONTEXT

Once the worker has a picture of the 'good client' it will be possible to construct the narrative around service users' situations accordingly. Taylor and White (2000) give some very good examples of how service users construct themselves as deserving of services. For example, in a women's refuge network, it helps if the woman is seen to be 'in dire need, not complicit in her victimisation, and is morally worthy' (2000: 83). If we are operating in an 'enterprise culture', as Cannan (1994) argues underpins the contemporary delivery of services in the UK, then it may help to establish the service user as a passive victim of circumstances, or as someone who is normally independent, but has been struck by crisis outside their control. In this narrative, the delivery of services is constructed as simply needing to return the person to their normal state of independence.

Exercise

For the following scenario, construct a professional narrative which you think will be effective. Try to incorporate the five elements we have just discussed.

You are working as a student counsellor in a university. A student social worker seeks your assistance in gaining extensions from university teaching staff on all assignments. She is a single mother and says she finds it impossible to juggle all the demands of study and parenting. She feels she will be able to manage if she has long extensions. There is a whole range of subjects involved – two social work practice subjects, a psychology subject and an economics subject. You agree to approach each staff member on her behalf.

Will the narratives you construct be different for the different staff you approach? How? What assumptions and beliefs guided the ways you constructed each narrative?

STRATEGIES

In some ways we have already hinted at the specific practice strategies involved in constructing a professional narrative. However, in this section I want to delve into a little more detail, particularly in relation to adapting research strategies for gaining a complex understanding of people and their situations.

ETHNOGRAPHIC AND OBSERVATIONAL METHODS

As mentioned earlier, Rodwell (1987) likened the process of assessment making to that of naturalistic inquiry, implying that a whole set of methods associated with qualitative approaches and ethnographic methods can be used appropriately to further our understanding of service users and their experiences.

Much has been written about observational methods, how specific items in situations or incidents are selected for identification and recording. Types of observation include: exterior physical signs; expressive movement; physical location; language behaviour; time duration (Kellehear, 1993: 116). Observation can assist us in making connections between the context and specific behaviours, and especially making connections between different sets of interactions. It can be a useful device for providing some different perspectives other than those of specific players, who may not be able to see the overall set of interactions from their own place within them.

Ethnographic methods may involve researchers immersing themselves, as participant observers, in the situation. Researchers may attempt to understand the experience of people from their point of view by placing themselves in the same situation. Obviously there are limits to this, since researchers can never really be in the same social situation as the people they are researching, but immersing yourself in similar experiences as much as possible goes some way further than trying to understand experience in a disembodied kind of way. A home visit may be seen as a type of ethnographic study in a sense, since it is an attempt to enter the physical world of the service user a little more. Many community development workers work and live within the same geographic environments as the people with whom they work, in order to understand and align themselves with the experiences of service users.

BIOGRAPHICAL METHODS

The resurgence of interest in biographical methods is associated with the postmodern turn (Merrill and West, 2009) and the emphasis on identity politics, in which the reflexive making of self and experience become an important life project. In simpler terms, it is also becoming more politic to value the data derived from personal experience and service user perspectives in policy development and decision making.

'Biographical methods' loosely refers to those methods which rely on people's life histories or personal stories as an integral part of the research. Some other methods discussed in this section might also be included under this rubric (ethnographic and reflexive methods), as well as oral histories, auto-ethnographies, narrative work and memory work (e.g. Haug et al., 1999). Many of these methods may be easily adapted for use in social work practice, as they encompass approaches and techniques which focus on both valuing and eliciting the person's own view of themselves and their lives. In this sense, biographical research methods make an important link between social work practice and social work research.

Narrative methods will be discussed in more detail in the following chapter. Memory work is a very interesting group method, designed to explore individual memories in order to create and rewrite collective memories, having made links between personal experience and social context (McLeod and Thomson, 2009). Memory work is thus also potentially transformative. Stephenson and Papadopoulos (2006) also illustrate how memory work can be used to identify new modes of being and acting from the experiences of marginal groups (in this case people with HIV/AIDS).

REFLEXIVE METHODS

The whole area of ethnographic methods raises the issue of reflexivity as a research tool in understanding and making sense of the worlds of service users. To what extent are our own views and perspectives unduly colouring the perspectives of our service users, and can such awareness be used to advantage? I think an understanding of how we reflexively create knowledge in a research process has direct application to how we construct a professional narrative in assessment making.

For instance, we may design ways of understanding service user situations and experience which allow us to be aware and critical of how our own constructions frame our understanding. Steier (1991: 166–7) gives an example of a technique of studying family therapists' constructions of family by co-viewing videotapes of family interviews and asking the therapeutic team to stop the tape at critical moments and discuss the reasons for actions taken at these points.

Many of the research designs developed under the 'new paradigm' of Reason and Rowan (1981), participative action research (Whyte, 1991) and co-operative inquiry (Heron, 1996) are designs which are congruent with the demands of reflexivity. They allow for researcher interaction with participants and for research respondents to participate as researchers in a joint process of data creation. Their designs often model reflective loops, in which information is elicited and reviewed through a number of processes which model the everyday research processes of information retrieval and processing that thinking individuals undertake in coping with daily decisions in the research process. These types of processes could be modelled in collaborative interactions with service users, where the object is to co-construct a narrative which 'works' for the service user within a professional culture.

Goodman (1998) makes a number of suggestions about the 'reflexive' collection of data which might be adapted for use in professional practice settings. These would assist in uncovering multiple and perhaps hidden perspectives. She selected research assistants with diverse social and cultural backgrounds and spent time debriefing by exploring their unique and different perceptions of similar events. She also made a conscious effort to avoid preconceived ideas, by avoiding too much prior reading and by trying to enter empathically the world of the research participants. Last, the researchers paid attention to phenomena which seemed to challenge initial observations, conceptions and experiences. They tried to look beyond what seemed initially obvious.

Being reflexive involves a recognition of how we ourselves, as whole people, influence the situations and contexts in which we interact. In ethnographic work, anthropologists have introduced the idea of the researcher as instrument, the whole person as the medium by which information is obtained, selected and interpreted. This idea of the 'self as instrument' has application to the ways in which workers might see and use themselves in co-constructing a narrative with service users.

Briggs conducted an ethnographic study of Eskimos (Rosaldo, 1993) in which she lived for a time with an Eskimo family, under conditions of severe cold. She felt at times extremely depressed, angry, frustrated and humiliated. She used these experiences as points of insight into the emotional life of the Eskimo family, as they struggle to understand her. 'Their perception of her "tiredness" revealed much about their views of emotions, particularly as experienced in the informal practices of everyday life rather than as articulated in abstract context-free statements' (Rosaldo, 1993: 178). Through the prism of her own experience and in daily interaction with her research participants in specific contexts, she is able to develop an understanding of their experience in relation to her own. As they struggle with an 'outsider' coping in their everyday context and as Briggs the person struggles with them and their context, the researcher is able to translate their story in relation to her own (Fook, 1999b).

OTHER UNOBTRUSIVE METHODS

In trying to build up a picture of multiple perspectives on service user experience and situations, it is important to remember that other people might not be the only sources of understanding. Often written or visual documents may exist which can provide yet another interpretation of a situation. Case files, past reports, service directories, referral notes, policy documents and manuals, meeting minutes, impact analyses and proposals, programme submissions and evaluations are all examples of documents which can be seen not as definitive sources of information, but as sources of potentially different perspectives, which may indicate something further about the discourses surrounding a situation. In these cases, many of the methods regarding document analysis (e.g. Kellehear, 1993) may be of use in building up a professional narrative which takes into account the perspectives presented in documents.

In this chapter I have focused on how the making of problems and assessments have discursive functions and how we can frame problems and assessments in ways which are effective for service users in different contexts. In this sense all the strategies we use in making knowledge are relevant. In the next chapter we focus more specifically on how narrative techniques might be used in a range of practice situations.

Chapter summary

A postmodern and critical approach to the way problems are conceptualised and assessments constructed is based on criticism of traditional approaches, which are seen as static, rational and linear. Such traditional approaches tend to position the professional as passive and objective, often simply fitting the service user's experience into preconceived problem (or service related) categories. Such approaches also have a discursive power function and tend to direct blame towards the service user.

An alternative approach is to see assessment as a 'construction of professional narrative' in which the worker enters into a more collaborative dialogue with service users, takes account of complexities and changes, resists traditional labels, and may co-create new narratives and labels which better frame the service user's view of themselves. An essential aim of a professional narrative is to construct a narrative about the service user which works to empower them (in the professional context of the worker).

The chapter also covered how such an approach affects how situations are problematised (it may be better to label them as 'situations' or 'circumstances' rather than 'problems') and how to set up the appropriate climate. The main element of a professional narrative are:

- service user perspective/story;
- the perspectives of other players;
- contexts and changes;
- how the narrative will be interpreted and enacted in the professional context of the worker;
- constructing a narrative to be effective in this context.

The remainder of the chapter detailed some specific research methods which might be adapted for use in practice, to assist in constructing professional narratives in a collaborative way. These included: biographical methods, ethnography, observational methods, reflexive methods and unobtrusive methods. Readings are provided to follow up on some of these methods in more detail.

FURTHER READING

McLeod, J. and Thomson, R. (2009) *Researching Social Change*. London: Sage. Ch. 2 'Memory work', pp. 15–32.

A good, simple introduction to this method.

Merrill, B. and West, L. (2009) *Using Biographical Methods in Social Research*. London: Sage. Ch. 7 'Interviewing and recording experience', pp. 113–27.

A good overview of a collaborative approach to conducting biographical research interviews, which has ready applications to social work practice.

Orme, J. and Shemmings, D. (2010) *Developing Research-based Social Work Practice*. Basingstoke: Palgrave Macmillan. Ch. 8 'Talk and discourse', pp. 138–55.

This chapter provides a good overview of and introduction to 'talk' methods (including discourse analysis and grounded theory).

Hall, C., Slembrouck, S. and Sarangi, S. (2006) *Language Practices in Social Work Categorisation and Accountability in Social Work*. London and New York: Routledge.

The whole book is a study of child welfare practices, based on an analysis of language used in different 'texts' such as conversations, interviews, media portrayals. Chapter 6 is based on an analysis of case notes. The book is useful for an in-depth illustration both of language-based research methods, but also for the illustration of the details of practice which emerge using such methods. It helps provide a detailed picture of how social workers actually do construct narratives and stories about service users, and is therefore a useful resource for seeing how these might be constructed in more empowering ways for service users.

10

NARRATIVE STRATEGIES

The idea of narrative, the notion that meanings (and social arrangements) are made, from various perspectives, through discourses, is central to a postmodern and critical approach to social work. Using the term 'narrative' in this sense implies a recognition of the ways in which we make and use knowledge to create and preserve our social worlds and places within them. We construct and tell ourselves and others stories which function to preserve our social positions. This is perhaps a common understanding which is shared by the many different traditions that have developed the concept of narrative to inspire many different strategies for use in many different fields. For instance, narrative techniques are used in research as narrative analysis (Manning and Cullum-Swan, 1994; Reissman, 1993 and 2008) or in therapy through, for example, the work of the critically acclaimed Michael White (Monk et al., 1997; Duvall and Beres, 2011) and David Epston (White and Epston, 1990). Narrativity also holds more direct political potential for different social groups who have previously lacked social voice (Agger, 1998). In this chapter I will pull together some aspects of these different traditions, in order to develop a repertoire of strategies which might be used by social workers in a variety of settings.

WHAT IS NARRATIVE?

In simplest terms a narrative is a story which performs social functions. They are a form of making meaning of experience (Polkinghorne, 1998: 36), and because meaning frameworks are normally derived from social or cultural contexts, there is necessarily a social and political element. Narratives can also be a way of communicating about oneself and events in a social situation, so that one's social self also takes form, through the form of a narrative. This understanding of narrative has important implications for bringing about change, and therefore for therapeutic interventions.

Any individual or social grouping may construct or use many different narratives at any one time, some of which may be in conflict and change according to context.

In general, however, narratives are usually understood as stories that have a basic structure involving a succession of events, organised in a culturally coherent way, which lead to a finale (Ricoeur, 1986; Sands, 1996). As Polkinghorne says:

> Narrative recognises the meaning of individual experiences by noting how they function as parts of the whole. Its particular subject matter is human actions and events that affect human beings, which it configures into whole according to the roles these actions and events play in bringing about a conclusion. The narrative scheme serves as a lens through which the apparently independent and disconnected elements of existence are seen as related parts of a whole. (quoted in Brophy, 2009: 34)

The three main elements of narratives are as follows:

1   They aim to establish credibility or acceptance within a particular social or cultural context.
2   There is usually a linear, logical or causal link between different incidents in the narrative which leads to a conclusion or end.
3   The incidents are organised to create a coherent sequence and view (identity) of the narrator.

SUMMARY

We might summarise the elements of narratives succinctly as 'coherence, continuity, closure' (Solas, 1996) and credibility.

There can of course be many different types of narratives (as there can be many different types of discourses), depending on who is using and creating them and in what contexts. They may vary in content from the use of a particular name or label and its connotations, to a grand metanarrative which sows many specific elements together (such as those which characterise the major forms of thinking in different historical periods of human civilisation, like humanism or positivism). Individuals might have different narratives about themselves, some about their own past, some about their future. They might take the form of personal stories or stories of specific incidents. Narratives may function to incorporate adverse experiences, or to justify controversial activities. There may be family, organisational or even national narratives, or broad cultural narratives characteristic of the Western world, such as beliefs about 'orientalism' (Said, 1995).

In this sense, narratives and discourses are similar phenomena in the social and cultural functions they perform. Discourses might be said to be broader in that they can also incorporate structural elements. In this book I am using the term 'narrative' to focus primarily on the language, verbal and conversational aspects of discourses.

ELEMENTS OF NARRATIVES

There are many different elements of narratives. Different approaches to analysis may indicate focusing on different elements. For instance, Manning and Cullum-Swan

(1994: 464) suggest that narratives can be analysed according to codes, syntax, grammar or form and in more or less structured ways. More structured approaches might focus on using a preformulated set of rules and principles to understand the narrative, such as reducing a story to a set of propositions (divided into 'prerequisites' and 'events'). Less structured approaches might define a narrative as a story 'with a beginning, middle and end that reveals someone's experiences'. As Manning and Cullum-Swan suggest:

> Narratives take many forms, are told in many settings, before many audiences, and with various degrees of connection to actual events or persons. Thus themes, principal metaphors, definitions of narrative, defining structures or stories (beginning, middle and end), and conclusions are often defined poetically and artistically and are quite context bound. (Manning and Cullum-Swan, 1994: 465)

Burke uses drama-related terms to suggest focusing on 'act, scene, agent, agency and purpose' (1966). Taylor and White (2000: 57–8) focus on the conversational strategies which form part of people's narratives in establishing the credibility of themselves and their stories. They note that any description of a phenomenon represents a selection of descriptors which is variable and context dependent.

Exercise

Describe *where* you are right now.

What choices did you exercise about the kinds of descriptions you used?

Taylor and White (2000) note how even this simple type of description involves choices about level and type of detail ('at my computer', 'in my study', 'in Bramble Cottage', 'working at home', 'in Whaddon, Salisbury', 'in the UK', 'in a stressed state', 'in limbo'), depending on how you want to present yourself, what you think your audience wants to know and what you think they will understand. I am always struck by the level of choice of description (and confusion) involved for me when I am asked by someone, 'Where are you from?' This may seem a relatively simple question, but when I take into account one of my identities as a later generation Australian-born person of Chinese descent, I am never really sure what I am being asked, or how the questioner is seeing me. Do I respond 'Salisbury', 'the University of London', or that I am 'an Australian who lives in the UK'? Sometimes when I have been asked this question when I lived in Australia I have responded 'Geelong West'. Then they say, 'No, where are you *really* from?' If I say I was born in Sydney, they might say, 'Well, where are your parents from?' When they ask this, I usually assume they are asking a question about my racial or ethnic background and usually I then say, 'I am third generation Australian-born Chinese.' On one level this might simply be seen as an exercise in communication, but it is also an exercise in trying to construct a narrative about my identity, in response to a particular context. A delicate balance is involved, because in most instances people are simply asking about where I live. Assuming that they are asking more than this can make me look overly conscious of my ethnicity and 'differentness' which does not make me appear credible in a professional social work setting, for instance, where the culture is one which values shared experiences.

SUMMARY

Taylor and White (2000: 59–70) identify several conversational devices commonly used by people in everyday talk to establish the credibility of their narratives. First, they note devices for framing the credibility of the narrator.

- Establishing the 'disinterest' of the narrator – this involves trying to show the narrator does not stand to gain anything from their position in the story. A dilemma arises however of how to establish disinterest when it is clear that the narrator is involved. Taylor and White term this the 'dilemma of stake' (p. 59). Some of the devices we might use could include portraying ourselves as 'impartial bystanders' or 'ordinary people' to whom something happened 'out of the blue'.
- Stake inoculation – this involves the narrator establishing her or himself as a 'fair and independent person' (p. 62). Sometimes openly acknowledging interest may effectively establish a 'fair' identity for the narrator, as opposed to being seen as someone who has deliberately hidden an interest.
- Category entitlement – this involves establishing that certain categories of people may be more authoritative or knowledgeable, and then claiming membership of this group. For instance, people who have experienced a phenomenon are often privileged in the telling of the story of it.

Second, Taylor and White discuss how credible accounts are established:

- externalising devices (p. 66) – this involves drawing attention away from the narrator to the 'facts' of the story.
- Using detail – this involves filling in more detail to make it seem as if the narrator was 'really there', and sometimes filling in 'active voice' (p. 69) by constructing snippets of 'real' conversation to describe the scene and make it seem as if the narrator is only telling 'what happened'.
- Extreme case formulations – this involves framing the story in extreme terms (p. 69), for example, saying 'I would never …'; or minimising ('I only ignored him for a second …') (p. 70).

THE BROAD USES OF NARRATIVE STRATEGIES – NARRATIVE RECONSTRUCTION

In a broad sense, an understanding and analysis of narratives and the role they play in the politics of people's lives, at macro and micro levels, can be used effectively in changing the politics of situations. The process of change involved can be characterised quite simply as one of narrative reconstruction. Problematic narratives are deconstructed, and then reconstructed along more desired lines. This is, of course, similar to the process of deconstruction and reconstruction of discourses except that, as noted earlier, the analysis and recreation of discourses may also involve material elements. The primary focus in narrative reconstruction is the verbal and language elements of discourses.

With this approach in mind, it is easy to imagine processes of narrative reconstruction working at many different levels and in many different settings. The following are some of the main ways in which narrative reconstruction might be used by social workers.

IDENTITY RECONSTRUCTION AND IDENTITY POLITICS

As discussed earlier, people's identities, their subject positions, their own view of themselves and where they 'fit' in the social order are a major aspect of how discourse and narratives exercise social and power functions. It therefore follows that an ability to recreate identities in ways which are more empowering is an important part of critical social work practice. Identity reconstruction can be as effective at an individual level as it can at group, community, organisational or even national level. It is probably most applied at individual or group level, but in this section I will develop several applications of the idea.

At *individual level*, the idea of identity reconstruction provides a guiding reference point for therapeutic work. Given that disempowerment might be associated with a disempowered self-image and a devalued perspective, reconstructing personal identities along more powerful and valued lines can be an important aspect of assistance. For instance, Sands (1996: 180–3) discusses the example of a woman whose more positive views of herself were outweighed by more negative psychiatric labels. Simply validating her own views and helping her sort through the different perspectives so that she could develop a coherent picture of herself allowed her to develop a personal narrative, a positive reconstructed identity.

At *group level*, the potential for marginalised groups to rediscover and validate identities which have previously been unrecognised is known as identity politics (Agger, 1998: 73). The process of expressing, legitimating and creating a social identity for previously marginalised groups, using a narrative process, is widely recognised as an important step in changing the power positions of these groups and creating a more inclusive society. A narrative approach is seen as particularly helpful in assisting groups previously without voice to articulate their experience. It is an enabling approach, because it is the group's own experience, and the group's own way of expressing this experience, which are valued. Therefore people who have previously been marginalised because they were unable to communicate their experience in terms determined by dominant groups are becoming empowered in expressing themselves. They are then able to participate in defining themselves in their own terms, rather than against norms determined outside their experience and culture.

The social movements associated with identity politics include feminism, of course, but disability and gay rights activists are also major groups which potentially benefit from such an approach. The relevance for indigenous groups and ethnic minorities is also self-evident. The political potential of such movements, in terms of structural change, might be ambiguous (Agger, 1998: 73). However, I think it is a vital stage, whatever the political process, that relatively marginalised groups contribute to ongoing debate through having their perspective added and through becoming empowered during the process.

At organisational levels it is easy to imagine how processes which allow the living enactment of organisational ideals to be articulated might assist in strengthening employees' commitment to the organisation. A process of organisational identity reconstruction, which allowed the different voices of all members to be expressed and valued, might potentially construct a very different organisational identity. At the same time it might establish a process whereby individual members learnt to reconstruct their identities in relation to their employing organisation.

ACTION RESEARCH

As discussed earlier, narrative analysis has developed as a major set of social research strategies (e.g. Reissman, 2008) and also approaches to practice (e.g. Brophy, 2009). The assumption underlying these approaches is that much can be understood about the narrator's social orientation and cultural position from an analysis of the stories they tell about themselves. Earlier I mentioned that there are many varied approaches to narrative analysis. It is important to remember that the analysis of narratives alone does not necessarily constitute narrative reconstruction. Although narrative reconstruction must incorporate a component of narrative deconstruction or analysis, many research activities might not take that further step of creating a new narrative in place of the deconstructed one.

Action and collaborative types of research, however, would incorporate such a step (Reason and Bradbury, 2001). These types of approaches, which include a component of changing or developing new practices as part of the research process, may be seen as a type of narrative reconstruction process, whereby the research participants are actively engaged in creating a new narrative. Such an understanding of narrative reconstruction, and its use in collaborative and action research, allows us to draw quite flexibly on the two fields in developing new sets of strategies for practice.

NARRATIVE THERAPY

This is probably recognised as the major way in which narrative strategies have been used in the helping field to date. Michael White is credited with having developed the narrative therapy approach (Monk et al., 1997; Brown and Augusta-Scott, 2006; Duvall and Beres, 2011). Using a number of influences, ranging between Foucault and strategic family therapy (Hart, 1995), White's narrative therapy is largely based on the idea of examining and changing narratives which are harmful to service users. The situations in which his work has been used constitute an impressive list, including child behavioural problems, grief, separation anxiety, encopresis, anorexia nervosa, intellectual disability, schizophrenia, children in residential care, sexual abuse and men who are violent (Hart, 1995: 181). In addition, a plethora of people have taken and developed specific aspects of his work further (e.g. Duvall and Beres, 2011). In later sections I will outline in more detail some of the major specific strategies which are involved in narrative therapy and can be adapted for practice in many different settings.

THE PROCESSES OF NARRATIVE RECONSTRUCTION

There is a common set of processes involved in reconstructing narratives. In simple terms, the process moves from uncovering and/or deconstructing the narrative (as appropriate) to externalising and creating an alternative narrative. Whether or not the initial narrative is validated or deconstructed will depend on the setting and the purpose of the interaction between the worker and service users. For instance, if the setting is therapeutic, then the narrative uncovered may have undesirable aspects which need to be challenged and changed. If however the social worker is working with a group of people whose story needs validating so that they can be empowered, then the process might involve simply legitimating the group's narrative. It may well be that most situations require elements of both. For instance, even in therapeutic clinical settings, aspects of service users' narratives may simply need validation, rather than challenging. Alternatively, the narratives of some marginal groups may incorporate aspects which are detrimental to their self image and may need to be challenged if the group is to be empowered.

With these varied situations in mind, I have constructed the following stages of the process to be as broadly applicable as possible. Narrative reconstruction is an interactive process in which all parties participate in creating a narrative about the situation which is empowering and changes the inequitable power relations which contribute to the problem situation. I have based these processes on several different versions (O'Hanlon, 1994; Parton and O'Byrne, 2000) and collapsed them into the major features below:

1 Uncover the narratives involved, taking care to identify those which are dominant, those which belong to key players and those which are devalued.
2 Identify the functions of different narratives, including the empowering and disempowering functions.
3 Validate the narratives (or aspects of narratives) that are performing a positive and empowering function and/or those which are marginalised; externalise the narratives (or aspects of narratives) that work against the interests of or are disempowering of service users.
4 Uncover or build alternative narratives, retell the story in a new way ('restorying') which is empowering.
5 Create further social validation by creating an audience for the new narratives.

TECHNIQUES OF NARRATIVE RECONSTRUCTION

The following are some specific strategies or techniques which might assist in the process of narrative reconstruction.

UNCOVERING THE NARRATIVES

- Look for the 'missed bits' which don't fit the main narratives.
- Ask about other, multiple perspectives (e.g. the perspectives of other people, other possible interpretations) and compare these to the story of the person.
- Use circular questioning – ask about the observations of other people who are present in the situation.

Exercise

Write up a brief description (no more than half a page) of an incident which you felt was problematic for you in some way. Try to uncover the main narratives in your story of the incident.

CHALLENGING ASSUMPTIONS THAT ARE UNHELPFUL

This might involve being mindful of whose the narrative is, where it came from and what functions it performs. For example, asking what 'so and so gets out of it' can help to focus the narrative on other players. Asking how/where this leaves the service user can help to externalise, but also alert the person to counter-productive functions.

Exercise

Identify the unhelpful assumptions in your narrative.

EXTERNALISING THE PROBLEM NARRATIVE

This might involve naming the problematic narrative and giving it agency. Parton and O'Byrne (2000: 89–90) quote O'Hanlon's (1995) useful list of metaphors which helps to attribute external agency to the problem. For example, images of *oppression* can help in asking how the problem 'forces' or 'frightens'. Alternatively, images of *imprisonment* (how does it 'brainwash'), *spying* (how does it 'undermine'), *crime* (how does it 'rob' or 'cheat'), *supernatural* (how does it 'haunt') and so on can provide colourful ways of expressing how a problem is experienced and naming the hold it has as something inherent to the problem itself, rather than the person who experiences it. Another technique for externalising problems is to include the *context* in narratives (White, 1996). Narratives might be retold with reference to the context, thus placing emphasis on the circumstances of the problem situation, rather than just the person involved (e.g. 'The circumstances forced you to ...').

Exercise

Invent a name or image for your problematic narrative.

SHIFTING THE STORY TO NARRATIVES THAT ARE ENABLING OR EMPOWERING

For example, below are some major ways in which discourses can become more empowering:

- From 'cause' to 'effect': rather than 'how did I cause this?' to 'what effect did this have on me?'
- From 'blame' to 'responsibility': rather than 'who can I blame for this in the past?' to 'what responsibility can I take now?'
- From 'guilt' to 'care'.
- From 'passive' to 'active'.
- From 'failure' to 'success'.
- From 'negative' to 'positive'.
- From 'weakness' to 'strength'.

Parton and O'Byrne (2000: 89–90), again quoting O'Hanlon (1995), also suggest that externalising images can be used to restory the narrative in more empowering ways. For example, if someone has a problem which 'imprisons' them, then they can be asked how they can 'get time out for good behaviour'. In effect this is building the person back into the story, 'restorying' the narrative so that they have agency and power.

Exercise

Create a more empowering label or image than the problematic one you have named.

Other techniques which might be effective in restorying are:

- retelling the story, incorporating the missing bits, e.g. the emotional or too painful aspects;
- using rituals and actions to retell some aspects which might be too difficult to verbalise;
- reworking the identity to incorporate an empowered identity (e.g. 'the new me', 'the old me');
- retelling the story, picking out all the positive bits from the past;
- rewriting the 'ideal' story.

Exercise

Now rewrite your narrative, incorporating the more empowering images.

CREATING AN AUDIENCE

It is useful to build in a stage of further social validation whereby the new narrative becomes socially sanctioned through being accepted by a further audience. This can be done in many ways. For example, telling the story to another person or group could help further legitimate that story. Writing about the story, so it can be seen in an externalised way and revisited constantly, may be helpful. Going more 'public' with the story, perhaps through media exposure, could gain support and more social legitimation, as well as creating a social space for the story and experience. Any form of more public expression could be explored as being useful in this stage.

Exercise

Find some way in which you can socially validate your story, and do this. What did you do, and what changes in your story and thinking occurred?

OTHER NARRATIVE TECHNIQUES

Duvall and Beres (2006) develop the use of conversational maps as a way of giving voice to people's experiences through developing and discussing their storylines. This acts as a guide to the therapeutic conversation. The map includes five main elements: (1) points of stories (what the person feels it is most important to talk about); (2) the backstory (or context); (3) pivotal events; (4) evaluation of effects; and (5) the summary. The process of discussing these elements of people's stories allows them to re-author their lives in more empowering ways.

Brophy (2009) develops narrative practices in organisational settings. In particular he applies a narrative approach to training methods, using narrative interviews, inter- and intra-organisational case studies, learning histories, collective sense-making, and naturalistic or informal story-gathering (pp. 135–6).

Chapter summary

The idea of narrative is well-developed and has spawned many different techniques and strategies, ranging from therapeutic, to research, to those which are more overtly political. Much of the social work literature to date has focused on therapeutic uses of narrative techniques. However, in this chapter I have tried to draw together some of the major usages, including political and research strategies, to provide a stimulus for thinking about how they might be used in the broad variety of ways which social work practice should include. The chapter has covered a broad five-stage process of narrative reconstruction, summarised as follows:

1 Uncover the narratives involved, taking care to identify those which are dominant, those which belong to key players, those which are devalued.
2 Identify the functions of different narratives, including the empowering and disempowering functions.
3 Validate the narratives (or aspects of narratives) that are performing a positive and empowering function and/or those which are marginalised; externalise the narratives (or aspects of narratives) that work against the interests of or are disempowering of service users.
4 Uncover or build alternative narratives, retell the story in a new way ('restorying') which is empowering.
5 Create further social validation by creating an audience for the new narratives.

FURTHER READING

Brophy, P. (2009) *Narrative-Based Practice*. Farnham: Ashgate.

This book is applicable to practice in a wide range of disciplines and professions, and therefore is particularly useful for applications outside the therapeutic context. As such it offers a fresh, and perhaps more easily socially and organisationally applicable orientation to practice.

Brown, C. and Augusta-Scott, T. (eds) (2007) *Narrative Therapy*. Thousand Oaks, CA: Sage.

This book is an edited collection. The introduction is especially helpful as a more recent account of postmodernism, reflexivity and narrative therapy. Chapter 9 by C. Brown 'Dethroning the suppressed voice: unpacking experience as story' is an excellent development of the notion of story and its relationship to experience.

Duvall, J. and Beres, L. (2011) *Innovations in Narrative Therapy: Connecting Practice, Training and Research*. New York: W.W. Norton.

The book is based on extensive research on narrative therapy, but as such also uses a critically reflective approach to develop narrative practice and theory further.

11

CONTEXTUAL PRACTICE
STRATEGIES FOR WORKING IN AND WITH CONTEXTS

If practices and knowledge about practices are contextual, what alternative ways might there be for framing our discourse about practice reflecting this emphasis on contextuality? Throughout this book, there has been an implicit emphasis on seeing social work practice in a holistic and generic way, as involving a similar orientation and set of skills, which are transferable between different settings and levels of practice. This is an alternative view to more traditional, 'modernist' conceptions of practice, which have tended to categorise practice in terms of the levels of 'intervention' (individual, group, family or community); population or problem groupings (for example, child and family work; aged care; health services); or other formulations (e.g. 'direct' or 'indirect' practice, clinical, policy, management or research).

A postmodern and critical analysis does not deny that practice might differ according to the contexts and types of people with whom we work. However, it does suggest alternative ways of understanding practices, based more on an understanding of how practices and thinking change in relation to context, rather than assuming that the knowledges or practices involved are inherently different between contexts.

In this chapter I will explore this alternative way of conceptualising social work practice in more detail, discussing some of the specific strategies which might be developed from this critical and postmodern approach. In Chapter 2 we outlined some of the ways in which the changing contexts of practice are influencing the profession, its autonomy and power base. In this chapter I want to explore ways in which these understandings can be used to transform the way we see our practice, role and mission, which lead to specific strategies in the concrete contexts in which we work every day.

A NEW WAY OF CONCEPTUALISING SOCIAL WORK PRACTICE: CONTEXTUAL PRACTICE

Since social work is a profession practised in context and we recognise that one of the distinctive features of our profession is that our work is situational, it is important to frame our practice in ways which represent this orientation. Many studies of social work practice which have focused on what is actually enacted, rather than theoretical ways of framing it, have shown that professionals work with a range of players in complex situations. Often it is not possible to identify one single 'client' who is and should be the clear beneficiary of social work practice (Fook et al., 1997, 2000). In some areas, such as child protection work, there may be several 'clients' whose interests clash. Of course there is constant debate about whether the service users or our employing agencies are our 'true' clients. Given the complexity of our work and myriad mixtures of players with whom we interact, it may be useful to conceptualise it as about working *with* context, as well as *within* context. Indeed, there are indications that this is in fact how experienced workers do see their practice (Fook et al., 2000).

SUMMARY

This idea of contextual practice – practice both with and within context – places an emphasis on several new ways of seeing our practice:

- the need to understand the nature of contexts in developing relevant practice strategies;
- the idea of positionality – being able to assume a reflexive stance, simultaneously outside and within contexts;
- the need to develop an ability to work with whole contexts, rather than simply a number of disparate players within a context;
- the need to develop practice and practice theory/knowledge which is transferable across different contexts;
- the need to reframe our skills in contextual terms.

I will discuss each of these in more detail.

THE NATURE OF CONTEXTS

Postmodern thinking recognises that contexts are 'habitats in which autonomous agents act in an environment characterised by chronic indeterminacy, ambivalence and contingency' (Leonard, 1997: 108). Contexts are uncertain, unpredictable and changeable; it is not possible to identify which and whether different elements of contexts 'cause' or 'determine' other elements. Furthermore, as Bauman succinctly notes:

> Postmodern contexts are complex because there is no single agency with an overall totalising ability to organise the different elements; and, worse still, there are a large number of different agencies of varying sizes and with different purposes, none of them large enough to determine the behaviour of others. (Bauman, 1992: 192)

Contexts therefore vary in size and degree of complexity. The contexts in which social workers practise range from broader levels of historical period, national and global situations, to the more localised community, employing organisational, personal or service user contexts. Of course there may be a variety of ways of understanding (and certainly many different discourses about) different contexts. In Britain, changing policies greatly influence the practice of social work, particularly the modernising agenda of more recent years (Lymbery, 2007).

However it is one thing to be aware of context as general background to practice, and another to be aware of how many specific contexts themselves actively shape our own understandings of what we are and do as social workers. It is part and parcel of being critical and reflexive that we understand how this context shapes the way we think about ourselves, and in particular our own ability to influence the situations in which we practise. As noted earlier, this understanding involves awareness of how a range of contexts have a role in shaping our behaviour and thinking.

The role of organisational context is one which has received much attention in social work literature (Jones and May, 1992; Lymbery, 2007), and is perhaps the one which we tend to be most highly aware of in day-to-day practice. Leonard (1997) discusses in some detail the features of the organisation as a particular work context. From a postmodern perspective, the whole idea of the 'organisation' can be seen as a modernist attempt to control and impose order on disparate elements. In this type of culture, differentiation is devalued. Yet with any change in the organisation, there is resistance and defence, as well as opportunity to create power (p. 106). One of the defensive responses is to create more and more boundaries between professions and areas of expertise. While this may appear to be increasing differentiation, it effectively acts to delimit areas of knowledge and expertise within an increasing number of narrowing fields (p. 107). Any transformation of organisational context and professional roles and identities therefore needs to take into account how our contexts might offer us opportunities to create more powerful discourses, rather than trapping us in terms of the old debates.

Yet there are also many more specific contexts which we carry inside ourselves which are often harder to access, and which can involve the frameworks we use to make meaning of situations. I often become aware of these when I conduct critical reflection workshops, and I can see how people sometimes make meaning of a past crucial incident in their lives depending on the frameworks and experiences which are available to them at the time. For example, I may find that a person frames workplace authority issues in a certain way because of what they learnt about authority when they were an adolescent, or a newly qualified practitioner, or when they were working under an authoritarian manager. Often they carry this meaning into later life and work and it colours the way they see and relate to power. What critical reflection reveals, though, is that they may have had many subsequent different experiences of authority, which they have not incorporated into their current meaning framework – they are effectively carrying around a framework which was developed in a different context. This context may, or may not, still be relevant. This appreciation of how specific past contexts can influence present day practice is also vital to a contextual perspective.

SUMMARY

In order to be more aware of context the following list of differing contexts and their influence may be helpful (starting from the broader to the more specific):

- global;
- international/national;
- regional/local;
- community;
- policy;
- historical;
- political;
- social;
- cultural;
- economic;
- professional;
- personal;
- biographical.

The list is not meant to be exhaustive, nor are the categories mutually exclusive. However it does give some pointers as to what we need to be mindful of in understanding how we are creatures of context.

Exercise

Think of something which you did, or which happened to you recently. Note down aspects of the context in which it occurred and how you think they influenced it, using the list above. How do you think your understanding might be different if any aspect of the context was different? Do you think you might interpret it differently, or indeed act differently, if something similar occurred in the future? If so, why might this be the case?

POSITIONALITY

If we recognise that we and the people with whom we work, live and practise within a number of different contexts simultaneously, then our ability to work with and within several different contexts is crucial. This recognition allows us to see from different positions at the same time, and therefore to position ourselves in a number of different ways simultaneously. These multiple positions allow us to take multiple perspectives, to recognise our relative positions both *within* and *outside* our every-day working and living contexts. This ability to be located in, and at the same time not totally bound by, our work contexts, allows us the privilege of both seeing the critical possibilities for changes in any one situation, while at the same time being located in a position to help bring them about. Our relative positionality, with the multiple perspectives this entails, thus allows us (and the people we work with) to interact reflexively and responsively within our work contexts.

WORKING WITH WHOLE CONTEXTS

The ability to recognise simultaneous multiple positions and perspectives also allows us to work *with* whole contexts, while at the same time working *within* them. This involves being able to recognise the different players in a situation, that their inter-ests and identities may be complex and primarily influenced by a particular context. Therefore, it is important to recognise that service users might not always necessar-ily be 'disadvantaged', 'victims' or 'disempowered'. At the same time, organisations and managers might not always represent the more powerful groups. The most accurate way, in this sense, is to understand that people and contexts differ – it is the particular people within this particular context with whom the worker is involved. In this sense, it is the whole context which is the focus of the worker's practice, rather than individuals within it. Elsewhere my colleagues and I have termed this a type of 'connected practice':

> This involves the ability to work with the whole person, group, organisation or community within the whole context in which they or it is situated. This involves specifically an ability to recognise a variety of different players as 'clients', rather than necessarily those who are traditionally defined as 'disadvantaged'. In this sense, the true 'client' of the social worker is the *context*, rather than only specific identified individuals, although individual parties may benefit from the practitioners' work. An example of this might be the worker who perceives as their client, the whole organisa-tion, and the culture of ways in which services are delivered to service users. Such an orientation might result in a more responsive service delivery to individual service users, but it will be the whole context of service delivery which has also changed and benefitted. (Fook et al., 2000: 193)

TRANSFERABILITY

If, according to a postmodern way of thinking, knowledge is developed in relation to changing contexts and must be responsive and relevant given their unpredictabil-ity and multiplicity, then our understandings of how we create and value different types of knowledge need to be transformed accordingly. This involves, in broad terms, recognising that knowledge which has been developed from one situation might not necessarily apply to another. At the same time, however, professional social workers need to learn from past situations, in order to practise effectively in new situations. So how do we differentiate between knowledge which is applicable between different situations and that which is not?

The term 'transferability' has been coined to refer to knowledge which is developed in such a way as to be useful in new situations (Fook, 2000b, 2001c). This occurs in an inductive process, whereby theory is created from an amalgam of preconceived thinking and changing experience, to be more easily *transferred across contexts*. This skill of transferability – the ability to modify, change and develop theory and knowledge in ways that make it readily relevant in different contexts – involves the practitioner being open to changes in contexts, rather than assuming and imposing preconceived orientations. Relevance, rather than generalisability is important.

In more modernist ways of understanding knowledge, the emphasis is on deducing generalisable theories, those which can subsequently be readily applied from an objective standpoint. Abstract, preconceived and generalised theories are imposed on new contexts and new experiences are fitted into pre-existing categories, in order to make meaning of them. The concept of transferability, however, is about creating meaning inductively from each new situation and translating prior thinking into terms which make the practitioner more easily able to engage with new situations. The emphasis is on *elucidating meaning* rather than *preserving the 'truth'*. Transferability thus involves the reinterpretation of meaning in new contexts, rather than the imposition of one truth across contexts. This process encapsulates the ability to make new contextual meanings out of old (Fook et al., 2000: 191). Effectively this means that 'old' understandings are not lost, but simply constantly reworked, sometimes in ways which may make them unrecognisable. In this sense, a new meaning may have been created in response to a new context.

Bourdieu (1999: 221–3) makes a point in relation to the transfer of ideas over international contexts which may be helpful here. He refers to the context of origin of the idea, and the context of reception of the idea. He notes how different features of each of the contexts (for example, the politics of publishing) may have specific influences on the form of the expression of the idea, and of course its interpretation. These concepts might be employed when we analyse the relevance of our own practice theories, how they came about (their origin) and how they might be received or applied in a different context.

REFRAMING SKILLS IN CONTEXTUAL TERMS – CONTEXTUAL COMPETENCE

If we see ourselves as working with and within context, then it is important to reframe the way we see our skills in these terms. This may mean resisting discourses of interpersonal or intrapsychic helping, instead thinking of the ways in which our work makes connections between people and contexts. One major set of skills that has been proposed, which has some bearing on this way of thinking, is the idea of developing 'cultural competence' (Baldwin, 2000a; Jones and May, 1992: 223–4). This is taken to refer to the set of skills involved in assessing the cultural climate of an organisation and being able to practise in a strategic manner within it. There is, of course, a more recent (and popular) trend to develop 'cultural competence', but the bulk of this literature seems to refer to a more narrow use of the idea. Much of this literature appears to relate cultural competence to skills of working with social diversity (for example, Lum, 2003; Nylund, 2006; Perry and Tate-Manning, 2006; Williams, 2006; Allen-Meares, 2007; Sakamoto, 2007). Ben-Ari and Strier (2010) provide an overview of recent uses of the term in social work. They draw out a common tendency to focus on practitioner understanding of cultural and ethnic differences, and an ability to shape this understanding into appropriate cross-cultural practices at all levels of practice.

I am however more concerned to emphasise a broader understanding of context, which involves an appreciation of all aspects of context, including cultures – both those of people we might regard as socially different, and of course, being reflexive, an awareness of our own cultural backgrounds. Culture, in the sense I am referring to here, embraces all the more taken-for-granted sets of ideas to which we might adhere, not just those pertaining to ethnicity or religion. This of course is in line with a critically reflective approach to practice, in that critical reflection entails, on one level, becoming aware of the hidden influences of assumptions which emanate from cultural contexts.

If we broaden our vision to include any type of context (and culture) in which the worker operates, then we need to develop an understanding of the cultural climate of all contexts. Therefore cultural competence could refer to the set of skills involved in appreciating the cultural climate of all contexts. I refer to this as *contextual competence* – the ability to 'read' the cultural climate of contexts and to practise effectively with and within this climate.

RESISTING DOMINANT CULTURAL CONTEXTS

Many postmodern and critical analyses have focused on the dominance of managerialist cultures and agendas in the human services, as a direct result of the globalisation of markets. In Chapter 2 I discussed the influences of such cultures on the professional role and identity, and in particular the challenges faced by social workers in maintaining a 'social justice' perspective in the face of seemingly purist economic concerns. Many of the tensions and dilemmas have been framed in oppositional ways, so it seems as if workers are caught in impossible binds, with dichotomous and mutually exclusive choices about whether to meet the needs of powerless clients or subjugate themselves to the demands of organisations and managers.

A first step in resisting what are seen as the overriding demands of managerialism is to deconstruct the debate and question whether the choices must necessarily be framed in impossible terms. Baldwin's study of care management practice illustrates how framing the demands of managerialist culture in oppositional terms can limit the creative possibilities we see in our practice. His study, which was conducted with a number of practitioners who were collaboratively engaged in researching their practice, shows how workers actually exercised a considerable amount of discretion in the ways they implemented policy. While initially seeing themselves as controlled by policy imperatives, they came to recognise how they actually exercised a degree of choice about how it was applied with different people. They came to see the way they practised policy as quite a bit more complex than their original conceptions suggested (Baldwin, 2000a, 2000b). They actually built up a practice theory of how it was possible to subvert policy. Baldwin's findings are supported by the findings of a later study (Evans, 2010). This showed that many forms of 'street-level bureaucracy' were practised in a mental health and older persons team in a particular local authority in England, and that many managers participated in enabling this to happen.

Once the demands of contexts are not necessarily seen as mutually exclusive with worker interests and, indeed, if the worker sees the context as the focus of her or his work, then it is easy to shift the focus to how aspects of the predominant culture might be expropriated by the worker for use in different ways. For example, Jones and May (1992) discuss an extensive list of different managerialist concepts like efficiency and effectiveness and how they might be used positively in the worker's repertoire. Similarly, there are many other shared aspects of discourse between managers and workers which might be used to mutual benefit. 'Consumer satisfaction' is a prime example.

BUREAUCRATIC PRACTICE

RECONSTRUCTING ROLES AND IDENTITIES

In broad terms this might involve constructing organisational, professional and service user roles and identities in ways which represent complexity and multiple perspectives, and upset taken-for-granted assumptions, structures and power imbalances. In earlier chapters we discussed strategies such as constructing professional narratives which help to represent the service user perspective, rather than simply fitting service user experience into predetermined bureaucratic categories.

It may be helpful to develop a practice of always thinking of several different terms or categories which represent the multiplicity and complexity of people's jobs. For example, a 'front line' worker might also be a 'public relations' worker or a 'service user relations' worker. A social worker might be a 'care manager', 'team relations builder' and 'policy implementer'. Care might also be taken to ensure that perspectives which are often missing (like service user perspectives) are always represented in the language of the bureaucracy. So for instance, it might introduce an awareness of the control element of care management if workers were called 'service user managers' rather than 'care managers'.

In a sense, part of the task of constructing roles and identities, through creating different discourses, is the role of *translation*. Workers might see part of their role as transforming bureaucratic culture by valuing and translating between different discourses. For instance, the practice of always naming at least two different terms or categories not only alerts people to different perspectives, but also allows different groups to learn and understand the meaning of different discourses used by different groups. This should increase the possibilities for dialogue and negotiation. For example, constantly coupling 'care management' and 'service user management' together not only draws attention to the idea that there are different perspectives on the one activity, but also begins to enculturate people in seeing both perspectives, in order to allow them to communicate successfully in both. We could add a third called 'budget management', perhaps representative of management perspectives. This adds a further dimension to naming the context in which the 'management' activity is carried out and perhaps also makes more obvious a hidden perspective which actually drives the agenda.

CHALLENGING DICHOTOMIES AND IMPOSSIBLE DILEMMAS

Because of the need to categorise and impose order within a bureaucracy, bureaucratic culture often includes clearly dichotomous categories. This makes it easier to dispense appropriate services. For example, service users are often divided into 'voluntary' or 'involuntary' groupings, making it clearer as to rights and obligations. Social work culture, and the way its practice is categorised within organisational contexts, is replete with examples of these dichotomies. We have discussed many of them earlier throughout this book. In this section I wish to draw attention to particular ones which seem to arise more directly from organisational cultures, or at least the profession's response to the imperatives of the employing organisation.

A major problem with dichotomies is that they often lead the practitioner to frame her or his practice in such a way as to pose impossible dilemmas, so that they feel they have no choice about how to act. Often they are framed implicitly in terms of the moral high or low ground, with the low ground being associated with the pragmatic and more self-serving options. For example, professional practice is often categorised as being a choice between 'values' or 'money', and in a related way to categorise practitioners as performing a 'professional' or a 'functionary' role. Are our service users 'clients' or 'consumers' and are we 'carers' or 'controllers'? Are we engaged in the macro-level politics of 'policy' or the micro-level band-aid work of 'practice'?

Many of these impossible dichotomies lie at the heart of practice dilemmas conceived by practitioners themselves. It is only by deconstructing them and recreating more complex visions that workers are able to move beyond the dilemma and become re-energised in their work. For example, some workers found professional rules limiting – they had created a dichotomy in which the 'personal' and the 'professional' were kept separate. It was through realising that the two categories were not dichotomous, that the 'personal and professional' could be integrated, that they undertook some groundbreaking practice (Harvey and Harvey, 2000; Lowth and Bramwell, 2000).

CRITICAL CASE MANAGEMENT

Case management has become a common feature of Western professional social work practice in the current global context. I include a discussion of it here because it seems to have superseded the idea of 'casework' in much of the social work literature. This indicates to me an example of a piece of managerialist discourse which has ousted a piece of professional discourse, and for that reason deserves some particular discussion in relation to how we develop strategies to challenge overly bureaucratic cultures.

There are many different perspectives on case management. In simple terms, however, case management is about co-ordinated and planned care, based on sound assessments of service user needs and rights and a sound knowledge of (and ability to use) the context of existing services. This obviously requires some professional interpersonal competence in relationship building, assessment, co-ordination, budget management and evaluation (Parton, 1998: 79). In itself, case management sounds like a necessary and valuable form of practice which is little different from the practice of casework (except perhaps for budget management). However, in a climate of increased government and management control over professionals and service users, it is likely that case management is a practice which will:

- be system rather than service user focused;
- serve management rather than professional or service user interests;
- be technocratic and simplistic rather than complex, holistic or long term and as a consequence, less responsive to personalised, individual needs;
- be driven by an economic rationalist imperative.

The practice of case management therefore decreases the likelihood that existing systems will be criticised, that newer more responsive systems might be developed or created, and that individual service users will question the relevance of services and/or become empowered in the process of being case managed. There are also increased possibilities that individual professional workers or case managers, whatever their occupational background, will bear the brunt of the blame/responsibility for the effectiveness of the case management process, regardless of the level and appropriateness of the resourcing available or authority they hold.

The danger, in short, is that the case management model and the individualising focus it entails are seen as the answer to the shortfalls of our existing care systems. In this way the focus shifts from whether the service user needs have been met or whether adequate services exist, to whether service users have been managed or co-ordinated properly.

Since many worker roles, regardless of occupational training, background or expertise, are simply case management ones, the danger is that professionals from disparate backgrounds also shift the focus from problematic services by competing against each other to be the legitimate case managers within respective contexts.

But must case management, by definition, be conservative, controlling and managerial? It must depend, at least to some extent, on the value base from which people work, the levels of autonomy they are able to negotiate, the ways in which resources are used and distributed and the types of processes and relationships set up.

Case management can therefore be more critical if services are co-ordinated so as to give the best possible entitlements and access to service users; if resources can be used or redistributed to fill gaps in services; if service users are able to participate in decision making about which and how services are used; and if attention is paid to the longer term, holistic and complex situations in which people live, rather than concentrating on the quick fix with measurable results.

Case management can also be critical if workers resist the idea that it is the one neat solution to inadequacies in our systems of service delivery. It is in the interests of all professionals that we show that it is only through a holistic and multidisciplinary understanding of people's situations and a critical matching and creation of services that cases will most effectively be 'managed'.

ADVOCACY

In many ways the idea of advocacy arises out of a modernist way of thinking. The idea of the advocate as someone who 'acts for' another, in order to ensure their rights against opposition from others, is replete with binary assumptions. Although most situations are more complex than this however, there are still needy people caught in situations where the actions of a more powerful person might assist in changing the situation in more beneficial ways. In short, there may still be a need for advocates, a need for people more articulate or more powerful to act on behalf of those who cannot. So how can the idea of advocacy be reworked in ways which recognise complexity?

Some of the responses to these questions relate to issues we have already discussed, particularly to our analysis of power and empowerment. I will discuss these again as they relate specifically to a practice of advocacy.

First, we need to recognise that there are both *outcome* and *process aspects of advocacy*. While the ultimate outcome of advocacy may be to ensure the rights or entitlements of the person or group for whom we are acting, the process itself should be experienced as an empowering one by the people we are working for. Sometimes advocating for someone can be experienced by them as disempowering, since it may effectively define them as incapable or inadequate, assigning to them a 'victim' or 'powerless' identity. As well, while someone else speaks for them, they are not actually developing or practising the skills of speaking for themselves. The 'glory' may go to the advocate, rather than the person they are acting for.

Second, it is important to identify multiple points of contradiction, alliance, complexity and resistance. Not all people we encounter as advocates will oppose the interests of the person we are advocating for. We may share some points of commonality with them. Nor should we assume that the people we are advocating for are necessarily blameless. Often people with 'victim' identities can be difficult or unpleasant to deal with. Other people in that person's situation have rights and responsibilties as well. In trying to sort through the complexity of competing rights and interests, it is helpful to remember that the main aim is to change the situation for the benefit of your service user in some way so that as many of these are respected as possible. Taking the context into account and looking for different perspectives helps to shift blame from particular people and creates a context for shared responsibilities. This allows you to form alliances with potential enemies, rather than setting them up as an impossible opposition. Using the 'language of alliance' can help here (e.g. 'How can we help you?' 'How can you help us?' 'What can we do about this?' 'What do you advise us?' 'What would you do in this situation?'). To refrain from assuming the moral high ground is also a useful strategy. This might involve making an alternative assumption that everyone in the situation may feel equal concern to act morally but that some people may feel more constrained in this than others. The challenge therefore becomes how to create ways in which all players feel they can act morally.

Last, the act of empowering may involve simply not assuming that we know best what the people we are advocating for actually want. I remember when working with people with disabilities that for many their greatest wish was to 'be normal'. This invariably meant getting married and having a family. For me in the late 1970s, this was anathema, especially as I thought the route to liberation was in freeing people from social conformities. However, from their perspective a 'normal' identity would have freed them from the stigma of their disabilities. The act and process of empowerment may also involve ensuring that people always participate as much as possible in their own empowerment. So whatever actions are taken, it may be important to break these down into different aspects so that the people we are advocating for can take part in some, and can see how their contributions are involved in the whole process. Empowerment in advocacy might also involve not 'othering' the people we are advocating for – not feeling a need to differentiate our identity from theirs in order to feed our own powerfulness, but instead drawing our own power from other sources.

CONSTRUCTING ENEMIES AND ALLIES

Because of the critical social worker's strong emphasis on social justice, there is a tendency for us to assume the moral high ground and to conceptualise our practice as a 'war' in which there are only two sides – those for or against social justice. We discussed some of these ideas in Chapter 8. The idea of 'justice' itself implies a moral component, a 'right' and 'wrong', of those 'wronged against' and those enacting the injustices. This tendency to create two sides effectively divides different players in our work contexts into only two groups – 'enemies' or 'allies'. I discussed this idea in my personal reflection about an incident involving an assessment of an Asian student's interviewing skills (Fook, 2000d) in Chapter 8 as well. The incident involved myself and two colleagues who disagreed with me that an Asian student's performance was adequate. I felt that his performance should be assessed on cultural grounds and that if these were taken into account the performance was satisfactory. I reflect upon how I take the moral high ground, assuming that other colleagues, simply because they don't agree with me, must necessarily be against me and therefore racist.

In my case, I discuss how this type of thinking can have very powerful self-protective functions, because it effectively makes me less responsible for change, because I am able to blame those who disagree with me. It also allows me to keep the moral high ground and in so doing the possibilities for change are lessened, because I am stuck in defining the differences between myself and my colleagues. In effect, constructing myself as the 'lone crusader', sole inhabitant of the moral mountain, means that I am also protected from bringing about and having to bring about change.

In this story and my reflection upon it is a powerful image for the ways in which critical social workers might construct workplace contexts so that politics become stalemated. In my reflection, I go on to develop alternative ways of seeing colleagues and situations which might allow me to change the situation. These include an ability to re-theorise the 'enemy' by trying to construct potential 'allies' – perhaps setting up a climate where views are debated more freely, rather than differences or similarities being assumed and identities therefore 'frozen', would help. Framing the debate in a number of different ways, so that we can find a common way of seeing, might allow us to work together more effectively. Not assuming difference, but working to identify various points of commonality (and difference) as part of a complex picture may help to identify points where we can form alliances. This type of conceptualisation can be used appropriately in many types of workplace settings.

SUPERVISION, MANAGEMENT, EDUCATION AND ORGANISATIONAL CHANGE

Similarly, the way of thinking built up in this chapter – the idea of contextual practice – can be used to help us transform the ways we work with supervision, management and education, and for organisational change. If we see ourselves as working in and with complex contexts, then our practice becomes that of working to change that context. Because the context is often expressed in discourse, in the culture and structures which are implicit in that context, then contextual change involves a process of reconstruction through re-enculturation – an ability to interpret cultural context and your place within it, and to practise strategically on the basis of that understanding.

So, for example, good supervision practice, from a postmodern and critical perspective, might simply involve the forming of a partnership to explore shared and different meanings of practice, with a view to jointly creating meanings which might grapple with some of the dilemmas of practice. Management of staff and organisations might involve the establishment of a culture which enables and expresses the joint concerns of the organisation. Leonard pursues this idea to some extent in his discussion of the postmodern organisation as 'process' (1997: 109).

In this type of enculturation model, the issue of organisational change also becomes an issue of organisational culture and how it is created and preserved. Conscious efforts to change organisational culture are involved, which might be expressed at the most mundane and seemingly trivial level. Yet it is often at this level that everyday patterns of thinking and behaviour become most strongly inculcated. New ways of relating between management and staff, over pleasantries expressed in the tea room, might go as far in changing agency culture as a new policy about which staff feel little ownership. Structures and practices, formal policies and informal actions, need to work together to communicate the values and direction of the organisation. As a dynamic process, organisational change is ongoing and happens despite conscious and rational efforts of staff. In creating planned change, however, it is important to tap into and use the dynamics which are already operating.

EDUCATION – ESTABLISHING THE APPROPRIATE LEARNING CLIMATE

Educational techniques might be most effective and learning best achieved when a learning environment is established which is most congruent with the culture desired. I discuss this issue in some detail in relation to establishing an environment conducive to social work education (Fook, 2001b). The whole learning environment and culture must attempt to communicate the most important messages about social work. Implicit messages in the behaviour of staff, in relations which are set up with outside organisations, in the ways students are related to in and outside the classroom, are as important as the specific content in the curriculum, particular teaching strategies, formal selection policies, or grades achieved by students. In this way of thinking, staff need to model the kinds of ways of relating which they feel are integral to social work.

The particular approach I am outlining here might be likened to education as being about establishing the appropriate learning climate. This sounds easier to do than it is, as often the learning climate which is unwittingly communicated is based on aspects of an internalised learning culture which may or may not be consciously intentional. For example, I discuss some of the difficulties of establishing a climate of 'critical acceptance' – a climate which generates enough safety to challenge accepted ways of thinking, which is conducive to critical reflection (Fook, in press). This involves being open to new and multiple perspectives, and suspending judgement enough to give due consideration to conflicting interpretations. However, when much of our traditional cultures are inspired by 'management inspired' cultures which exhort us to identify and address singular causes of problems, it is difficult for us to simply adopt different orientations. Sometimes these orientations involve deep-rooted cultures regarding what we recognise as legitimate forms of knowledge and ways of knowing.

In *Women's Ways of Knowing*, the celebrated study by Belenky et al. (1986) of 135 women students in higher education, they develop the idea of 'connected teaching'. This is a nice example of an approach to teaching which encapsulates abilities to incorporate the context and process of teaching into particular strategies. They note 'connected' features like creating a culture for growth, through interaction and dialogue; allowing uncertainty and sharing a process of learning; recognising diversity; situating oneself in the learning and also seeing through the student's eyes (being both 'objective' and 'personal'). Seeing the teacher as 'midwife' is a nice phrase that encapsulates the role of a connected teacher, which is primarily one of encouraging women to develop their own authentic voices (pp. 214–29).

Dore (1994) makes similar points which also emphasise the contextual and processual aspects of education. She notes the three overarching goals of feminist pedagogy as: (a) the empowerment of all participants in the learning process (students and teachers); (b) a sense of community in which all share in the learning process; (c) a development of leadership capacity as a result of taking responsibility for learning.

DECONSTRUCTING EDUCATIONAL PRACTICES

One of the interesting aspects of the *Women's Ways of Knowing* study is the attention drawn to the learning climate, as opposed to simply the content of what is taught and learnt. This underscores the point I have been making throughout this chapter. In postmodern terms we might refer to the learning climate as the 'subtext'. 'Text' might refer to the content and organisation of the curriculum, the actual words and language used, but 'subtext' covers the range of messages communicated through the process, climate and context of the situation. These distinctions are important in analysing the experience of education – often there are unintentional contradictions between text and subtext. As well, it might be that the most lasting impressions are those implicit in the subtext. As we have said earlier, the implicit assumptions and therefore discursive functions of the educational experience may often run counter to explicit intentions of education.

Exercise

Think about your experience of social work education to date, or even what you are experiencing right now as you read this material. Think, for example, about the structures and practices which you are using to learn about the material in this book.

(Cont'd)

- What do they communicate to you about yourself as a learner and about the lecturer?
- What assumptions are they based on?
- Are there discrepancies between the text and subtext?
- What overriding messages do you feel you have picked up and how have these been communicated?
- Are these different from the messages you think were intended, or that you thought you should have received?

From the experience of reading this material, as an example of an educational experience, you might pick up numerous different messages. For instance, aside from the specific ideas communicated there will also be messages about how to engage with ideas; that it is desirable to link personal experience with other types of learning; that it is possible to learn through self-reflection. Another (contradictory) message communicated from this chapter (which is short on self-reflective exercises compared to others) might be that didactic learning is best.

However, one of the main messages I hope you gain from reading this book is that the experience of learning, as influenced by the whole context and process of education, is as important to the learning process as the more specific content which is taught. So for example, students might learn to engage more easily with material if the teacher comes across as a less intimidating person, one who is unsure of their own conclusions, someone who hasn't 'worked it all out'.

One of the examples of anecdotes I am most fond of in the Belenky et al. study (1986: 215) is of the lecturer who stayed up late working out an elaborate argument which she put to her class, in an erudite and excited fashion, the next day. When she enthusiastically (and sincerely) asked for comment and debate, to her surprise the class remained silent. When asked why there was no comment, one student volunteered that people felt too intimidated because she had obviously worked it all out, it had taken hours, and who were they to think they could offer an intelligent criticism on the spur of the moment? The teacher had unwittingly created an intimidating environment, when her actual intention had been the opposite.

A contextual way of thinking can lead to very different methods of engaging with situations and therefore very different practices. In this chapter we have discussed several ways in which knowledge can be transformed in more contextually oriented ways (e.g. transferability, contextual competence) and also their implications for bureaucratic and more explicitly political practices.

Chapter summary

This chapter has set out the nature of *contextual practice* – practice both *with* and *within* context. Contextual practice emphasises five new ways of approaching practice:

- the need to understand the *nature of contexts* in developing relevant practice strategies;
- the idea of *positionality* – being able to assume a reflexive stance, simultaneously outside and within contexts;
- the need to develop an ability to *work with whole contexts*, rather than simply a number of disparate players within a context;
- the need to develop practice and practice theory/knowledge which is *transferable* across different contexts;
- the need to *reframe our skills in contextual terms* – contextual competence, and resisting dominant cultural contexts.

A number of different types of practices which might support contextual practice were outlined. These also included existing practices which might be modified to take on a more contextual approach:

- Bureaucratic practices (reconstructing roles and identities; challenging dichotomies and impossible dilemmas; critical case management);
- Advocacy;
- Constructing enemies and allies;
- Educational strategies: establishing the appropriate learning climate.

FURTHER READING

Ben-Ari, A. and Strier, R. (2010) 'Rethinking cultural competence: what can we learn from Levinas?', *British Journal of Social Work*, 40 (7): 2155–67.

This article provides an excellent overview of recent usages of the term 'cultural competence' but also attempts to develop the theoretical framework better by using Levinas' concept of 'other'.

Flyvberg, B. (2001) *Making Social Science Matter*. Cambridge: Cambridge University Press. Ch. 4 'Context counts', pp. 38–49.

This chapter is about the impossibility of creating relevant social science theory without attention to context. It is of use here as a rehearsal of the arguments about context, and how they might apply in the creating contextual social work knowledge and hence a contextual approach to practice.

Polkinghorne, D.E. (2004) *Practice and the Human Sciences: The Case for a Judgement-Based Practice of Care*. New York: State University of New York Press.

The whole book might be read on one level, as an argument for context-based practice. It is particularly useful for providing reviews of, and theoretical frameworks regarding, the concepts of practice, theory and context. It ties in an argument for, and approach to reflection.

12

ONGOING LEARNING

How do we, as social workers practising with critical and postmodern ways of thinking, maintain and create our practice so that it is responsive within changing contexts? What sorts of orientations will help us? What ongoing issues might we struggle with, and how can we make meaning of and incorporate these dilemmas into our continuing experiences? This chapter ends the book by posing some ways of conceptualising ourselves and our professional roles as postmodern critical social workers within changing levels of contexts, and in a context of some specific dilemmas posed by these new ways of thinking and how they are practised.

WORKING CRITICALLY IN UNCERTAINTY

One of the major dilemmas posed for current practice is the difficulty of acting effectively, through using learning from past experience, when the new situations we encounter are unpredictable and uncertain. In earlier chapters we have discussed the need to develop *contextual practice*, an orientation towards practice which involves working with whole contexts, and *transferability* – the ability to remake knowledge for relevance across different contexts. These are important elements of an ability to work with uncertainty, to respond to the unpredictable changes that are integral to all practice contexts. I and my colleagues have discussed these skills in detail elsewhere (Fook et al., 2000), and throughout this book I have drawn on some of the ideas developed from these studies of practitioners. In a broad sense, the idea of professional expertise developed from these studies has relevance to postmodern practice – our ideas of expertise incorporated notions of changing contexts and of expertise derived from experience, thus valuing new ways of knowing.

For our purposes here, however, it is useful to focus on how these sorts of skills might have specific relevance for critical practice as well. How is the idea of contextual practice, the ability to work creatively in uncertainty, useful in challenging ideas and structures of domination? As we have discussed and assumed throughout this book, critical reflection is central to the ability constantly to remake practice and practice knowledge and theory in relation to changing contexts. Critical reflection is a process which allows practitioners to reflect on experience so as to create new knowledge which is transferable to different contexts.

We have also shown how these processes, which I have likened, in this book, to processes of deconstruction and reconstruction, can be used to analyse and remake knowledge about, and relations of, power. Critical reflection in this sense, is both an approach (a way of understanding knowledge and its generation) and a process (a way of creating knowledge), which can assist the practitioner constantly to remake power relations in changing contexts. From a postmodern and critical viewpoint, we understand that power, and the way it is expressed and exercised, differs between contexts. Critical reflection allows the practitioner to change practice and understanding in relation to power accordingly. A critically reflective approach should allow social workers to interact with and respond to power dynamics in situations in a much more flexible, differentiated and therefore effective way. By making fewer 'blanket' assumptions about power, the critically reflective practitioner should be able to engage with the specific power dynamics of situations in more relevant and effective ways.

It is important therefore, if we are to practise effectively in uncertainty, to pay attention to, and link, both the 'critical' and 'reflection' aspects of critical reflection. The critical aspects pay attention to power, and provide a basis for analysis and change of situations and experience. They point up, if you like, the more intellectual ways of grappling with change. By contrast, reflection emphasises the more experiential side – the aspects where feelings, analysis, actions and meanings come together to forge a framework for future practice. The reflective level is where a person makes and remakes the meaning of their experiences in relation to ever changing contexts. In remaking this meaning, people are effectively remaking and reaffirming fundamental guiding values which form the bedrock of practice. This fundamental core of values is something which I believe to be crucial to good social work practice in uncertainty (Fook, 2007). This ability is also crucial to contextual practice, and therefore crucial to the ability to practise effectively in uncertainty.

CRITICAL REFLECTION: LINKING REFLECTION, EVALUATION AND RESEARCH

Not only does a process of critical reflection allow us to analyse and remake power relations in a contextually relevant way, but it is also relevant to practice because it constitutes an alternative approach to our understanding of knowledge and knowledge creation, which also upends traditional power hierarchies. It collapses the potential status divisions between practice, thinking and research by making it possible to see (and practise) them as integrated activities. In this sense, processes of critical reflection can function simultaneously as a way of evaluating practice and a way of researching that practice (by developing the practice theory which evolves from it). If we engage in systematic and honest processes of critical reflection, this also functions as an ongoing evaluation of our work (because it is constantly exposed to scrutiny). It is also a form of research, in that it involves ongoing documentation of practice and provides information (data) about how practice can and should be changed. This process therefore also functions as a process for redeveloping and changing practice and practice theories.

This is not to suggest that as a critical social worker you will not and should not engage in other forms of evaluation and research as well. It is important to remember, from a postmodern way of thinking, that many different research methods may be needed to engage with many different situations – an inclusive approach to the understanding and use of research methods is vital in social work (Fook, 2000b). However, unless you also engage in a critically self-reflective process in your practice (whether that be the practice of research, policy development and analysis, management or casework), the potential for actually developing your own practice theory through researching your own experience remains undeveloped. Therefore the relevance of your own learning to others and yourself in different situations remains undeveloped.

Millstein (1993) and Klein and Bloom (1995) weave together the processes of evaluation, reflection and research. Millstein gives some nice examples from practitioners' work – the process she describes is very similar to the one we have been using, except that she also integrates the example of single-case research design. Klein and Bloom talk about 'practice wisdom', a term sometimes used to refer to the theory which arises directly out of practitioners' experiences. Scott (1990) argues that this practice wisdom or theory is a worthy and relevant topic for research study. Klein and Bloom (1995) outline a model for the development of practice wisdom or theory which combines learning from reflective as well as empirical means. This type of model fits nicely with our understanding of knowledge development in critical social work, as social work from a critical perspective should incorporate knowledge developed by both reflective and empirical methods.

In line with this way of thinking, Rees (1991) points out that evaluation is more than the often assumed 'scientific' process which happens at the end of a piece of work. Making a similar point, Adams (1996: 138) talks about 'experiment in practice' rather than 'traditional experimental method' as a better way of understanding evaluation which is empowering.

LINKING LEARNING, THERAPY AND RESEARCH

In the same way that critical reflection links evaluation and research, it might also be said to perform simultaneously the three functions of learning, therapy and research. It is an important part of our ongoing learning as social workers, that we recognise the links between these three functions, and are able to pursue learning, if you like, on a number of fronts.

Elsewhere (Fook 2010) I have defined learning, therapy and research in the following ways:

- Therapy: Addressing some problematic aspect of emotional/personal life, in particular which might have derived from past experience;
- Learning: developing, and/or becoming aware of developing new knowledge which leads to new ways of thinking/being/doing;
- Research: Representing/translating some aspect of life/experience/practice so it can become seen (understood/explained) in new ways (or by other people) through systematic (and transparent) methods of investigation.

Critical reflection on experience follows a systematic process of investigating the assumptive basis of experience. This effectively allows its meaning to be remade (translated) in ways which are relevant to current situations. In the process new knowledge is developed, and 'sticking points' from past experience also become remade in a way which allows a person to re-engage with present situations in new ways.

The following paraphrases and quotes, taken from evaluation forms from a number of workshops I have run with my colleague Fiona Gardner (Fook and Gardner, 2007 and Fook, 2010) give a flavour of how some of these functions interrelate:

> 'I learnt about trust, shared meaning and experiences … about hope, power, the use of self … the power of self as opposed to theories. Hard to dig to the deep level required for this process but the rewards were huge. Really throwing away my assumptions/truths and being really open to the situation regardless of the vulnerability we feel.'

> 'Emotions are highly relevant to workplace practice and that unconscious attitudes can affect actions … also that recognising this can change practice.'

Participants spoke of the critical reflection process as a '*healthy*' way to view personal and professional boundaries and experience, and that it 'enabled me to gain strength and learn from incidents rather than drain me and reinforce negative thinking'. Through the process '*all is not lost*'; '*pain becomes gain*'. Many participants characterised the process as '*meaningful*', referring to the '*transformative nature of new meaning*'; its ability to help them integrate '*macro/micro*' and '*head/heart*' matters; and its assistance in finding satisfaction and direction.

A GROUNDED AND TRANSCENDENT VISION

How do we maintain a coherent sense of ourselves as responsible professionals who are at the same time able to respond to changing and unpredictable situations? What type of professional identity maintains a confidence in our own values and abilities and at the same time allows us the flexibility to adapt these to changing situations? Findings from the expertise study I mentioned earlier (Fook et al., 2000) indicated that workers who did not experience burnout were those who maintained a broader vision of the mission of social work. For them, being professional was more than being an employee. Their concerns transcended the everyday concerns of the workplace. They worked primarily because they believed in the values and ideals of the social work profession and saw their immediate jobs as simply being the current way in which they were able to express these ideals. Even if their jobs were conflict ridden and experienced as frustrating, ironically this broader vision allowed them to approach their workplace demands with vigour. They were less burnt out than workers without this vision because they saw their immediate struggles as part of a larger struggle. Instead of feeling defeated by daily dilemmas, they regarded them as opportunities for ongoing challenge. So their vision of practice, while *transcending everyday practice*, was still *grounded in the local and immediate context*. In a sense, we might say that they were able to see even small and ordinary activities as having a broader purpose, because they were contributing to a bigger picture. It was not a contradiction for them to be able to act on a number of levels; to recognise that seemingly insignificant activities might be of value, even if exactly how they contributed to a larger vision might not be immediately clear. This type of vision is related to Mathieson's idea of 'the unfinished' (Cohen, 1975) which we discussed earlier in the book. Rather than devaluing small levels of change as inadequate because they are small, it is better to recognise that even small levels of change may contribute, in the longer term, or even in unpredictably immediate ways, to larger scale levels of change.

This type of vision might go hand in hand with an ability to tolerate ambiguity and uncertainty – an ability to recognise and accept that situations might involve contradiction and conflict and that outcomes cannot necessarily be guaranteed. This recognition allows us to maintain a sense of ideals to which we are working, in spite of minor setbacks. This provides meaning and purpose to everyday activities, so that our ideals are not undermined by the vagaries and unpredictabilities of complex localised situations. The grounded yet transcendent worker is thus able to act and think on a number of different levels at the same time. They are able to use broad ideals to energise and give meaning to, but not necessarily prescribe, concrete practice. At the same time they are able to change and modify both concrete practice and broad ideals, through a reflective interaction with their experience in specific situations. This dual *grounded* and *transcendent* vision means that critically reflective practitioners are able to work at both local and idealistic levels simultaneously, because they can see both levels simultaneously. In fact, they do not see them as separate levels, but as an integrated whole, a way of understanding how actions and thinking interact at many levels and in complex ways.

UNITY IN DIVERSITY?

One of the dilemmas of postmodern and critical practice we have posed throughout is how we value diversity and at the same time present a united political front in order to achieve critical aims. In our approach to postmodern critical social work, we have acknowledged the politicising benefits, for marginal individuals and groups, of recognising and expressing their perspectives and of developing publically accepted identities. But how do the identity politics of specific individuals and groups, whose empowerment may at the same time lie in their differentiation from other people, actually contribute to the common struggle for all marginalised groups, to change the dominant structures which create their disadvantage? How do we celebrate diversity at the same time as emphasising the collective? Are they necessarily contradictory or mutually exclusive activities?

In discussing this seeming dilemma, first it is important to deconstruct it. In some ways it appears as a dilemma because the two elements have been constructed in oppositional terms, as if somehow 'unity' is the opposite of 'diversity'. It may be helpful to reconceptualise the issue as one of 'unity in diversity' or 'diversity in unity'. For instance, what unifies people from diverse backgrounds could be the common experience of marginalisation, the fact that they have all been assigned a devalued identity. It may be that this commonality can only be established through a process of dialogue which recognises and values this experience (Fook and Pease, 1999: 226).

In this sense 'unity' and 'diversity' may actually both be integral aspects of the same experience. It is possible, for instance, simultaneously to have and experience an identity which incorporates elements of commonality with some groups and difference from others. Given that, in a postmodern way of thinking, identities are fluid, changing and complex, it may be possible to have seemingly contradictory aspects of one identity at the same time. As well, people do not necessarily feel completely defined by only one identity. For example, ethnicity is often not a complete identity – class and gender may be equally important considerations for people. In my own personal reflections, as a later generation Australian-born Chinese person, I noted how ethnic identity can change and be remade according to circumstance (Fook, 2001a). Sometimes I can feel a common identity with Australian Chinese groups (when they speak about common experiences of racism), and sometimes not (when male-dominated hierarchies are supported). I feel differentially 'diverse' from or 'unified' with other Australian Chinese people, depending on the circumstances. I may unite with other Australian Chinese people to combat racism, but I may act against some Australian Chinese colleagues who disempower women. All the while I still see myself as Australian Chinese – my identity is coherent.

Recognising the possibility of coherent yet contradictory aspects of identity means that diverse groups can be unified around some aspects of identity. In a sense this involves a recognition of the possibilities of diversity even within marginal groups themselves. Unity can perhaps be made stronger through this recognition of diversity. This more complex appreciation of identity means that political efforts are potentially more inclusive – able to incorporate the interests of many different individuals and groups.

RELATIVISM?

Postmodernism is probably most criticised for its dangerously relativist stance (Piele and McCouat, 1997). Critics argue that the postmodern denial of claims to universal truths runs directly contrary to the ideals of critical social work (Ife, 1999). There is the added possibility that a postmodern perspective leaves the situation open to be co-opted by any sort of political interest. On a more practical note, there seems to be little guidance for concrete action when knowledge and practice must be contextually relevant.

We discussed these doubts in the first chapter of the book, pointing out that if we see postmodernism as primarily an epistemology (theory about ways of knowing) and critical theory as primarily a structural theory (a theory of underlying explanations implying a moral element), then it is possible to combine the two approaches. Thus critical perspectives provide the moral and directional element to postmodern thinking and postmodern thinking adds complexity to our understanding of how domination is created and maintained, at different sites and in different contexts. Thus they are potentially complementary ways of thinking. A critical perspective provides a broad vision of ideals, of values which are abstract and generalised. It provides the meaning and purpose for our actions, a guide and yardstick by which we are able to improve and value our practice. A postmodern way of thinking allows us to translate these ideals into practice in local contexts and to respond effectively in differential and complex ways.

In this sense critical postmodern practice is relativistic, in that it recognises that abstract ideals will have specific meaning in specific contexts. Yet it is not relativistic in that it also recognises that abstract ideals are needed as a starting point for guiding and providing meaning for specific situations. Both standpoints are necessary for effective practice.

CRITICAL PRACTICE IN HOSTILE ENVIRONMENTS?

In a sense this question is related to our foregoing discussion. How can we work from an abstract vision of ideals if specific situations seem to run counter to these? Is it possible to bring about social justice in an unjust environment? How can I be critically reflective in my work if it is not encouraged in my job? How can I empower service users when my practice is prescribed by the organisation? How can I challenge and change structures when it is those same structures which employ me?

REFRAMING OUR PRACTICE AS CONTEXTUAL

The first point to make in discussing this dilemma is again that it is worthwhile to deconstruct the dilemma. Why is the debate framed in these terms? There seems to be an assumption that practice is *determined* by context, and that therefore it is not possible to counter the influence of context. There is also an assumption that 'contexts' are unified in their influence. For instance, it is everything about the context that is 'socially unjust', 'hostile' or 'prescribed'. Yet from discussions throughout this book we have acknowledged that contexts are complex, contain contradictory and conflicting elements and that it is impossible to identify one-way, linear causal relationships. In fact, from a postmodern and critical standpoint, we have reframed our idea of context and our idea of practice within it. In fact, if *practice is contextual* then this dilemma (of opposition between practice and environment) is no longer a dilemma. Our practice is simply defined as *working with the context*, no matter what that context may be. If we perceive our environments as hostile, then we simply work to change this, rather than trying to work in spite of it. The focus becomes one of changing the environment or aspects of it, rather than seeing ourselves in a 'crusader' or 'victim' role, as the lone person being prevented from doing their job because of their environment. We are always part of (within) our contexts and it is this position which also, ironically, allows us to change them.

Reframing our practice as contextual therefore means we reframe our practice as working *with* environments, rather than working *despite* environments. We see ourselves as part of a context, ourselves responsible for aspects of that context. In this way, we see possibilities for change, for *creating different microclimates within broader contexts*.

CHALLENGE AND RESISTANCE IN A VARIETY OF WAYS

Such an understanding of contextual practice means, as we have already discussed in the book, the ability both to challenge and resist different aspects of the contexts in which we work, in a variety of ways. Some may seem small and consist of simply changing the language we use in everyday conversation, or the way we greet our colleagues. We may not even know how such changes may contribute to the larger scale, yet because we know that all aspects of contexts interact and influence each other, we can assume that some kind of change will occur.

Sometimes we may be able to identify aspects of our contexts which we can more easily and directly influence. Therefore we may strive actively to create more enabling microclimates within more hostile macroclimates. Every person has a sphere of influence, small or large. It may be a matter of identifying that sphere of influence, and working initially with that.

EXPROPRIATING AND TRANSLATING THE DISCOURSE

Again, this was discussed earlier, but it is useful to remind ourselves that in working with contexts we should not assume that everything about the discourse of our dominant contexts is bad, or that it cannot be changed. By identifying aspects of the dominant discourse of the context which may be turned to other ends, we can actually use accepted ideas but in different ways. For instance, it is useful to remember that terms like 'social justice', 'empowerment' and 'participation' have often been expropriated by more conservative groups. 'Community participation', for instance, is often used to justify less government responsibility for public needs. The term might be expropriated back and translated as 'joint participation', whereby communities define the agenda and work with governments to resource needs.

'Critical reflection' might pose a threat to organisations because it appears time consuming. At the same time, it might well assist organisations because of its potential to improve workers' practice. So the discourse around critical reflection can be created which emphasises organisational benefits. It can be termed 'practice improvement', 'practice evaluation', 'supervision', 'practice review' or even 'practice research'. With these types of discourses, the conditions are created in which critical reflection is seen as something desirable that should perhaps be resourced, because it can help achieve the organisational goals. Rather than constructed as a marginal or luxury activity, the discourse around critical reflection can be reconstructed so that it becomes central to the concerns of the organisation. Research on critical reflection suggests that organisations might derive the following benefits from critically reflective workers (Fook, 2000d; Fook and Gardner, 2007):

- the ability to reframe debates in non-dichotomous terms so that creative ways are found to work with managers (Taylor, 1996);
- the clarification of boundaries (Walton, 1999);
- increased accountability and creativity;
- better staff morale;
- increased commitment to clients in a holistic and preventative way;
- increased openness to multiple perspectives and greater ability to work with difference;
- improved practice;
- better ability to tolerate ambiguity (Tsang, 2003);
- better sense of professionalism (Yip, 2006);
- improved ability to articulate the bases of practice.

IDENTIFYING CONTRADICTIONS, COMPLEXITIES AND POINTS OF ALLIANCE

If we assume contexts are complex then, no matter how hostile or unforgiving, there will be aspects which will be ambiguous or in conflict. There will be people who feel more or less strongly about the pervasive culture, those who fit to greater or lesser degrees. There will be some who are articulate about their dissension, others who are less open. It is possible to identify potential allies or weak spots in the system. By finding a common discourse, points of alliance may be set up with people who were potential enemies. If, for instance, we are working in a climate which seems antithetical to social justice, we may want to ask:

- What do we mean by social justice?
- What is social justice in this situation?
- Which aspects of this situation, or which people in this situation might support these ideas?
- What are the different ways I can work with these people or these aspects?

CONTRIBUTING TO CHANGE WHILE BEING PART OF THE PROBLEM?

In the first chapter we raised the issue of how a postmodern perspective brings an awareness of our own positionality, of the fact that we as social workers are implicated in the act of defining and creating our services user's positions of powerlessness (Rossiter, 2001). It is ironic in this sense that postmodernism both helps us understand and locate our power in a way which helps us create and exercise it more effectively, but at the same time shows us how any action in our role as social workers actually preserves the conditions which we hope to change. This poses a challenge to us. How can we simultaneously locate ourselves in situations and at the same time work to change them? Can we actually work to change a situation when we are in fact part of the problem?

In a sense this is a similar dilemma to the one I raised earlier, regarding the possibilities for critical practice within hostile environments. However, this is also a question about how and whether we can separate ourselves as social workers from the conditions and cultures which create the identities and powerlessness of our service users. Rossiter (2001) talks about how these questions became very real for her in the act of giving a homeless man some soup in a soup kitchen. She was aware that although this act would feed the man, it was also a significant act in defining his inequality, his 'differentness' from her, his relative powerlessness.

I think there are two important points to make in regard to this dilemma. First, it does bring home the fact that we are all part of the same social fabric (Fook and Napier, 2000). Everyone is part of a social situation, structure, culture. These are only ever partially of our own making and much of them is established and taken for granted prior to our own participation. However, we also choose to continue our participation in the ways assumed within this social fabric. In other words, there are some aspects we have choices about, some we do not.

Situations are also defined by the ways others act and choose to participate. We do not control it all. Presumably the homeless man receiving soup might not have liked being defined as powerless, but he may also have wanted soup. The situation was defined so that to receive one was to accept the other. In that immediate situation, these definitions could not be resisted. There were not any other choices of actions immediately possible to Amy – she could either give the soup or withhold the soup. The second choice presumably would have been a far worse action (it would have made him even more powerless) for the man in this immediate context. So there was only a small extent to which Amy could resist the culture of this particular situation. Her choice was either to define the man as powerless or deny him soup (which might have defined him as even more powerless and certainly hungry).

Second, the idea that Amy was defining the man as powerless is Amy's (and our) perspective on the situation. Presumably there may be other perspectives, given that social contexts are complex and contradictory. Although Amy felt keenly that she was defining this man as powerless, his concerns may have been more about his hunger. Even if he felt both, his choice might have been his hunger over his power. At the same time, it is possible that he felt cared for as well as made to feel powerless; two potentially contradictory identities being created by the one act. There are other things he might have felt and thought, as might Amy. Amy could have felt self-righteous or humbled, nurturant or frustrated by the situation. Although the situation might be analysed as a simple social definition of roles, it may carry several different layers of meanings for the different parties involved.

What do these points mean in terms of our dilemma? Can we carry out the mission of social work with and in a social climate which potentially defines our actions in counter-productive terms? Can we work to change the problem while at the same time being part of it? If we understand that each specific context in which we work, and even each specific act within it, has the potential to function in a number of ways simultaneously, then this indicates that we need to engage with people or situations in ways which minimise the harmful functions and maximise the empowering ones. For instance, although Amy may not have had much choice about whether she gave the man soup or not, she might have had a choice about how she gave it. She might choose to place emphasis on her care for the man as an equal, rather than on the fact she was giving him soup. Perhaps maximising his choice about the type of soup and giving it in a respectful way might help to emphasise this part of the role. Noting his needs about how he wishes to be related to and engaging with him in this way would also reinforce his equality. Although the social situation defines him as needy and unequal, there is no need for the details of interpersonal interactions to do this as well. So there is room for ambiguity, for resistance, even in simple situations.

HANDLING DIFFERENCES IN AN ACCEPTING WAY

CREATING A CLIMATE OF CRITICAL ACCEPTANCE

One of the very practical dilemmas involved in postmodern critical social work is how we deal with perspectives which fly in the face of social justice principles. How do we respect differences if these contravene our basic social work values and ideals? This problem is of course not exclusive to postmodern critical practice. All social workers grapple with the issue of respecting service users, even when they might be contravening the rights of others. However, it is more of an issue from a postmodern perspective, in which the importance of multiple perspectives is given primacy.

Some of these issues occur in the teaching situation. Both Featherstone and Fawcett (1995) and Rossiter (1995) see the dilemma as one of how we value individual perspectives and create a climate which is mutually respectful, 'while engaging in discussions which potentially jeopardise our unexamined assumptions' (Rossiter, 1995: 13).

For example, how should we deal with racist views in the classroom if we are trying to create a climate of acceptance of different viewpoints? Are there non-oppositional ways of challenging unhelpful or wrong thinking? When I have asked this question in my own classrooms, some of the students' suggestions have been very creative. For instance, one idea was that instead of 'challenging' such views in a confrontational way, that if we have created an accepting and reflective climate, the class can 'challenge' such views by encouraging the person's own reflection on their views, and ask questions which might enable this. In this way, the 'reflective team' might ask self-reflective, enabling sorts of questions, rather than foreclosing on discussion with statements of strong disagreement. For example, a person with racist views might be encouraged to talk about where the 'racist' views have come from, to trace the experiences and thinking which have helped construct these views. This could open the way for dialogue in which other group members might air their experiences of how they have arrived at different ways of thinking. This might help create a climate in which all views can be aired and reformulated in relation to each other and in the light of each other's experiences, rather than forcing people into oppositional positions. In this sense, illustration and sharing of experience can be a much more powerful argument than intellectual debate.

Elsewhere I have termed this type of climate, in which different perspectives are expressed and examined through mutual dialogue, a climate of *critical acceptance* (Fook et al., 2000: 231; Fook and Gardner, 2007: 78–84; Fook, in press). In this type of climate, different viewpoints are explored through the prism of different experiences and are self-evaluated in the context of other perspectives, rather than defended or challenged in opposition to other viewpoints. There are of course particular challenges for practitioners and educators who hold a social justice orientation, but must sometimes suspend the logical judgements which flow from these values, in order to be open to new or other ways of thinking. I discuss some of the reigning cultures which make this difficult, and posit that seeing this mutual dialogue as a form of 'co-researching' can help establish the kind of climate which enables it (Fook, in press).

A reflective way of thinking and expressing viewpoints can also foster a similar climate. In an excellent example of reflective writing by Dubus (1997), '*Why I gave up the gun*', shows how illustration from storytelling about personal experience can act as powerfully as intellectual argument on an issue. He tells of his reasons for wanting to carry a gun ('protection') and of a series of incidents through which he came to question the possibility of 'protecting' himself and others without the possibility of also doing harm. Thus he 'gave up the gun'.

In this article Dubus provides a nice example of one of the ways in which critical postmodern techniques and processes can be just as effective as more oppositional ones, if not more so, in challenging and changing undesirable viewpoints. Such processes, rather than being seen as 'going soft' on unwanted views, might in fact be more effective in changing them because they actually appeal to the *whole* person (emotions and intellect) and potentially engage the whole person in taking some responsibility to change their views. It is probably better that change comes from personal choice, rather than from external pressure (although of course one does not preclude the other).

Another issue is the potential power of descriptive/illustrative (as opposed to explicitly analytical) argument. By this I mean the ability to portray different viewpoints and perspectives through more literary, as opposed to more academic, intellectual means. This, of course, is the approach taken by narrative therapies.

POLITICISING SERVICE USERS?

These points have implications for how we see and effect change in service users. One of the dilemmas for critical practitioners is the issue of whether their assistance of service users is simply the same as politicising them, and whether we can actually help them effectively if they do not come around to our political way of thinking. Do we really need to 'convert' them in order to help them (Fook, 1993: 148)? If this is the case, what does it mean for self-determination? If change, from a critical perspective, involves a change in the political perspective of service users, does this contravene their right to self-determination?

From a critical reflective viewpoint, if we place importance on processes of dialogue and communication, in a climate of mutual respect, then the issue is not so much about us as professionals bringing about change in service users, but one in which we all mutually participate in a joint reconstruction of different viewpoints. Not only do our service users change, but so do we. We all create new ways of seeing through interactions with each other. The change which occurs in this way is as much self-directed as it is brought about by the viewpoints of other people.

STRUCTURAL OR PERSONAL POWER?

I want to end this book on a reflective and more personal note. One of the ongoing questions for me, raised by my practice and thinking on postmodern and critical social work, is the issue of just how much my critical analyses, my ability to be reflective, my flexibility in handling change and uncertainty, can really substitute for what I feel is my relative lack of structural power. I am sure this is an issue for most of us. There always seems to be some higher position to attain from which we could do so much more. Even if I recognise and maximise the ways in which I exercise personal power, could I be more effective if I was actually assigned a higher social status? Would I be more effective if I was a white man perhaps, or came from a more 'establishment' background? Would my job be done any better if I had more resources at my disposal, or commanded more influence? It is tempting for me, for many of us I suspect, to fantasise about ways in which our work could be made easier, our influence more widespread or long lasting. This is one reason why structural power seems so much more attractive than personal power exercised at the micro level.

Yet I also reflect that if I was someone different, working from a different social position, I would have different challenges and opportunities open to me. If I had a more senior position than the one I have now, for instance, I might have more resources to make the changes I want at my university, but equally I might have more responsibilities and other factors to take into account, which could restrict me in other ways. If I was a man, people might not relate to me in the same open fashion they do now. I would get a different picture of my situation and it is that picture I would need to work with, not the one I have now. Perhaps, I reflect, it is my relative social position, my identity and place as a marginal person, a woman of Chinese descent working in a predominantly white male culture, that has forced me to find other ways in which to be influential or to change structures.

The point I am making from my experience is that it is not what type of power (structural or personal) I have at my disposal which is important, but how I use, engage with and create the opportunities available to me. Each social position that we inherit or occupy (some we can change, like jobs, others we cannot, like our bodily appearance) carries challenges and opportunities for the exercise of different types of power. At the end of the day, the major promise for me of postmodern and critical perspectives on practice is that they give me access to these opportunities.

CELEBRATING SOCIAL WORK

My final reflections lead me back to the place I started with in this book. Social work begins and ends with the seminal struggles that concern humankind, even as structures and contexts melt and rebuild. I have always counted myself lucky to be paid to work at the cutting edge of what defines our personhood and our civilisation. Sometimes though it is easy to forget this as we feel swamped by bureaucracy, managerial requirements, or just the emotional demands of the work. Unfortunately it is all too easy *not* to celebrate what we do, as our contribution feels like it becomes reduced to having to avoid blame, minimise risk, tiptoe around political sensitivities, or defend minute decisions. Celebrating social work is about reminding ourselves that it is important that we, as social workers, retain the right to define the profession, what we do, what we see as important and our contribution towards that. We have the right to construct how we do this in both the small and large activities we engage in. We have the right to celebrate social work.

FURTHER READING

Rossiter, A. (2005) 'Where in the world are we? Notes on the need for a social work response to power', in S. Hick, J. Fook and R. Pozzuto (eds), *Social Work: A Critical Turn*. Toronto: Thompson Educational Publishing. Ch. 12, pp. 189–202.

This chapter includes some thoughtful reflections on where social work is at in global terms, and reconsiders our position, and some of the things we can do, in a climate of increased power disparities.

Dubus, A. (1997) 'Why I gave up the gun', *The Age*, 17 May: 1, 4.

This article provides a personal account of a series of incidents which led the writer to relinquish carrying a gun. It is a moving example of reflective writing, in which he manages to remake the meaning of successive experiences into a broader guiding principle about gun-carrying.

Fook, J. (in press) 'Challenges of creating critically reflective groups', *Social Work with Groups*.

This article discusses the difficulties that social workers with social justice orientations sometimes have in trying to hold onto social justice values whilst at the same time being open to other people's perspectives, and also new interpretations of their own experience (as necessary conditions for critical reflection). It posits a new way of labelling a critically reflective climate as one of 'co-researching'. It is useful for thinking through how to create micro-cultures for critical reflection in different contexts.

GLOSSARY

Agency   A person's power or ability to influence a situation, and their own sense of this.

Binary oppositional thinking (see also dichotomous thinking)   Thinking which involves categorising phenomena into two opposing categories only (the whole population of the phenomenon in question must belong to one or other of the categories) which are mutually exclusive and in which one is usually defined in terms of criteria which define the other, and therefore is seen in terms of what it is not, and also therefore devalued.

Commodification   Refers to the process whereby a phenomenon is spoken about, and treated as if it is a physical or material entity, which can be exchanged or traded. The commodification of power is a major way in which power is conceptualised in modernist thinking.

Complicity with oppression   A term associated with the idea of false consciousness. People are 'complicit' with their own oppression when they willingly take on beliefs which are self-defeating, or which contribute to keeping them in relatively powerless or disadvantaged positions. They may thus hold ideological beliefs which contribute to a 'false consciousness' about their own situation, which functions to keep them in that oppressive situation.

Critical acceptance   Refers to the climate which is essential to enable critical reflection. It is a culture or climate which provides enough safety so that people can risk vulnerability and exposure in order to feel safe enough to challenge their existing views in order to learn from the process.

Critical approach   In this book it encompasses both critical and postmodern thinking. A critical approach on its own refers to an approach based on an analysis of how power (relations and structures) is created and maintained at all levels, but in particular how personal and social power is linked.

Critical incident   In relation to the approach to practising critical reflection used in this book, a critical incident (used in 'critical incident technique') refers to an incident, or something which happens to or is experienced by a person, which they believe is significant to their own learning. In broad terms it may be critical for many different reasons. It does not necessarily involve a crisis or emergency, but does usually represent some kind of turning point, or encapsulate some kind of issue or tension which a person feels they need to reflect on further because of its implications for future work or living. The 'critical' in this case means 'significant'.

Critical reflection   A process of reflecting on experience in order to learn from it. The process may be stimulated by searching for tacit and taken-for-granted assumptions. It becomes critical when fundamental assumptions are exposed (and reworked) and new meaning is made, which can serve as principles or guidelines for further action. It is also critical when a critical analysis of power is applied in order to provide further understanding, so that new meanings which are made are also potentially transformative. In the workplace, critical reflection can function to help improve practice, but also to create new practice theories, and therefore to help practitioners function in situations of uncertainty.

Contextual practice   Practice that locates itself in context, and is able to work effectively both with and within context. It involves a number of shifts of thinking, which are detailed in this book.

Contextual competence   The ability to read contexts appropriately, understand their influence on practice, and to modify practice accordingly.

Cultural competence   Normally refers to the ability to practise effectively on the basis of awareness of different ethnic or religious cultures, but can be taken more broadly to refer to any social differences or sets of cultures (e.g. organisational) which may be involved in the context of practice.

Deconstruction/deconstructive methods (see also 'Discourse/s' and 'Discourse analysis')   Involves uncovering dominant ways of thinking (discourses), particularly by searching for hidden, multiple or suppressed discourses. Deconstruction typically 'unsettles' or 'decentres' dominant discourses.

Dichotomous thinking (see 'Binary oppositional thinking' above)

Dilemma of difference   This involves the problem of how to name (validate) difference without perpetuating further discrimination because of that naming. It is argued that it is important politically to locate the source of the difference in social relations (i.e. the need to name it for political reasons) rather than an inherent difference in the named people themselves. The dilemma of difference is also tied up with identity politics.

Discourse/s   The ways in which social phenomena are spoken about, which implies thinking about power arrangements, and how these are constructed. Typically language, and the specific terms and phrases which are used, are focused on as the major element of discourses. However other communications may also be included (such as communications implied in physical arrangements, non-verbal communication, and so forth). Discourses which are dominant tend to be those held or perpetrated by dominant groups, which means that their view of situations is maintained, and so therefore their relative power is maintained.

Discourse analysis   Involves analysing the implied thinking about power (and how it is constructed) which is communicated in all the various ways phenomena are communicated about. Discourse analysis invariably involves also an analysis of power and how it is maintained through discourses.

False consciousness (see also 'Ideology')   When the thinking of a person or group of people is 'ideological', i.e. when their beliefs hold political functions, particularly functions which serve to keep them in their place and keep them from challenging the status quo or existing power arrangements, they are said to be in a state of 'false consciousness'.

Globalisation   Processes whereby the world is said to be 'shrinking' through increased technology and mobility. There are economic, social, cultural and political aspects to globalisation. Debate is rife about the deleterious effects of globalisation, particularly in increasing the social chasms between 'haves' and 'have nots' through exaggerated forms of capitalism which have emerged. The corresponding break-down of familiar structures has led to greater uncertainty. Postmodernism is often associated with globalisation, as being one type of thinking which has emerged.

Ideology   Ideas, or sets of ideas, which hold a social and political function (regardless of their truth or falsity).

Identity politics   Power plays which are involved in issues of who defines the identity of groups. Typically this is an issue for marginal groups whose identity is normally determined by more powerful groups, such as policy makers. It is seen as an integral site for marginal groups to create more power for themselves.

Logocentrism   Refers to the modernist tendency to believe that there is one unified 'truth' which is unchangeable, and can be arrived at through progressive and cumulative approaches to knowledge (i.e. successive research attempts can build upon knowledge which has come before, and each successive attempt yields better and more accurate knowledge).

Narrative/s   Narratives are regarded as particular constructions of a situation or event, told from the perspective of whoever is constructing the story, and for particular purposes. It is recognised that, in one sense, everybody creates narratives or 'stories', as they can only be communicated through language, whose meanings are limited by time and context. Narratives in this sense can normally only represent one perspective, or version of what happened. They may or may not be regarded as true, depending on the perspective of the listener.

Narrative identity   Narrative identities are the versions of how people see themselves, through the narratives they construct about themselves.

Othering   A process in which social difference is constructed. Binary categories are created (usually 'us' and 'the other') and differences are constructed in binary oppositional ways (see '**Binary oppositional thinking**' above). Social differences are then usually constructed as oppositional and in relation to characteristics of 'us', therefore becoming automically defined in terms of the first group ('us') and also by definition, devalued.

Positionality   Involves an ability to recognise one's social position and its influence in any one context, and therefore to act in ways which take this into account. Awareness of social position should allow reflexive practice, and an ability to act from both within and outside a situation.

Postmodernism   Refers to both a way of thinking, and also a label for the current period of history. In simple terms it refers to a critique of logocentrism, or the belief in unified theories or ways of thinking. Postmodern thinking opens the way to accept many different perspectives and ways of knowing.

Poststructuralism   Often related to postmodern thinking but refers more specifically to the analyses of language and discourse aspects. It is a critique, in particular, of structural thinking, i.e. that phenomena can be completely explained in terms of underlying structures or thinking. Poststructuralism essentially argues that meanings are much more open, and subject to interpretation in context.

Reflection   Learning from experience by being able to (re-)examine the fundamental bases on which it is interpreted.

Reflexivity   Being able to locate one's influence in context, and to understand how one's self and actions are constructed in relation to context.

Reflective practice   The ability to reflect on the assumptions (hidden theory) embedded in practice, and to expose these for examination, in order to improve practice.

Situated subjectivity   The notion that people's ideas about themselves and how they are made or constituted, are subject to changing contexts and interpretations. Their own subjectivity is therefore dependent on changing situations.

Transferability   The notion that ideas or knowledge or theories which are formulated in relation to a specific context need to be reworked for applicability in different contexts, i.e. are transferable between contexts.

REFERENCES

Adams, R. (1996) *Social Work and Empowerment*. London: Macmillan.

Adams, R., Dominelli, L. and Payne, M. (eds) (2009a) *Social Work: Themes, Issues and Critical Debates*, 3rd edn. Basingstoke: Palgrave Macmillan.

Adams, R., Dominelli, L. and Payne, M. (eds) (2009b) *Critical Practice in Social Work*, 2nd edn. Basingstoke: Palgrave Macmillan.

Adams, R., Dominelli, L. and Payne, M. (eds) (2009c) *Practising Social Work in a Complex World*, 2nd edn. Basingstoke: Palgrave Macmillan.

Addams, J. (1910/1990) *Twenty Years at Hull House: With Autobiographical Notes*. Urbana and Chicago: University of Illinois Press.

Agger, B. (1991) 'Critical theory, poststructuralism, postmodernism: their sociological relevance', *Annual Review of Sociology*, 17: 105–31.

Agger, B. (1998) *Critical Social Theories*. Boulder, CO and Oxford: Westview Press.

Albury, R. (1976) 'Ideology: the origin of the term', *Tharunka*, 13 October: 3–4.

Allan, J., Briskman, L. and Pease, B. (2009) *Critical Social Work: Theories and Practices for a Socially Just World*, 2nd edn. Sydney: Allen & Unwin.

Allen-Meares, P. (2007) 'Cultural competence: an ethical requirement', *Journal of Ethnic and Cultural Diversity in Social Work*, 16: 83–92.

Alvesson, M. and Sköldberg, K. (2009) *Relexive Methodology: New Vistas for Qualitative Research*, 2nd edn. London: Sage.

Argyris, C. and Schön, D. (1976) *Theory in Practice: Increasing Professional Effectiveness*. San Francisco: Jossey-Bass.

Bailey, R. and Brake, M. (eds) (1975) *Radical Social Work*. London: Edward Arnold.

Bailey, R. and Brake, M. (eds) (1980) *Radical Social Work and Practice*. London: Edward Arnold.

Baines, D. (ed.) (2007) *Doing Anti-Oppressive Practice: Building Transformative Politicised Social Work*. Halifax, BC: Fernwood Publishing.

Baistow, K. (1994/5) 'Liberation and regulation? Some paradoxes of empowerment', *Critical Social Policy*, 42: 34–46.

Baldwin, M. (2000a) *Care Management and Community Care*. Aldershot: Ashgate.

Baldwin, M. (2000b) 'Learning to practice with the tensions between professional discretion and agency procedure', in L. Napier and J. Fook (eds), *Breakthroughs in Practice*. London: Whiting and Birch. pp. 131–42.

Bauman, Z. (1992) *Intimations of Postmodernity*. London: Routledge.

Beck, U. (1992) *Risk Society: Towards a New Modernity*. London: Sage.

Belenky, M.F., Clinchy, B.M., Godberger, N.R. and Tarule, J.M. (1986) *Women's Ways of Knowing*. New York: Basic Books.

Ben-Ari, A. and Strier, R. (2010) 'Rethinking cultural competence: what can we learn from Levinas?', *British Journal of Social Work*, 40 (7): 2155–67.

Benner, P. (1984) *From Novice to Expert: Excellence and Power in Clinical Nursing*. Menlo Park: Addison-Wesley.

Berlin, S. (1990) 'Dichotomous and complex thinking', *Social Service Review*, March: 46–59.

Best, S. and Kellner, D. (1991) *Postmodern Theory: Critical Interrogations*. New York: Guilford Press.

Blanchard, A., Wearne, A. and Carpenter, J. (1994) 'Where are the men? Gender imbalance in social work', in J. Ife, S. Leitmann and P. Murphy (eds), *Advances in Social Work and Welfare Education*. Papers from the National Conference of the Australian Association for Social Work and Welfare Education, University of Western Australia. pp. 5–11.

Boud, D., Keogh, R. and Walker, D. (eds) (1985) *Reflection: Turning Experience Into Learning*. London: Kogan Page.

Bourdieu, P. (1999) 'Social conditions of the international circulation of ideas', in R. Shusterman (ed.), *Bourdieu: A Critical Reader*. Oxford: Blackwell. pp. 220–8.

Brook, E. and Davis, A. (eds) (1985) *Women, the Family and Social Work*. London: Tavistock.

Brookfield, S. (1995) *Becoming a Critically Reflective Teacher*. San Francisco: Jossey-Bass.

Brophy, P. (2009) *Narrative-Based Practice*. Farnham: Ashgate.

Brown, C. (1994) 'Feminist postmodernism and the challenge of diversity', in A. Chambon and A. Irving (eds), *Essays on Postmodernism and Social Work*. Toronto: Canadian Scholars' Press. pp. 35–48.

Brown, C. and Augusta-Scott, T. (eds) *Narrative Therapy*. Thousand Oaks, CA: Sage.

Burke, K. (1966) *A Rhetoric of Motives and a Grammar of Motives*. Cleveland, OH: World.

Butler, J. (1995) 'Contingent foundations', in L. Nicholson (ed.), *Feminist Contentions: A Philosophical Exchange*. London: Routledge.

Cannan, C. (1994) 'Enterprise culture, professional socialisation, and social work education in Britain', *Critical Social Policy*, 14 (3): 5–18.

Carniol, B. (2010) *Case Critical: Social Services and Social Justice in Canada*, 6th edn. Toronto: Between the Lines.

Carroll, J. (1992) 'Economic rationalism and its consequences', in J. Carrol and R. Manne (eds), *Shutdown: The Failure of Economic Rationalism and How to Rescue Australia*. Melbourne: Text Publishing. pp. 7–26.

Charnley, H., Roddam, G. and Wistow, J. (2009) 'Working with service users and carers' in R. Adams, L. Dominelli and M. Payne (eds), *Themes, Issues and Critical Debates*, 3rd edn. Basingstoke: Palgrave Macmillan. pp. 193–208.

Clarke, J. (1996) 'After social work?', in N. Parton (ed.), *Social Theory, Social Change and Social Work*. London: Routledge. pp. 36–60.

Cohen, S. (1975) 'It's alright for you to talk', in R. Bailey and M. Brake (eds), *Radical Social Work*. London: Edward Arnold. pp. 76–95.

Cohler, B.J. (1991) 'The life story and the study of resilience and response to adversity', *Journal of Narrative and Life History*, 1: 169–200.

Compton, B. and Galaway, G. (1999) *Social Work Processes*. Pacific Grove, CA: Brooks Cole.

Conway, J. Ker (1992) *Written by Herself: Autobiographies of American Women*. London: Vintage.

Corrigan, P. and Leonard, P. (1978) *Social Work Practice Under Capitalism: A Marxist Approach*. London: Macmillan.

Crinall, K. (1999) 'Challenging victimisation in practice with young women', in B. Pease and J. Fook (eds), *Transforming Social Work Practice*. Sydney: Allen & Unwin. pp. 70–83.

Dalrymple, J. and Burke, B. (2006) *Anti-Oppressive Practice: Social Care and the Law*, 2nd edn. Maidenhead: Open University Press.

Davies, H. and Kinloch, H. (2000) 'Critical incident analysis: facilitating reflection and transfer of learning', in V.E. Cree and C. Macauley (eds), *Transfer of Learning in Professional and Vocational Education*. London: Routledge. pp. 137–47.

de Maria, W. (1993) 'Exploring radical social work teaching in Australia', *Journal of Progressive Human Services*, 4 (2): 45–63.

de Montigny, G. (2005) 'A reflexive materialist alternative', in S. Hick, J. Fook and R. Pozzuto (eds) *Social Work: A Critical Turn*. Toronto: Thompson Educational Publishing. pp. 121–36.

Denzin, N. and Lincoln, Y.S. (1994) *Handbook of Qualitative Research*. Newbury Park, CA: Sage.

Department of Education, Employment and Training (DEET) (1995) *Australia's Workforce 2005: Jobs in the Future*. Canberra: Australian Government Publishing Service.

Derrida, J. (1978) *Writing and Difference*. Chicago: University of Chicago Press.

Dominelli, L. (1996) 'De-professionalising social work: anti-oppressive practices, competencies and postmodernism', *British Journal of Social Work*, 26: 153–75.

Dominelli, L. (1999) *Sociology for Social Work*. London: Macmillan.

Dominelli, L. (2002a) *Feminist Social Work: Theory and Practice*. Basingstoke: Palgrave Macmillan.

Dominelli, L. (2002b) *Anti-Oppressive Social Work: Theory and Practice*. Basingstoke: Palgrave Macmillan.

Dominelli, L. (ed.) (2007) *Revitalising Communities in a Globalised World*. Aldershot: Ashgate.

Dominelli, L. (2009) 'Repositioning social work', in R. Adams, L. Dominelli and M. Payne (eds) *Social Work: Themes, Issues and Critical Debates*, 3rd edn. Basingstoke: Palgrave Macmillan. pp. 13–25.

Dominelli, L. and Hoogevelt, A. (1996) 'Globalisation and the technocratisation of social work', *Critical Social Policy*, 16 (2): 45–62.

Dominelli, L. and McLeod, E. (1989) *Feminist Social Work*. London: Macmillan.

Dore, M.M. (1994) 'Feminist pedagogy and the teaching of social work practice', *Journal of Social Work Education*, 30 (1): 97–106.

Dreyfus, H. and Dreyfus, S. (1986) *Mind Over Machine*. Oxford: Blackwell.

Dubus, A. (1997) 'Why I gave up the gun', *The Age*, 17 May: 1, 4.

Duvall, J. and Beres, L. (2006) 'Movement of identities: a map for therapeutic conversations about trauma', in C. Brown and T. Augusta-Scott (eds), *Narrative Therapy*. London: Sage. pp. 229–50.

Duvall, J. and Beres, L. (2011) *Innovations in Narrative Therapy*. New York: W.W. Norton.

Evans, T. (2010) *Professional Discretion in Welfare Services: Beyond Street-Level Bureaucracy*. Farnham: Ashgate.

Evans, T. and Hardy, M. (2010) *Evidence and Knowledge for Practice*. Cambridge: Polity.

Ernst, J. (1996) 'Privatisation and competition in the human services', in J. Fook, F. Lindsay and M. Ryan (eds), *Advances in Social Work and Welfare Education*. Papers from the National Conference of the Australian Association for Social Work and Welfare Education, La Trobe University, Bundoora. pp. 36–44.

Fabricant, M.B. and Burghardt, S. (1992) *The Welfare State and the Transformation of Social Service Work*. New York and London: M.E. Sharpe.

Fawcett, B. (2000) 'Researching disability: meaning, interpretations and analysis', in B. Fawcett, B. Featherstone, J. Fook and A. Rossiter (eds), *Practice and Research in Social Work*. London: Routledge. pp. 62–82.

Fawcett, B. (2009) 'Postmodernism in social work', in V.E. Cree (ed.), *Social Work: A Reader.* London: Routledge. pp. 227–35.

Fawcett, B. and Featherstone, B. (2000) 'Setting the scene', in B. Fawcett, B. Featherstone, J. Fook and A. Rossiter (eds), *Practice and Research in Social Work.* London: Routledge. pp. 5–23.

Featherstone, B. (2000) 'Researching into mothers' violence: some thoughts on the process', in B. Fawcett, B. Featherstone, J. Fook and A. Rossiter (eds), *Practice and Research in Social Work.* London: Routledge. pp. 120–35.

Featherstone, B. and Fawcett, B. (1995) 'Oh no! Not more "isms" ', *Social Work Education,* 14 (3): 25–43.

Ferguson, H. (2001) 'Social work, individualization and life politics' , *British Journal of Social Work,* 31: 41–55.

Ferguson, I. (2008) *Reclaiming Social Work: Challenging Neo-Liberalism and Promoting Social Justice.* London: Sage.

Finlayson, J. and Anderson, I. (1996) 'The Aboriginal self', in A. Kellehear (ed.), *Social Self, Global Culture.* Melbourne: Oxford University Press. pp. 45–56.

Fitzgerald, J. (2007) *Big White Lie: Chinese Australians in White Australia.* Sydney: UNSW Press.

Flyvberg, B. (2001) *Making Social Science Matter.* Cambridge: Cambridge University Press.

Fook, J. (forthcoming) 'Critical reflection in unreflective environments', paper delivered at the joint IFSW/IASSW conference. Montreal, July/August 2000.

Fook, J. (1987) 'Empowerment as a goal in casework: structural perspectives in casework: can they guide practice?', *Australian Social Work,* 40 (3): 43–4.

Fook, J. (1993) *Radical Casework: A Theory of Practice.* St. Leonards, NSW: Allen & Unwin.

Fook, J. (1995) 'Beyond structuralism?', paper presented at the 'Narratives of Change' Conference, Monash University, Gippsland, 28 November.

Fook, J. (ed.) (1996) *The Reflective Researcher: Social Workers' Theories of Practice Research.* Sydney: Allen & Unwin.

Fook, J. (1999a) 'Critical reflection in education and practice', in B. Pease and J. Fook (eds), *Transforming Social Work Practice.* London: Routledge. pp. 195–209.

Fook, J. (1999b) 'Reflexivity as method', in J. Daly, A. Kellehear and E. Willis (eds), *Annual Review of Health Social Sciences,* vol. 9, La Trobe University, Bundoora. pp. 11–20.

Fook, J. (2000a) 'Deconstructing and reconstructing professional expertise', in B. Fawcett, B. Featherstone, J. Fook and A. Rossiter (eds), *Practice and Research in Social Work.* London: Routledge. pp. 104–17.

Fook, J. (2000b) 'Critical perspectives on social work practice', in I. O'Connor, P. Smyth and J. Warburton (eds), *Contemporary Perspectives on Social Work and the Human Services.* Melbourne: Addison-Wesley Longman. pp. 128–37.

Fook, J. (2000c) 'Critical reflection in an unreflective environment'. Unpublished paper presented at the International Association of Schools of Social Work Conference, Montreal, July–August.

Fook, J. (2000d) 'The lone crusader: constructing enemies and allies in the workplace', in L. Napier and J. Fook (eds), *Breakthroughs in Practice.* London: Whiting and Birch. pp. 186–200.

Fook, J. (2001a) 'Emerging ethnicities as a theoretical framework for social work', in L. Dominelli, W. Lorenz and H. Soydan (eds), *Beyond Racial Divides.* Aldershot: Ashgate. pp. 9–22.

Fook, J. (2001b) 'What is the aim of the bachelor of social work?', *Australian Social Work*, 54 (1): 20–2.

Fook, J. (2001c) 'Identifying expert social work: qualitative practitioner research', in I. Shaw and N. Gould (eds), *Qualitative Research in Social Work*. London: Sage.

Fook, J. (2007) 'Uncertainty: the defining characteristic of social work?', in M. Lymbery and K. Postle (eds), *Social Work: A Companion to Learning*. London: Sage. pp. 30–9.

Fook, J. (2010) 'Critical reflection: integrating therapy, learning and research', 'Catching the Winds of Change', Maritime Collaborative Therapies Conference, Halifax (June).

Fook, J. (2011) 'Critical reflection and power in social work', in T. Okitikpi (ed.), *Social Control and the Use of Power in Social Work with Children and Families*. Lyme Regis: Russell House Publishing. pp. 126–40.

Fook, J. (2011) 'Developing critical reflection as a research method', in J. Higgs, A. Titchen, D. Horsfall and D. Bridges (eds), *Creative Spaces for Qualitative Researching*. Rotterdam: Sense Publishers. pp. 55–64.

Fook, J. (in press) 'Challenges of creating critically reflective groups', *Social Work with Groups*.

Fook, J. and Askeland, G.A. (2006) 'The "critical" in critical reflection', in S. White, J. Fook and F. Gardner (eds), *Critical Reflection in Health and Social Care*. Maidenhead: Open University Press. pp. 40–53.

Fook, J. and Gardner, F. (2007) *Practising Critical Reflection: A Resource Handbook*. Maidenhead: Open University Press.

Fook, J. and Kellehear, A. (2010) 'Using critical reflection to support health promotion goals in palliative care', *Journal of Palliative Care*, 26 (3): 295–302.

Fook, J. and Morley, C. (2005) 'Empowerment: a contextual perspective', in S. Hick, J. Fook and R. Pozzuto (eds), *Social Work: A Critical Turn*. Toronto: Thompson Educational Publishers. pp. 67–86.

Fook, J. and Napier, L. (2000) 'From dilemma to breakthrough: re-theorising social work', in L. Napier and J. Fook (eds), *Breakthroughs in Practice*. London: Whiting and Birch. pp. 212–17.

Fook, J. and Pease, B. (1999) 'Emancipatory social work for a postmodern age', in B. Pease and J. Fook (eds), *Transforming Social Work Practice*. Sydney: Allen & Unwin. pp. 224–9.

Fook, J., Ryan, M. and Hawkins, L. (1997) 'Towards a theory of social work expertise', *British Journal of Social Work*, 27: 399–417.

Fook, J., Ryan, M. and Hawkins, L. (2000) *Professional Expertise: Practice, Theory and Education for Working in Uncertainty*. London: Whiting and Birch.

Fook, J., White, S. and Gardner, F. (2006) 'Critical reflection: a review of contemporary literature and understandings', in S. White, J. Fook and R. Gardner (eds), *Critical Reflection in Health and Social Care*. Maidenhead: Open University Press. pp. 3–20.

Foucault, M. (1984) 'In the interview with Paul Rabinow and Hubert Dreyfus', in P. Rabinow (ed.), *The Foucault Reader*. Harmondsworth: Penguin.

Francis, D. (1997) 'Critical incident analysis: a strategy for developing reflective practice', *Teachers and Teaching: Theory and Practice*, 3 (2): 169–88.

Furlong, M. (1987) 'A rationale for the use of empowerment as a goal in casework', *Australian Social Work*, 40 (3): 25–30.

Galper, J. (1980) *Social Work Practice: A Radical Perspective*. Englewood Cliffs, NJ: Prentice Hall.

Garner, H. (1995) *The First Stone*. Sydney: Picador.

Giddens, A. (1991) *Modernity and Self Identity*. Oxford: Polity.

Gilgun, J. (1994) 'Hand in glove: the grounded theory approach and social work practice research', in E. Sherman and W.J. Reid (eds), *Quantitative Research in Social Work*. New York: Columbia University Press. pp. 115–25.

Gilligan, C. (1982) *In a Different Voice: Psychological Theory and Women's Development*. Cambridge, MA: Harvard University Press.

Goodman, J. (1998) 'Ideology and critical ethnography', in J. Smyth and G. Shacklock (eds), *Being Reflexive in Critical Educational and Social Research*. London: Falmer Press.

Grosz, E. (1989) *Sexual Subversions: Three French Feminists*. Sydney: Allen & Unwin.

Hamilton, G. (1951) *Theory and Practice of Social Casework*. New York: Columbia University Press.

Harrison, G. and Melville, R. (2010) *Rethinking Social Work in a Global World*. Basingstoke: Palgrave Macmillan.

Hart, B. (1995) 'Re-authoring the stories we work by situating the narrative approach in the presence of the family of therapists', *Australian and New Zealand Journal of Family Therapy*, 16 (4): 181–9.

Harvey, M. and Harvey, J. (2000) 'When the labels are off', in L. Napier and J. Fook (eds), *Breakthroughs in Practice*. London: Whiting and Birch. pp. 91–103.

Haug, F., Andresen, S., Bunz-Elfferding, A., Hauser, K., Lang, U. and Laudan, M. (1999) *Female Sexualisation: A Collective Work of Memory* (trans. E. Carter). London: Verso.

Hawkins, L., Ryan, M., Murray, H., Grace, M., Hawkins, G., Mendes, P. and Chatley, B. (2000) 'Supply and demand: a study of labour market trends and the employment of new social work graduates in Victoria', *Australian Social Work*, 53 (1): 35–41.

Healy, B. and Fook, J. (1994) 'Reinventing social work', in J. Ife, S. Leitman and P. Murphy (eds), *Advances in Social Work and Welfare Education*. Papers from the National Conference of the Australian Association for Social Work and Welfare Education, University of Western Australia. pp. 42–55.

Healy, K. (2000) *Social Work Practices*. London: Sage.

Healy, K. (2005) *Social Work Theories in Context: Creating Frameworks for Practice*. London: Sage.

Hearn, G. (1987) *The Gender of Oppression: Men, Masculinity and the Critique of Marxism*. London: Wheatsheaf.

Heron, J. (1996) *Co-Operative Inquiry: Research into the Human Condition*. London: Sage.

Hick, S. (2005) 'Reconceptualising critical social work', in S. Hick, J. Fook and R. Pozzuto (eds), *Social Work: A Critical Turn*. Toronto: Thompson Educational Publishing. Ch. 3, pp. 39–51.

Hogan, T. (1996) 'Globalisation: experiences and explanations', in A. Kellehear (ed.), *Social Self, Global Culture*. Melbourne: Oxford University Press. pp. 275–88.

Hoogeveldt, A. (2009) 'Globalisation and imperialism: wars and humanitarian intervention', in L. Dominelli (ed.), *Revitalising Communities in a Globalising World*. Aldershot: Ashgate. pp. 17–42.

Hough, G. (1994) 'Post-industrial work? The use of information technology in the restructuring of state social work', in J. Ife, S. Leitman and P. Murphy (eds), *Advances in Social Work and Welfare Education*. Papers from the National Conference of the Australian Association for Social Work and Welfare Education, University of Western Australia. pp. 56–62.

Houston, S. (2001) 'Beyond social constructionism: critical realism and social work', *British Journal of Social Work*, 31: 845–61.

Howe, D. (1986) *Social Workers and their Practice in Welfare Bureaucracies*. Aldershot: Gower.

Hugman, R. (1991) *Power in Caring Professions*. London: Macmillan.

Humphrey, C. (2009) 'By the light of the Tao', *European Journal of Social Work*, 12 (3): 377–90.

Ife, J. (1997) *Rethinking Social Work: Towards Critical Practice*. Melbourne: Addison-Wesley Longman.

Ife, J. (1999) 'Postmodernism, critical theory and social work', in B. Pease and J. Fook (eds), *Transforming Social Work Practice*. Sydney: Allen & Unwin. pp. 211–23.

Ife, J., Healy, K., Spratt, T. and Solomon, B. (2005) 'Current understandings of critical social work', in S. Hick, J. Fook and R. Pozzuto (eds), *Social Work: A Critical Turn*. Toronto: Thompson Educational Publishing. Ch. 1, pp. 3–24.

Ingersoll, V. and Adams, G. (1986) 'Beyond organisational boundaries: exploring the managerial metamyth', *Administration and Society*, 18: 360–81.

Jayasuriya, L. (1997) 'Understanding diversity and pluralism for education and training', in L. Jayasuriya (ed.), *Immigration and Multiculturalism in Australia*. Perth: University of Western Australia. pp. 1–19.

Jeffrey, L. (2011) *Understanding Agency: Social Welfare and Change*. Bristol: Policy Press.

Johnson, K. (2009) 'Disabling discourses and enabling practices in disability politics', in J. Allan, L. Briskman and B. Pease (eds), *Critical Social Work: Theories and Practices for a Socially Just World*. Sydney: Allen and Unwin. pp. 188–200.

Johnson, M. (1987) *The Welfare State in Transition*. Brighton: Wheatsheaf.

Jones, A. and May, J. (1992) *Working in Human Service Organisations*. Melbourne: Longman.

Jones, K., Cooper, B. and Ferguson, H. (2008) *Best Practice in Social Work: Critical Perspectives*. Basingstoke: Palgrave Macmillan.

Jones, M. (1990) 'Understanding social work: a matter of interpretation?', *British Journal of Social Work*, 20: 181–96.

Jordan, B. (1998) *The New Politics of Welfare*. London: Sage.

Jordan, B. (2009) 'Re-affirming the value of social work', in R. Adams, L. Dominelli and M. Payne (eds), *Social Work: Themes, Issues and Critical Debates*. Basingstoke: Palgrave Macmillan. pp. 65–73.

Jordan, B. and Jordan, C. (2000) *Social Work and the Third Way: Tough Love as Social Policy*. London: Sage.

Kearney, J. (2004) '"Knowing how to go on": towards situated practice and emergent theory in social work', in R. Lovelock, K. Lyons and J. Powell (eds), *Reflecting on Social Work: Discipline and Profession*. Aldershot: Ashgate. pp. 163–80.

Kellehear, A. (1993) *The Unobtrusive Researcher*. Sydney: Allen & Unwin.

Klein, W.C. and Bloom, M. (1995) 'Practice wisdom', *Social Work*, 40 (6): 799–807.

Laragy, C. (1996) 'Social work and welfare work in the Year 2000', *Advances in Social Work and Welfare Education*, 2 (1): 104–13.

Laragy, C. (1997) 'Social and welfare workers in the Year 2000', in J. Fook, F. Lindsey and M. Ryan (eds), *Advances in Social Work and Welfare Education*, 2 (1): 104–13.

Leicht , K.T. and Fennell, M.L. (2001) *Professional Work: A Sociological Approach*. Oxford: Blackwell.

Leonard, P. (1997) *Postmodern Welfare: Reconstructing an Emancipatory Project*. London: Sage.

Lewin, F. (1991) 'Theoretical and political implications of the dynamic approach to aboriginality', *Australian Journal of Anthropology*, 2 (2): 171–8.

Lincoln, Y.S. and Guba, E.G. (1985) *Naturalistic Inquiry*. Newbury Park, CA: Sage.

Lowth, A. and Bramwell, M. (2000) 'Dedicated to the memory of Susan', in L. Napier and J. Fook (eds), *Breakthroughs in Practice*. London: Whiting and Birch. pp. 79–90.

Lum, D. (2003) *Culturally Competent Practice: A Framework for Understanding Diverse Groups and Justice Issues*. Pacific Grove, CA: Brooks-Cole Publishers.

Lymbery, M. (2007) 'Social work in its organisational context', in M. Lymbery and K. Postle (eds), *Social Work: A Companion to Learning*. London: Sage. pp. 179–88.

Lymbery, M. and Millward, A. (2000) 'The primary health care interface', in G. Bradley and J. Manthorpe (eds), *Working on the Fault Line: Social Work and Health Services*. Birmingham: Venture Press.

MacDonald, C. (1999) 'Human service professionals in the community services industry', *Australian Social Work*, 52 (1): 17–25.

McBeath, G. and Webb, S. (2005) 'Post-critical social work analytics', in S. Hick, J. Fook and R. Pozzuto (eds), *Social Work: A Critical Turn*. Toronto: Thompson Educational Publishers. pp. 167–86.

McLeod, J. and Thomson, R. (2009) *Researching Social Change*. London: Sage.

Mailick, M.D. (1977) 'A situational perspective in casework theory', *Social Casework*, 58 (7): 401–11.

Manning, P.K. and Cullum-Swan, B. (1994) 'Narrative, content and semiotic analysis', in N. Denzin and Y. Lincoln (eds), *Handbook of Qualitative Research*. Thousand Oaks, CA: Sage. pp. 463–78.

Marchant, H. and Wearing, B. (eds) (1986) *Gender Reclaimed*. Sydney: Hale and Iremonger.

Marcia, J.E. (1980) 'Identity in adolescence', in J. Edelson (ed.), *Handbook of Adolescent Psychology*. New York: Wiley. pp. 159–87.

Merrill, B. and West, L. (2009) *Using Biographical Methods in Social Research*. London: Sage.

Midgley, J. (2001) 'Issues in international social work: resolving critical debates in the profession', *Journal of Social Work*, 1 (1): 21–36.

Miles, M.B. and Huberman, A.M. (1994) *Qualitative Data Analysis*. Newbury Park, CA: Sage.

Millstein, K.H. (1993) 'Building knowledge from the study of cases', in J. Laird (ed.), *Revisioning Social Work Education*. New York: Haworth. pp. 255–79.

Minow, M. (1985) 'Learning to live with the dilemma of difference', *Law and Contemporary Problems*, 18 (2): 157–211.

Mishler, E.G. (1986) *Research Interviewing: Context and Narrative*. Cambridge, MA: Harvard University Press.

Moffat, L. (1999) 'Surveillance and government of the welfare recipient', in A.S. Chambon, A. Irving and L. Epstein (eds), *Reading Foucault for Social Work*. New York: Columbia University Press. pp. 219–45.

Monk, G., Winslade, J., Crocket, K. and Epston, D. (1997) *Narrative Therapy in Practice*. San Francisco: Jossey-Bass.

Moreau, M. (1979) 'A structural approach to social work practice', *Canadian Journal of Social Work Education*, 5 (1): 78–94.

Mullaly, B. (1993) *Structural Social Work*. Toronto: Oxford University Press.

Mullaly, B. (1997) *Structural Social Work: Ideology, Theory and Practice,* 2nd edn. Toronto: Oxford University Press.

Mullaly, B. (2007) *The New Structural Social Work,* 3rd edn. Toronto: Oxford University Press.

Napier, L. and Fook, J. (eds) (2000) *Breakthroughs in Practice: Social Workers Theorise Critical Moments.* London: Whiting and Birch.

Newton, J. (1988) 'History as usual? Feminism and the new historicism', *Cultural Critique,* 9: 87–121.

Nipperness, S. and Briskman, L. (2009) 'Promoting a human rights perspective on critical social work', in J. Allan, L. Briskman and B. Pease (eds), *Critical Social Work: Theories and Practices for a Socially Just World.* Sydney: Allen and Unwin. p. 58–69.

Nylund, D. (2006) 'Critical multiculturalism, whiteness, and social work: towards a more radical view of cultural competence', *Journal of Progressive Human Services,* 17: 27–42.

O'Hanlon, B. (1994) 'The third wave', *Networker,* Nov/Dec: 19–29.

O'Hanlon, B. (1995) 'Breaking the bad trance'. London conference.

Okitikpi, T. (ed.) (2011) *Social Control and the Use of Power in Social Work with Children and Families.* Lyme Regis: Russell House Publishing.

Padgett, D. (1998) 'Does the glove really fit? Qualitative research and clinical social work practice', *Social Work,* 43 (4): 373–81.

Parton, N. (1994) '"Problematics of government", (post)modernity and social work', *British Journal of Social Work,* 24: 9–32.

Parton, N. (1998) 'Advanced liberalism, (post)modernity and social work: some emerging social configurations', in R.G. Meinert, J.T. Pardeck and J.W. Murphy (eds), *Postmodernism, Religion and the Future of Social Work.* New York: Haworth. pp. 71–88.

Parton, N. (2004) 'Post-theories for practice: challenging the dogmas', in L. Davies and P. Leonard (eds), *Social Work in a Corporate Era.* Aldershot: Ashgate. pp. 31–44.

Parton, N. (2008) 'Changes in the form of knowledge in social work: from the "social" to the "informational"', *British Journal of Social Work,* 38: 253–69.

Parton, N. and O'Byrne, P. (2000) *Constructive Social Work.* London: Macmillan.

Patton, P. (1995) 'Mabo and Australian society and toward a postmodern republic', *Australian Journal of Anthropology,* 6(1–2): 83–94.

Payne, M. (2006) *What is Professional Social Work.* Bristol: Policy Press.

Payne, M. (2009) 'Management and managerialism', in R. Adams, L. Dominelli and M. Payne (eds), *Practising Social Work in a Complex World,* 2nd edn. Basingstoke: Palgrave Macmillan. pp. 143–57.

Payne, M. and Askeland, G.A. (2008) *Globalisation and International Social Work.* Aldershot: Ashgate.

Perry, C. and Tate-Manning, L. (2006) 'Unravelling cultural constructions in social work education: journeying toward cultural competence', *Social Work Education,* 25: 735–48.

Piele, C. and McCouat, M. (1997) 'The rise of relativism: the future of theory and knowledge development in social work', *British Journal of Social Work,* 27: 343–60.

Polkinghorne, D.E. (1998) *Narrative Knowing and the Human Sciences.* New York: State University of New York Press.

Polkinghorne, D.E. (2004) *Practice and the Human Sciences: The Case for a Judgement-Based Practice of Care.* New York: State University of New York Press.

Powell, F. (2001) *The Politics of Social Work*. London: Sage.

Pugh, R. and Gould, N. (2000) 'Globalization, social work and social welfare', *European Journal of Social Work*, 3 (2): 123–38.

Purvis, T. and Hunt, A. (1993) 'Discourse, ideology, discourse, ideology, discourse, ideology …', *British Journal of Sociology*, 44 (3): 473–99.

Raber, M. (1996) 'Downsizing the nation's labour force and the need for a social work response', *Social Work*, 20 (1): 46–58.

Reason, P. and Bradbury, H. (eds) (2001) *Handbook of Action Research*. London: Sage.

Reason, P. and Rowan, P. (eds) (1981) *Human Inquiry: A Sourcebook of New Paradigm Research*. Chichester: Wiley.

Rees, S. (1991) *Achieving Power*. Sydney: Allen & Unwin. pp. 799–807.

Reich, R. (1991) *The Work of Nations*. New York: Knopf.

Reissman, C.K. (2008) *Narrative Methods for the Human Science*. Thousand Oaks: Sage.

Reissman, C.K. (1993) *Qualitative Studies in Social Work Research*. Thousand Oaks: Sage.

Richmond, M. (1922) *What is Social Casework?* New York: Russell Sage.

Ricoeur, P. (1986) 'Life: a story in search of a narrator', in M.C. Doeser and J.N. Kray (eds), *Facts and Values: Philosophical Reflections from Western and Non-Western Perspectives*. Dordrecht: Martinus Nijhoff. pp. 121–32.

Riley, A. (1996) 'Murder and social work', *Australian Social Work*, 49 (2): 37–43.

Robertson, R. (1992) *Globalisation*. London: Sage.

Rodwell, M.K. (1987) 'Naturalistic inquiry: an alternative model for social work assessments', *Social Service Review*, June: 233–46.

Rodwell, M.K. (1998) *Social Work Constructivist Research*. New York: Garland.

Rosaldo, R. (1993) *Culture and Truth*. London: Beacon Press.

Rossiter, A. (1995) 'Entering the intersection of identity, form and knowledge: reflection on curriculum transformation', *Canadian Journal of Community Mental Health*, 14 (1): 5–14.

Rossiter, A. (1996) 'A perspective on critical social work', *Journal of Progressive Human Services*, 7 (2): 23–41.

Rossiter, A. (2001) 'Innocence lost and suspicion found: do we educate for or against social work?', *Critical Social Work*, 2 (1): www.criticalsocialwork.com/CSW_2001_1.html.

Rossiter, A. (2005) 'Where in the world are we? Notes on the need for a social work response to global power', in S. Hick, J. Fook and R. Pozzuto (eds), *Social Work: A Critical Turn*. Toronto: Thompson Educational Publishers. pp. 189–202.

Rowe, W., Hanley, J., Moreno, E.R. and Mould, J. (2000) 'Voices of social work practice: international reflections on the effects of globalisation', in *Social Work and Globalisation*, special issue; *Canadian Social Work*, 2 (1); supplementary issue, *Canadian Social Work Review*, 17; special edition, *Intervention*: 65–87.

Said, E. (1978) *Orientalism*. London: Routledge and Kegan Paul.

Said, E. (1993) *Culture and Imperialism*. New York: Alfred A. Knopf.

Said, E. (1995) *Orientalism: Western Conceptions of the Orient*. London: Penguin.

Sakamoto, I. (2007) 'An anti-oppressive approach to cultural competence', *Canadian Social Work Review/Revue Canadienne de Service Social*, 24: 105–14.

Sands, R. (1996) 'The elusiveness of identity in social work practice with women', *Clinical Social Work Journal*, 24 (2): 167–86.

Sands, R. and Nuccio, K. (1992) 'Postmodern feminist theory and social work', *Social Work*, 37 (6): 480–94.

Sawicki, J. (1991) *Disciplining Foucault: Feminism, Power and the Body*. New York: Routledge.

Schön, D. (1983) *The Reflective Practitioner*. London: Temple Smith.

Schön, D. (1987) *Educating the Reflective Practitioner*. San Francisco: Jossey-Bass.

Scott, D. (1990) 'Practice wisdom: the neglected source of practice research', *Social Work*, 35 (6): 564–8.

Solas, J. (1996) 'Reviewing and reconstructing the clients' story in social work', *Australian Social Work*, 48 (3): 33–6.

Steier, F. (ed.) (1991) *Research and Reflexivity*. London: Sage.

Stephenson, N. and Papadopoulos, D. (2006) *Analysing Everyday Experience: Social Research and Political Change*. Basingstoke: Palgrave Macmillan.

Steyaert, J. (2005) 'Web-based higher education, the inclusion/exclusion paradox', *Journal of Technology in Human Services*, 23 (1/2): 67–78.

Steyaert, J. and Gould, N. (2009) 'Social work and the changing face of the digital divide', *British Journal of Social Work*, 39 (4): 740–53.

Taylor, C. and White, S. (2000) *Practising Reflexively in Health and Welfare*. Buckingham: Open University Press.

Taylor, I. (1996) 'Reflective learning, social work education and practice in the 21st century', in N. Gould and I. Taylor (eds), *Reflective Learning for Social Work*. Aldershot: Arena. pp. 153–61.

Thompson, N. (2006) *Anti-Discriminatory Practice*, 3rd edn. Basingstoke: Palgrave.

Throssell, H. (ed.) (1975) *Social Work: Radical Essays*. St Lucia: University of Queensland Press.

Torstendahl, R. (1990) 'Introduction: promotion and strategies of knowledge-based groups', in R. Torstendahl and M. Burrage (eds), *The Formation of Professions*. London: Sage.

Tsang, A.K.T. (2003) 'Journalling from internship to practice teaching', *Reflective Practice*, 4 (2): 221–40.

Turner, B.S. (1992) *Regulating Bodies*. London: Routledge.

Uttley, S. (1994) 'Professionals "moving down": rationalisation, routinisation and displacement', in J. Ife, S. Leitmann and P. Murphy (eds), *Advances in Social Work and Welfare Education*. Papers from the National Conference of the Australian Association for Social Work and Welfare Education, University of Western Australia. pp. 46–58.

Walton, P. (1999) 'Using competence as a basis for developing reflective practice', *Journal of Practice Teaching in Health and Social Work*, 2 (2): 63–76.

Ward, D. and Mullender, A. (1991) 'Empowerment and oppression: an indissoluble pairing for contemporary social work', *Critical Social Policy*, 32: 21–30.

Webb, C. (1992) 'The use of first person in academic writing: language, objectivity and gatekeeping', *Journal of Advanced Nursing*, 17: 747–52.

Weedon, C. (1987) *Feminist Practice and Post Structuralist Theory*. Oxford: Blackwell.

White, M. (1996) Doncaster 2-day Training Conference.

White, M. and Epston, D. (1990) *Narrative Means to Therapeutic Ends*. New York: Norton.

Whyte, W. (1991) *Participatory Action Research*. Newbury Park: Sage.

Williams, C.C. (2006) 'The epistemology of cultural competence', *Families in Society*, 87: 209–20.

Williams, F. (1996) 'Postmodernism, feminism and the question of difference', in N. Parton (ed.), *Social Theory, Social Change and Social Work*. London: Routledge. pp. 61–76.

Yee, J. (2005) 'Critical anti-racism praxis: the concept of whiteness implicated', in S. Hick, J. Fook and R. Pozzuto (eds), *Social Work: A Critical Turn*. Toronto: Thompson Educational Publishers. pp. 87–103.

Yip, Y.S. (2006) 'Reflectivity in social work practice with clients in mental health illness', *International Social Work*, 49 (3): 245–55.

Young, I. (1990) *Justice and the Politics of Difference*. Princeton: University of Princeton Press.

INDEX

Added to a page number 'g' denotes glossary.

ability/disability 89, 90
Aboriginality 96–7
absolutism 10
academic theory 7
access 25
accountability 30
action 70
action research 146, 155
Adams, G. 23
Adams, R. 55
Addams, J. 3, 4
advantage 27
advocacy 171–2
age 89, 90
agency 17, 57, 88, 89, 124, 129, 140, 141, 193g
Albury, R. 66
alienation 17, 71
allies 172–3, 186
ambiguity 182
analysis 5, 18
anti-discriminatory practice 18, 124
anti-oppressive practice 5, 18, 19
applicability 44
Argyris, C. 45
Aristotle 44
assessment
    criticisms of traditional notions of 132–5
    establishing appropriate climate and process 137–8
    and narrative see professional narratives
    politics and context 139–41
    research orientation and strategies 138–9
assumptions
    challenging unhelpful 157
    relating to power 109, 125, 128–9
    taken-for-granted 106, 168
audience (narrative) 159
Australia 19, 23, 95, 96
authority 163–4
auto-ethnographies 146
autonomy 24, 84, 171
    see also professional autonomy
awareness 70

Bailey, R. 5
Baistow, K. 56
Baldwin, M. 126, 167, 168
'banking' models of education 9–10
Bauman, Z. 163

Beck, U. 88
Belenky, M.F. 42, 84, 175, 176
beliefs 17, 58, 68, 69, 107
Beres, L. 159
Berlin, S. 85
Big Society 24
binary oppositional relations 56–7
binary oppositional thinking 10, 13, 106–7, 193g
    disempowerment 56–7, 128
    fixed categorisation 93
    marginalisation 95
    Marxist ideology 72
    social work 85–6
    see also dichotomous thinking
biographical methods 145–6
Bloom, M. 180
bottom-up approach, knowledge generation 45
bottom-up view, of power 61
Boud, D. 113
boundaries, breakdown of 21–2
Bourdieu, P. 166
Brake, M. 5
Britain see United Kingdom
Brophy, P. 160
Brown, C. 96
bureaucratic practice 168–71
Burke, K. 152

Canada 19
Cannan, C. 91, 144
capitalist imperialism 22
Carniol, B. 31
case management 170–1
case managers 31
casework 5, 6, 7, 9, 66, 170, 180
categories 13, 59, 74, 83, 84, 87, 133
categorisation 27, 85, 86, 89, 92
    see also binary oppositional thinking
category entitlement, narrator credibility 153
'cause and effect', in narrative 77
centralisation 19, 23, 25
challenge 104, 110–11, 122, 185
chances 89
change 18, 88, 89, 182
    contextual 173
    contributing to 187–8
    global 22, 23, 27
    positioning 104

change *cont.*
   and responsibility 128
   see also organisational change; social change(s);
      total change
child protection, service users in 92
choice(s) 58, 59, 89, 138
Clarke, J. 30
class 59, 84, 87, 89, 183
closure 151
co-construction 146
co-operative inquiry 146
co-researching 189
coalition government 24
coherence 88, 151
collaborative narrative construction 137–8, 141
collaborative research 155
collective approaches 7
commodification 9, 10, 193g
commodity, power as 56–7
communication 17, 18, 32, 47, 190
   see also dialogue; discourse; language
community, sense of 88–9, 175
community contexts 140
community culture 124
community participation 185–6
competition, economic 22–3
complexity 14, 33, 186
complicity with oppression 17, 58–9, 88, 128, 193g
connected practice 165
connected teaching 175
connectedness 125
consciousness, action and 70
consciousness-raising 70
conservatives 6, 7
constructivist research 105
context(s)
   and assessment 139–41, 143
   emphasis on 32
   knowledge generation 47
   nature of 162–4
   positionality 164–5
   and power 60, 179
   professional 3
   working with whole 165
   see also cultural contexts; social context
contextual competence 166–7, 194g
contextual practice 162, 173, 184–5, 194g
contextuality 16, 33, 49–50, 178
continuity 151
contract culture 24
contradictions 58–9, 72, 88, 186
control
   identity construction 98
   organisational context 163
   over knowledge 29, 43
   see also centralisation; managerial control; social
      control
conversational devices 74, 112, 153
Corrigan, P. 5
Crinall, K. 57, 97
critical acceptance 174, 188–90, 193g

critical approach 5–6, 193g
critical case management 171
critical incidents 113–15, 193–4g
critical postmodern approach 18, 47, 51, 52, 95,
   161, 178, 184, 189
critical postmodern perspective 62, 78, 79, 86, 87,
   88, 179
critical realism 19
critical reconstructive process 106–12
critical reflection 45, 73, 194g
   benefits 186
   critical incident technique 113–15
   de/reconstruction 112–13
   discourse 186
   linking evaluation and research 179–80
   origins of reflective approach 45–6
   other approaches 116–17
   other perspectives 50
   in practice 46–7
   processes 48–9, 181
   reflexivity, reflective practice and contextuality
     49–50
critical social work 17–18, 98, 117
   contextualising other perspectives 18–19
   empowerment 53
   in hostile environments 184–8
   redeveloping 33–4
   see also critical postmodern approach
critical thinking 40
Cullum-Swan, B. 151–2
cultural competence 194g
cultural contexts 167–8, 173
cultural disrespect 27
cultural domination 27
cultural identities 26
cultural orthodoxy 58
cultural power 126
culture of poverty 91, 134
culture of powerlessness 125

data collection, reflexive 147
de Maria, W. 5
de Montigny, G. 19
decentralisation 23
decision-making, power 23
deconstruction/deconstructive methods 13, 14,
   106–9, 194g
   critical reflection 48–9, 112–13
   discourse analysis 104–6
   educational practices 175–6
   power 121–3
dependency (welfare) 91
deprofessionalisation 23
Derrida, J. 13, 93
descriptive/illustrative 189–90
detail, credible narrative 153
determinism 10
devaluation
   cultures 27
   dichotomous thinking 85
   identity categorisation 94

devaluation *cont.*
  marginalised groups 58
  professional knowledge 23
  in social work 7, 9, 76, 127
  of women 84, 92
development 22
dialogue 18, 47, 169, 190
diary records 48
dichotomies, challenging 169–70
dichotomous thinking 13, 14, 84–6, 128
  see also binary oppositional thinking
differance 93
difference(s) 13, 14, 26, 27
  allowance for 58
  diversity and inclusivity 95
  handling 188–90
  making 92–5
  politics of 33
  see also dilemma of difference
differentiation 84, 163, 183
digital divide 25
dilemma of difference 59, 95–7, 194g
dilemmas, challenging impossible 169–70
directionality 70–1
disability activists 154
disadvantage 27, 59, 71
disadvantaged 10, 58, 70–1, 97, 165
disaggregation 23
discourse analysis 195g
  deconstructive methods 104–6
  resistance, challenge and change 103–4
discourse(s) 13, 65
  assessment 134
  creating new 111
  defined 72–3, 194–5g
  and difference 96
  empowering 158
  expropriating and translating 185–6
  and identity 88
  ideology and 72
  language, power and 75–6, 104
  and narrative 76–7
  see also dominant discourses; hidden discourses; multiple discourses
discrimination 95
disempowerment 10, 86, 95
  empowerment as 59–60
  oppositional thinking 56–7, 128
  participation of self in 127–8
disinterest, narrator credibility 153
diversity 16, 26, 95, 96, 182–3
divided society 27
division 96
dominant discourses 13
  about service users 91
  compliance with 75, 79
  content and processes of assessment 135
  fixed categorisation 93
  unsettling 103–6, 109, 110, 111, 141, 185
domination 17, 72
Dominelli, L. 22

Dore, M.M. 175
downsizing 22
Dubus, A. 189
Duvall, J. 159

economic aspects 22–4
education
  women and 42
  see also social work education
effectiveness 23, 168
efficiency 23, 24, 168
elite knowledge 26
emancipation 5, 17, 47, 49
empathy 70, 71, 72
empirical knowledge 18, 47
empirical reality 17, 40
employment 30
empowerment 9, 10, 14, 27, 30, 53, 185
  in advocacy 172
  constructing personal theories of 129–30
  identity construction 97
  model, criticisms of 55–6
  narrative and 158
  new notions of 119–20
  problems in conceptions of 56–60
  process of 120
  reformulating the concept of 61–3
  see also disempowerment
enculturation model 174
the enemy, constructing 125–6, 172–3
enterprise culture 24, 91
episteme 44
equality 58, 94, 96
Eskimo study 89, 147
ethnicity 26, 27, 89, 96–7, 167, 183
ethnographic methods 139, 145, 146, 147
evaluation, linking reflection, research and 179–80
Evans, T. 126–7
excellence 23
exclusion 27, 28, 33
experience 5, 14, 105, 139
  devaluation of 7
  learning and 116–17, 176
  as narrative 48
  see also lived experience
'experiment in practice' 180
expert knowledge 29
external self 83
externalisation, problem narrative 157–8
externalising devices, credible narrative 153
extreme case formulations, credible narrative 153

false consciousness 17, 58, 69, 195g
  see also ideology
fatalism 17
Fawcett, B. 188
Featherstone, B. 188
feminism 46, 59, 84, 88, 92, 154
feminist approaches 5, 16, 70
feminist pedagogy 175

Ferguson, H. 89
Ferguson, I. 18
The First Stone 140
fixed categories 93
fixed identity 84, 85, 86, 87, 92, 96
fixed knowledge 51
Flyvberg, B. 44
Fook, J. 5, 126
formal theory 78, 79
Foucault, M. 13, 16, 73, 104
fragmentation 16, 22, 23, 26, 28
Freud, S. 13

Galper, J. 5
Gardner, F. 181
Garner, H. 140
gay rights activists 154
gender 5, 7, 54, 183
gender bias 14, 84
gender categorisation 84, 85, 87, 89, 90
generalisability 44, 166
Giddens, A. 88, 89
Gilligan, C. 84
globalisation 21–2, 195g
    challenges for social work 28–31, 34
    critical possibilities for social work 31–4
    economic aspects 22–4
    labour market 30–1
    political, social and cultural ramifications 26–8
    technological aspects 24–5
    theoretical aspects 25–6
Goodman, J. 147
Gould, N. 22, 24
government intervention 25
grand narratives 12, 106
group identity 67, 154

Harrison, G. 27
health 89, 90
Healy, K. 85
hidden discourses 110, 111
hierarchies, breakdown of 26
historical contexts 140
holistic approach 4, 28, 44, 46, 105, 161
holistic context 47, 49, 171
Hoogevelt, A. 22
Hough, G. 24
Houston, S. 19
Huberman, A.M. 44
Hull House 4
human rights perspectives 19

ideas 16, 67, 166
identity 26
    criticisms of traditional conceptions 83–4
    defined 82–3
    dichotomous thinking 84–6
    ethnic 96–7
    ideology 67
    perception and experience 89
    professional 30, 32, 181

identity *cont.*
    in reflexive modernity 88–9
    reformulating ideas of 86–8
    service users 91–2
    women's 84, 92
    see also cultural identities; political identity;
        politics of identity; powerless identity; victim
        identity
identity categories 84, 86, 90, 94, 95, 97, 134
identity construction 97, 98, 126
identity politics 27, 33, 97–8, 145, 154–5,
    183, 195g
identity reconstruction 154–5, 168–9
ideology 66–9, 195g
    and discourse 72
    limitations of concept 69–72
immersion, in research 145
in-person service workers 32
inclusion 25, 27, 33
inclusionary practice 44
inclusivity 33, 47, 50–1, 95
independence 24
indigenous issues, postcolonial world 26–7
individual identity reconstruction 154
individualisation 5, 170
individuation 84
inductive process 49, 166
inequality 22, 25, 53, 58, 96, 187
information and communication technologies 24, 25
informational culture 24
Ingersoll, V. 23
initiative 24
'innocent' knowledge 15
institutional level, ideology 66
intellectual virtues 44
interaction
    worker-service user 156, 190
    see also reflective interaction; social
        interaction
interests 70, 71, 85
internal self 83
interpretive approaches 77–8
interprofessional working 30
interviews 138–9, 142
intuition 45

Jeffrey, L. 95
joint participation 186
Jones, K. 18
Jones, M. 77
Jordan, B. 24, 76, 91
Jordan, C. 91
Judge Judy 77

Klein, W.C. 180
knowing, ways of 14, 16, 26, 33, 78
knowledge
    development 180
    and discourse 73
    empirical 18, 47
    modernist perspective 12

knowledge *cont.*
   nature of 39–41
   postmodern perspective 14, 15, 26, 39, 40, 43, 51
   transferability 32, 165–6, 196g
   see also professional knowledge; specialist
      knowledge
knowledge construction 17
knowledge generation 41–2, 45–6, 47

labels 59, 73, 74, 85, 110, 112, 133
labour market 30–1
Lacan, J. 13
language 73–5, 107
   of alliance 172
   discourse and power 75–6
   interpretation 13
   professional narratives 142
   social construction 105
Laragy, C. 125
learning
   and experience 116–17, 176
   therapy and research 180–1
legitimate knowledge 39, 40
Leonard, P. 5, 91, 163, 174
Lewin, F. 97
life histories 89, 146
life politics 88, 89
linear process, problem conceptualisation 132
lived experience 14, 72, 88
living, inclusive ways of 47
logocentrism 13, 92, 135, 195g

macro level work 7, 9
management 173, 174
managerial control 22, 24
managerial culture 23, 167–8, 174–5
Manning, P.K. 151–2
marginalisation 14, 84, 95, 183
marginalised groups 58, 86, 154, 155, 156
marketisation 23
Marx, K. 13
Marxism 16, 66, 70, 72
meaning 12, 13, 26, 74, 166
meaning-making 76, 77–8, 138, 141, 163
medical systems 90
Melville, R. 27
memory work 146
metanarrative 151
micro level work 6, 8, 9
Miles, M.B. 44
Millstein, K.H. 180
Minow, M. 59, 95
'modernising' agenda 19
modernism 12, 25, 39, 45, 56, 65
Moffat, L. 92
moral absolutism 10
moral high ground 172, 173
moral inaction 15
moral relativism 15
Moreau, M. 5
Mullaly, B. 5

Mullender, A. 56
multiple discourses 13, 14
multiple perspectives 12, 15, 80, 104, 141, 147,
   157, 165, 168, 174, 188
multiplicity 16
mutual respect 141, 190

naming 110, 111
narrative 76–7, 114, 146
   defined 150–1, 195g
   elements of 151–3
   postmodern perspective 48
   see also professional narratives
narrative analysis 150, 152, 155
narrative identity 87–8, 196g
narrative reconstruction
   processes 156
   techniques 157–60
   uses 153–6
narrative therapy 155–6
narrativity 98, 150
narrator credibility 153
nation-state(s) 12, 24, 26
naturalistic inquiry 139, 145
negotiation 169
neo-liberalism 22, 91
neo-Marxism 18
New Labour 19, 24, 91
new professionalism 30
New Right 91
non-essentialist view 87
non-feminist pathways 59
non-recognition 27
'non-service user' perspective 111
Nuccio, K. 13

objectivity 133
observational methods 139, 145
O'Byrne, P. 158
oppositional thinking *see* binary oppositional
   thinking
oppression 10, 56
   see also complicity with oppression
organisational change 173, 174
organisational contexts 160, 163, 169
organisational culture 174
organisational identity reconstruction 155
organisations, modernist 12
orientalism 27, 95
othering 13, 95, 196g
outcome of advocacy 171

Papadopoulos, D. 146
parochial thinking, breakdown of 21–2
participation 185–6, 187
participative action research 146
partnership 30, 174
Parton, N. 24, 30, 158
passivity 17, 133
patriarchy 84
pattern recognition 139

person-in-situation 4, 14, 32
personal power 126, 190
personal-professional dichotomy 169–70
phronesis 44–5
plurality 72
policy contexts 140
policy development 23
political correctness 9
political identity 19
political neutrality 15, 16
politics
    and assessment 139–41
    see also identity politics; life politics
Polkinghorne, D.E. 44, 151
positionality 15, 87, 164–5, 187, 196g
positioning 104, 130
positivism 17
postcolonialism 26–7
postmodern organisation 174
postmodern social work 18, 96
    addressing concerns of structural approach 14–15
    similarity with critical approach 17
    see also critical postmodern approach
postmodernism 12, 19, 25, 28, 145, 196g
    breakdown of hierarchies 26
    and context 162, 163
    and discourse 65
    doubts about 15–16
    and identity 86–7, 88, 98
    and knowledge 15, 26, 39, 40, 43, 51
    and language 74
    practice/experience as narrative 48
    and the reflective approach 46
    relativist stance 183–4
    theory and practice 43
postmodernism feminism 88
poststructural social work 14
poststructuralism 12–13, 16, 39, 58, 65, 92, 196g
poverty 27, 31, 91, 134
Powell, F. 27
power 53–63, 141
    assumptions relating to 109, 125, 128–9
    authority and perceptions of 163–4
    commodification 10
    constructing personal theories of 129–30
    constructions of, in social work 123–7
    and context 179
    decision-making 23
    deconstruction and reconstruction 14, 120–3
    of discourses 104
    and empathy 71
    language, discourse and 75–6
    managerial 24
    of narrative 77
    new notions of 119–20
    problems in conceptions of 56–60
    professional knowledge 42–3, 51
    reflecting on 53–5
    reformulating the concept of 60–1
    see also empowerment; professional power;
        structural power

power relations 18, 68, 107, 109, 156
powerful(ness) 55, 57, 60, 92, 120, 125, 126,
    128, 133
powerless(ness) 55, 57, 92, 109, 120, 124, 125,
    127, 187–8
powerless identity 57, 86, 127, 128, 171
practical knowledge 4, 44
practical level, ideology 66
practice(s) 107
    beliefs and 69
    dangerousness of 16
    narrative in 77
    theory and 9, 14, 43–5, 51
    see also professional practice
practice theory 45, 78, 113, 115–16, 120, 168, 180
practice wisdom 78, 180
praxis 44
presenting problems 133
privatisation 22, 23
privilege 27
problem narrative, externalising 157–8
problematising 136
problems, criticisms of traditional notions
    of 132–5
process, postmodern organisation as 174
process of advocacy 171
professional autonomy 23, 24, 28, 30, 161
professional expertise 24, 25, 26, 29, 125, 178
professional identity 30, 32, 181
professional knowledge 30, 51
    globalisation 23, 25
    masculinisation 4–5
    as phronetic 44
    and power 42–3
professional narratives
    assessment as construction of 135–6
    changing nature of constructing 141
    effective 144
    interpretation and enactment 143–4
    main elements 142–3
    reframing major concepts and language 142
    research strategies 145–8
    unobtrusive methods 147
professional power 29, 43, 45, 51
professional practice 169
    changing views of 32–3
    critical reflective approach 46–7
    globalisation 23
    reflective judgement in 44
    see also bureaucratic practice; connected practice;
        contextual practice; reflective practice
professional qualifications 30
professionalism 127
    changing views of 32–3
    as contested territory 29–30
professions 3, 29, 43
progress 17
Pugh, R. 22
purchase-provider split 23

questioning 48–9, 115–16, 142

race 26, 27, 84, 87, 89, 90
racism 27, 126, 183
radical approaches 5, 7, 8, 9, 10, 11, 16, 66,
    70, 84
rationalism 23–4, 26, 70
re-enculturation 173
'real' problems 133
reality 12, 13, 17, 40, 71, 73, 76, 77
Reason, P. 146
reconstruction 49, 111–12
    contextual change 173
    power 123
    of self and service users 129
    see also identity reconstruction; narrative
        reconstruction
Rees, S. 5, 180
reflection 196g
    see also critical reflection
reflective interaction 182
reflective judgement 44
reflective practice 49–50, 196g
reflective questions 48–9, 115–16
reflective writing 189
reflectivity 49
'reflexive materialist' position 19
reflexive methods 139, 146–7
reflexive modernity, self and identity in 88–9
reflexivity 49, 196g
Reich, R. 32
relativism 183–4
relevance 44, 166
research
    learning, therapy and 180–1
    linking reflection, evaluation and 179–80
    narrative in 77
    social work and 105
researcher as instrument 147
resistance 18, 103–4, 109–10, 122, 185
responsibility 24, 25, 57, 125, 128, 133
Richmond, Mary 3
Riley, A. 78
risk(s) 24, 26
Rodwell, M.K. 105, 139, 145
roles, reconstructing 168–9
Rosaldo, R. 89
Rossiter, A. 15, 94, 96, 126, 187, 188
routine workers 32
Rowan, P. 146

Said, E. 27, 95
sameness 58, 94, 96
Sands, R. 13, 83, 87, 89, 154
Schon, D. 45
scientific discourse 132
scientific knowledge 10, 39, 40, 41, 44
'scientistic' thinking 26
Scott, D. 180
self
    constructions in social work 90–2
    criticisms of traditional conceptions 83–4
    defined 82–3

self cont.
    embodied nature of 89
    as instrument 147
    reconstructing 129
    in reflexive modernity 88–9
    reformulating ideas of 86–8
    social workers' construction of 124–5
    see also whole self
'self-defeating' beliefs 17, 58
self-evaluation 30
self-hood 87
self-reflection 18, 47
self-reliance 24
semiotic analysis 105
service providers 22–3
service provision 23, 25
service user perspective 112, 143
service users
    construction of, in non-threatening ways 133
    empathy and power 71
    identity 91–2
    involvement and empowerment 30
    narratives, translating 135, 137
    politicising 190
    reconstructing 129
    relationships with 25
sexual harassment 140
sexuality 89
situated subjectivity 13, 14, 87, 196g
skills
    technocratisation 22–3
    see also contextual competence
social change(s) 5, 6, 17, 18, 25, 47, 54, 98
social constructionism 18, 19, 105
social context 4, 5, 6, 14
social control 6, 7, 66
social critique 6
social development approaches 33
social interaction 17–18, 27, 60, 89, 90, 92, 123,
    145, 146, 175
social justice 6, 15, 24, 29, 56, 167, 172,
    185, 189
social movements, identity politics 154–5
social reality 17
social relations 17, 18, 22, 47, 60, 71, 72,
    89, 90, 194
social structural categorisations 84, 85, 86, 87, 89
social superstructure 71
social work
    binary opposites in 85–6
    celebrating 191
    constructions of self in 90–2
    critical see critical social work
    critical origins 3–5
    culture 169
    femaleness of 69
    feminist approaches 5, 16, 70
    globalisation see globalisation
    identity politics 97–8
    postmodern see postmodern social work
    poststructural see poststructural social work

social work *cont.*
  power in 123–7
  practice *see* practice
  radical approach 5, 7, 8, 9, 10, 11, 16, 66, 70, 84
  and research 105
  structural approach 5, 6–12, 14, 16, 19,
    70, 84
  vision 181–2
social work education 67, 173
  appropriate learning climate 174–5
  banking models 9–10
  involvement of service users in 30
  and knowledge 15
  practices, deconstructing 175–6
social workers
  changing role of 30–1
  constructions of self 124–5
  identity 32
  interpretation and enactment of narrative 143–4
  objectivity/passivity in problem
    conceptualisation 133
  power 71
socio-economic structures 5
specialist knowledge 32, 42, 43
stake inoculation, narrator credibility 153
Steier, F. 146
Stephenson, N. 146
Steyaert, J. 24
stigma/stigmatisation 59, 84, 95, 96, 172
story *see* narrative
structural approach 5, 6–12, 14, 16, 19, 70, 84
structural power 126, 127, 190–1
structuralism 13
structures 18, 67, 68, 77, 107
subject positions 15, 77, 78, 91, 104, 107, 109
subjectivity 14, 86, 89
  see also situated subjectivity
subordination 71, 72
supervision 173, 174
symbolic analysts 32

taken-for-granted assumptions 106, 168
Taylor, C. 74, 92, 144, 152, 153
techne 44
technical absolutism 10
technological aspects, globalisation 24–5
text(s) 48, 76, 105, 107, 175
theoretical level, ideology 66
theory(ies)
  commodification 9
  development 45–6
  discourse and 78–9
  power accorded to 128–9

theory(ies) *cont.*
  of power, constructing 129–30
  and practice 9, 14, 43–5, 51
  see also academic theory; practice theory
therapy, research and learning 180–1
third way 24, 91
Throssell, H. 5
top-down approach, knowledge generation 45
total change 127
tough love 91
transferability 32, 165–6, 178, 196g
transformative reflection 117
translation 135, 137, 168
transparency 30
truth/falsity distinction 69

uncertainty 26, 58, 141, 178–9, 182
underclass 91
'the unfinished' 182
United Kingdom 18, 24, 30, 163
unity in diversity 182–3
Uttley, S. 29

value base 29, 32, 95, 171
values 10, 89, 117, 179
victim, service user as 92
victim identity 10, 84, 128, 172
victim-blaming 5, 97
victimhood 57
vision 181–2
voluntaristic, social work as 17

Ward, D. 56
Weedon, C. 73, 104
welfare clients 92
welfare dependents 91
welfare state 22, 24, 25
White, M. 155
White, S. 74, 92, 144, 152, 153
whiteness 27
whole self 89–90
Why I gave up the gun 189
William, C.C. 96
women's identity 84, 92
women's psychology 84
Women's Ways of Knowing 42, 175
workers
  Reich's categorisation 32
  see also social workers
workplace contexts 173

Yee, J. 27
Young, I. 98